CHICKEN SOUP FOR THE ADOPTED SOUL

Chicken Soup for the Adopted Soul
Stories Celebrating Forever Families
Jack Canfield, Mark Victor Hansen, LeAnn Thieman

Published by Backlist, LLC,
a unit of Chicken Soup for the Soul Publishing, LLC. www.chickensoup.com

Front cover design by Larissa Hise Henoch
Originally published in 2008 by Health Communications, Inc.

Back cover and spine redesign by Pneuma Books, LLC

Distributed to the booktrade by Simon & Schuster. SAN: 200-2442

Publisher's Cataloging-in-Publication Data
(Prepared by The Donohue Group)

Chicken soup for the adopted soul : stories celebrating forever families / [compiled by] Jack Canfield, Mark Victor Hansen, [and] LeAnn Thieman.

   p. : ill. ; cm.

   Originally published: Deerfield Beach, FL : Health Communications, c2008.
   ISBN: 978-1-62361-116-3

   1. Adopted children--Anecdotes. 2. Adoption--Anecdotes. 3. Parent and child--Anecdotes. 4. Adoptive parents--Anecdotes. 5. Anecdotes. I. Canfield, Jack, 1944- II. Hansen, Mark Victor. III. Thieman, LeAnn.

HV875 .C345 2012
362.734   2012945888

PRINTED IN THE UNITED STATES OF AMERICA
on acid free paper

22 21 20 19 18 17 16 15 14 13   01 02 03 04 05 06 07 08 09 10

CHICKEN SOUP FOR THE ADOPTED SOUL

Stories Celebrating Forever Families

Jack Canfield
Mark Victor Hansen
LeAnn Thieman

Backlist, LLC, a unit of
Chicken Soup for the Soul Publishing, LLC
Cos Cob, CT
www.chickensoup.com

Not flesh of my flesh
Nor bone from my bone,
But still miraculously my own.
Never forget for a single minute,
You didn't grow beneath my heart,
But in it.
—Anonymous

Contents

3. LOVE

4. DIVINE INTERVENTION

5. LESSONS

6. DEFINING MOMENTS

7. OVERCOMING OBSTACLES

Introduction

In every speech I give, I'm blessed to share the saga of adopting our son, Mitch. Every time, I declare, "I don't know why he was conceived in another womb or born in another land, but I know with all my heart that God created him to be ours." Reading the 3,000+ stories submitted for *Chicken Soup for the Adopted Soul* taught me that this is not just my conviction, but the universal belief of every adoptive parent. I was surprised at the consistent theme of parents identifying and claiming their assigned children from groups of dozens, hundreds, or even thousands. I was struck to realize that adoption is a calling, be it from a dream or a feeling deep in one's heart or gut. There is a knowing, a certainty, propelling us toward that assigned child, and a confidence and faith that in time—seemingly too much time—he or she will be shown to us. It is then we comprehend and believe the truth shared by the precious little boy who surmised, "I was born for you."

Every adoptive parent, child, and family member will find a piece of themselves in these stories. Take your time reading them—soak in the love, the privilege, and the glory of adoption.

And be prepared—if you haven't adopted yet, you will!

1

CLAIMING MY OWN

I will not leave you orphans. I will come to you.

John 14:18

The Stuffed Animal

What gift has Providence bestowed on man that is so dear to him as children?

Cicero

"This one is for my baby sister." She tossed a furry, spotted dog into the box. "For baby Annie," she said in her endearing voice.

We sealed the box shut and addressed it to a Romanian orphanage in the town of Buzau. We felt a need to give back to the place that had given us Juliana, our only child. Friends from our church and neighborhood helped collect supplies and fill the boxes.

With the doors to adoptions closed, my husband and I were disappointed that we couldn't adopt from Romania again. But two-year-old Juliana insisted each time we packed boxes of medical supplies, food, toys, and clothes that it was all going to her sister.

"Juliana, sweetie, you don't have a sister," I'd say as gently as I could.

My husband smiled. "We have all the paperwork completed for another adoption."

Indeed, our fingerprints were traced through the FBI.

Copies of our birth certificates, marriage license, and home study were already notarized and certified. Bank reference letters, police reports, and criminal records were officially compiled, waiting to be used again.

"Maybe we should adopt a sister for Juliana."

He was right. We called Elena, the Romanian lawyer who helped us with Juliana's private adoption. "The process is a lot longer and more difficult," she warned us in her delightful accent. "Americans are adopting through agencies now. No more private adoptions." She hesitated slightly before my heart had a chance to sink. "But send me your paperwork. I'll see what I can do. While I petition the courts, I'll visit the orphanages and try to find you a little girl."

I tried to be hopeful, but it wasn't easy. "Maybe we should use an agency," I confided in my husband. The agencies I contacted brought few children into the United States because of the mountains of bureaucratic red tape. There simply were no easy routes, no easy answers, and no guarantees.

Weeks turned into months. The agonizing wait was unbearable. The Immigration and Naturalization Service advised us to adopt from another country, one with easier laws. The U.S. State Department tried to persuade us against adopting a Romanian orphan, too, but their cautious words were left unheeded. Even though Juliana was only two, she constantly reminded us that somewhere out there she had a sister.

Finally, Elena called from Romania. "I have wonderful news. I found a baby girl. She's beautiful!" she cried. "Her name is Andrea."

A wave of relief washed over me as happiness bubbled out. I wanted to say something to let Elena know I was still there, listening, but I was unable to talk.

"I mailed a picture of her to you."

"You did?" I managed to say, my voice garbled over transatlantic phone lines. "What does she look like?"

"Well, she has big brown eyes, lots of dark, curly hair, chunky cheeks, and she smiles all of the time."

I closed my eyes, imagining the baby she was describing. I could see myself picking her up and cuddling her close. I couldn't wait to hold her and take her for long walks in the stroller. I couldn't wait to push her on the swing set in the backyard. "When can we fly to Romania to get her?"

"I'll have her paperwork complete in a month. You can come then."

"I can't wait a month!" I protested.

I could hear her laugh at my comment.

I hung up the phone, my excitement soaring. I knelt beside Juliana and told her the news. She began to dance around the kitchen in tiny, uncoordinated steps. "Baby Annie!" she said happily.

I watched her in amazement, nodding my head, even mimicking the words, "Baby Annie."

My husband asked through a cynical smile, "We're not calling her little orphan Annie, are we?"

"No. We're calling her Andrea." I frowned in mock disapproval while I thought about the names, how close Annie and Andrea were.

When the time came to fly to Romania, it was bittersweet. We didn't want to leave Juliana, but I had to find this little orphaned girl Juliana had predicted. We packed ruffled pink dresses, soft pastel blankets, and a teddy bear for our new daughter.

We arrived at the orphanage in Buzau, in the poverty-stricken countryside of Romania, wearing our hearts on our sleeves. Elena led us down the dimly lit corridor where our future daughter had spent practically the entire first year of her life. It was damp and eerily quiet, except for the buzzing of flies.

I noticed a few toys stacked near the wall. "Look!" I nearly shouted. "These are the toys we sent!"

Just then, a dozen little children ran to us for the one thing they got too little of at the orphanage—affection. I recognized their tattered Mickey Mouse shirts from the boxes of clothes I'd mailed months ago, hand-me-downs from my neighbors. I bent down to touch the children, each one eager to be held. As much as I wanted to spend the day holding them, I knew there was one special child I couldn't wait to hold.

The orphanage director urged me on, leading me into a room filled with endless rows of white metal cribs. Had I not known it was in a Romanian orphanage, I would have thought I had entered a cloning factory in the middle of Eastern Europe. My eyes scanned the tiny faces, searching for the one that matched the picture Elena had mailed to us. They were all beautiful babies, and I wanted them all.

They quietly rocked themselves because they had no one to rock them.

Mobiles dangled over most cribs, and the children looked away from them with inquisitive glances as we strolled past.

Across the room, farthest from the window, a baby lay propped against the side of the paint-chipped bedrail. She was the most beautiful child there. Rich curls spilled across her pale forehead, the first place I planned to kiss. I leaned into the crib and gingerly lifted our daughter into my arms. Her frail arms refused to release the toy she'd been clenching . . . the spotted dog Juliana had packed months before, claiming, "This is for my baby sister!"

Barbara S. Canale

And His Name Was Nicolas

Our fate is decreed, and things do not happen by chance.

Lucius Annaeus Seneca

As children, like most little girls, my big sister, Shannon, and I loved to play house. Before we could officially start our play, we would always decide on various important details, such as what our pretend husbands looked like, how many kids we had, and what their names were. Shannon always had a boy and a girl. The girl's name often changed, but the boy's name was always Nicolas.

When we grew older and my sister became pregnant with her first child, she had many names picked out for a girl, but only one boy's name: Nicolas. When she became pregnant with her second child, she still hoped she would be able to use the name Nicolas, but she was happy when she gave birth to another healthy baby girl.

After the birth of her two daughters, my sister discovered she would be unable to have any more biological children, so sadly, the name Nicolas went unused.

Shortly after I married my husband, we started trying to have children. After years of fertility treatments and many sad losses, we tentatively called an agency to inquire about the procedure for adoption. Due to my husband's deafness, we knew we could handle certain special needs, and we were very excited about the prospect of welcoming a deaf child into our home.

We decided to adopt from China. Just like when we were children, I felt like my sister and I were playing house again. We would excitedly call each other on the phone and talk about names for our little girl. What would she look like? Should we paint her room pink or purple? Should we name her Sophia or Olivia?

Shortly after submitting our application to our agency, I received a telephone call from our social worker. There was an eight-week-old baby boy in an orphanage in Bogota, Colombia, who was diagnosed at birth with a hearing loss. His birth mother named him Nicolas.

The social worker asked, "Are you interested?"

I immediately exclaimed, "Yes!" And only as an afterthought, I sent my husband an e-mail telling him of the exciting news.

The first telephone call I made was to my sister.

"Shannon," I said, "we might have a baby."

She excitedly replied, "Oh, but it's so soon. I thought you would have to wait longer. What part of China is she from?"

"Well, she's not from China, and 'she' is a 'he.' He's from Colombia, and he's deaf."

She hesitated.

"Oh, Erin, are you sure about this? A special-needs child can pose some real challenges."

I quietly said, "Shannon, his name is Nicolas."

And her reply? "That's your baby."

Erin Conroy

The Curly-Haired Girl

*Nothing so much convinces me of the bound-
lessness of the human mind as its operations in
dreaming.*

William Benton Clulow

My daughter came to me in a dream. Some might say it
was crazy to believe it, and I might have agreed with the
skeptics, except I'd seen both of my sons in dreams while
I was pregnant with them. The first time, my husband
was a bit skeptical, until our son grew into the baby I'd
described—exactly. So, the second time I dreamed about
my unborn baby, my husband believed. This little boy
also grew into the exact child I described after my dream.

When I had a dream about a child we were planning
to adopt in the far future, we both paid attention. This
toddler was beautiful, chubby, and curly-haired. In the
dream, she was sitting on the living-room floor, giggling and waving her chubby little hands. Oddly, she
was surrounded by red light. This child seemed perfectly at home, and when I woke up, I knew I had seen
my future daughter.

I was very confused by many things in the dream, though. We had finally decided, after several weeks of reading, discussion, and web searches, to adopt a baby from China. The girl in my dream did not look Chinese. For one thing, she had very curly hair. Did the red glow around her mean it was red? I couldn't remember what color the girl's hair was in the dream. Our friends and family speculated we should adopt from another country, someplace where children had red curly hair.

In the meantime, I fell in love with a special-needs orphan whose picture was on our agency's website. This toddler was adorable, Chinese, and her left hand was missing. Talk about switching gears! We had to consider if our family could handle something like that.

When a friend who lost her left arm in a childhood accident met with us to talk about what it takes to parent a child with a limb difference, we decided this little girl with short, straight black hair was going to come home to us.

When we started to submit the paperwork, we were sent updated photos of her. By now, she was many months older, and her hair had grown almost to her shoulders . . . a mass of curly black hair. Curly! She was chubby, happy, and had huge eyes.

When we received another package with translated materials, we found that her Chinese name meant very, very red, or, actually, red with lots of exclamation points after it. Our agency explained that red is a very lucky color, and the orphanage workers, when naming her, probably thought a little orphan girl without a left hand needed as much luck as they could give her.

But we are the lucky ones. The girl from my dream is ours.

Heidi Shelton-Jenck

Operation Babylift

*No language can express the power and beauty
and heroism and majesty of a mother's love.*

Edwin Hubbel Chapin

When I had agreed to be the next volunteer to escort six babies from Vietnam to their adoptive homes in the United States, there had been no increase in the war for many months. Still, the decision to leave Mark and our two chubby-cheeked little girls for two weeks was difficult, at best. When I asked Mark what he thought I should do, he only said, "You've gotta do what you gotta do, honey." But I knew the words, "Please, don't go!" were screaming inside him.

I considered how firsthand information would be helpful for our local Friends of Children of Vietnam (FCVN) chapter. Mark and I had applied for adoption of a son through FCVN and expected him in two to three years. I thought it might mean something to him someday to know that his mom had been to his homeland. Every call we made to the U.S. State Department gave the same encouraging advice: the war was not expected to escalate. Go.

So after much prayer and thought, I said I would.

One week later, a tremendous Viet Cong offensive began.

The day before I was to leave, I heard on the radio there was bombing within three miles of the city limits of Saigon. It was Easter Sunday, and I knelt in church, fearful and trembling, begging God for a sign I did not have to go. Instead, I was filled with a courage, conviction, and certainty. I *knew* I'd be safe. God would take care of me.

I couldn't explain my newfound strength to myself, much less anyone else. I lingered in Mark's arms, hoping his love and trust in me were greater than his fears.

Days later, when our plane finally circled Tan San Nhut airport and I saw camouflaged jets lining the runway, the question and doubts echoed again—until I was greeted by Cherie, FCVN's Saigon director. "Have you heard the news?" she exclaimed. "President Ford has okayed a giant orphan airlift! Instead of taking out six babies, you'll help take out 300, if we're lucky!"

All the questions, all the doubts, were answered.

As she drove through the overcrowded, chaotic streets, Cherie explained how dozens of babies were being brought to the FCVN Center to prepare for the evacuation. Still, my years as a pediatric nurse could not prepare me for what I witnessed there. Every inch of floor was covered with a mat, and every inch of mat was covered with babies! We spent the entire first day helping the Vietnamese workers diaper and feed scores of babbling, cooing, crying infants.

The next day, I learned that FCVN had been bumped from the first-place position in Operation Babylift. I fought and argued to reclaim the right to take the first planeload of orphans to the United States, but to no avail.

With disappointment still heavy in our hearts, we instead loaded babies destined for our Australia chapter. With twenty-two babies around me on the floor of a Volkswagen van, we headed to the airport. There, we saw an enormous black cloud billowing at the end of the runway. We heard the rumor—the first planeload of orphans, the one I had begged to be on, had crashed after takeoff, killing half of the adults and children onboard.

Stunned, we loaded the babies onto the Australian airliner, then returned to the FCVN Center where the rumor was confirmed. The office was awash with grief. I looked at my watch, still on Iowa time. The girls were having breakfast in their fuzzy pajamas. Mark was shaving and listening to the radio. He would hear the news and be terrified I was on that flight. And there was no way for me to call and spare him this horror and heartache. I slumped onto a rattan sofa and sobbed uncontrollably.

Finally, I went to Cherie, admitted my cowardice, and told her I had to go home. "Now." With sorrowful tears in her eyes too, she tenderly informed me that there were no flights out. My best and likely only way home was on an airlift plane.

I went back to the nursery, mustering a renewed faith and confidence. I rejoined the workers preparing the babies for our flight—whenever that would be.

The next day at breakfast, Cherie sat beside me. "LeAnn, you and Mark will be adopting one of those babies in the next room. All your paperwork is here and in order. You can wait and be assigned a son from across the desk in the States, or you can go in there and choose a son."

Speechless, I entered the next room and hopscotched through the sea of babies. Then, a little boy, wearing only a diaper, crawled across the floor and into my arms and heart. As I cuddled him, he nestled his head into my shoulder and seemed to hug me back. I carried him around the room, looking at and touching the other babies. I whispered a prayer for the decision I was about to make, knowing it would change many lives forever. "Oh, Mark, I wish you were here," I moaned. "How do I choose?" The little boy in my arms answered by patting my face.

"I know, Mitchell," I cooed, testing the name we'd picked. "You were created to be our son."

I knew then that this was why God had sent me to Vietnam. I'd been sent to choose a son—or had he chosen me?

Two days later, it was our turn to leave. The workers helped us load the babies onto a city bus taking them to their flight to freedom. Nine of us volunteers cared for 100 babies, placing three and four to a cardboard box. In spite of the stress, it was joyful work as we propped countless bottles and changed diarrhea diapers.

In the Philippines, we got a larger plane and more volunteers, then continued the next leg of our journey to Hawaii. There, every child was removed from the plane while it was refueled.

Finally, I could call Mark.

The noise around the phone booth was so loud that I had to shout instructions to the operator. I mumbled to myself, "Mark doesn't even know we have a son. He has no idea I'm bringing him home."

I had rehearsed how I would tell him the wonderful news, but when I heard his voice, I could only blurt out, "Honey, this is LeAnn," and I started to bawl.

I could hear him repeating my name as he sobbed, too. I tried to compose myself so I could tell him about Mitchell, but I couldn't catch my breath.

Then, still crying, he said, "Just tell me you're bringing me our son."

LeAnn Thieman

The Hidden Blessing

What the best and wisest parent wants for his own child, that must the community want for all its children.

John Dewey

In 1992, my husband and I entered into a contract with an adoption agency to assist us with the adoption of a child from Eastern Europe. Ultimately, we were assigned a nine-month-old boy residing in Szeged, Hungary.

After many months, it became evident that our adoption agency was both inept and powerless to assist us with finalizing the adoption of this little boy, whom our family had grown to love through videotape and pictures. I realized the only way we were going to be able to finalize it was to figure it out myself. So, I went to work talking to the U.S. State Department and having nearly daily conversations with American embassy officials in Hungary, working to find a way to adopt our son. I learned everything there was to know about international adoption. For purely political reasons, there were strong forces, both in the U.S. and Hungary, at work against the success of these adoptions.

In the end, I traveled to Hungary to try to bring to fruition the adoption of our son, as well as twenty-seven other orphaned children waiting for their American parents. I met with Hungarian parliament members. I wrote letters. I made speeches. I became a presence in the Hungarian media. I was followed by at least one person each time I left my hotel. I don't know who was following me, or why, but I suspect that I was creating discomfort for officials both in the Hungarian and the American governments. I could tell my telephone calls were being recorded and were likely being listened to by local authorities.

A week later, three other waiting mothers joined me, and our presence was something for which the government was not prepared.

During the six weeks I was in Hungary, my daughter, Laura, was celebrating her tenth birthday at home. The temperature was hovering near 100 degrees each day, there was no ice for our drinks, and I was both emotionally and physically exhausted. I missed my family and my daughter's first double-digit birthday. I considered giving up. I cried on the phone with my family, and Laura said to me, "Mom, don't come home without my little brother, Alex. He will be the best birthday present ever!" Her words gave me the will to stay and fight.

I went to a small courtyard behind the hotel and softly cried all alone. I asked God why he was allowing this to happen. *All I want to do is to take our little boy home and love him for the rest of my life. Why are you making this so difficult?*

Within a few seconds, a calm peace settled over me. I knew in that instant there was a reason for the trials of the past year. I also knew we would be successful in getting our children to their families.

Five days later, the American embassy told me the Hungarian government had given us permission to take our children home!

Although this sounds like the end of the story, it was really only the beginning. Two months after I returned to St. Louis, I was contacted by a pair of Russian-born American physicians who had a strong desire to assist orphaned children from their homeland, and to find loving American families. They'd learned of my efforts with the Hungarian children. I agreed to become their partner and to run the adoption program. I discovered in myself a driving need to make adoption easier for future families so that no one would encounter the pain, fear, and difficulty I experienced.

The rest, as they say, is history. Indeed, there was a reason for all these trials. As of August 2006, we have assisted approximately 1,600 Eastern European children in finding loving homes!

Brenda Henn

A Miracle of Joy

A miracle is a work exceeding the power of any created agent, consequently being an effect of the divine omnipotence.

Robert South

As I stood at the gate in the busy airport waiting for my plane, my mind went back to all the changes in my life during the past months. My marriage had crumbled, leaving me shattered and very confused. My dream of a happy home and children had been dashed. But somehow God was restoring my sense of purpose and desire to follow wherever he led.

It was just a few days before Christmas. In a matter of minutes, I would board the plane and be on my way to Russia to adopt a six-month-old baby girl.

How it had all happened was amazing in itself. I remember sitting in the living room with friends and quietly sharing my desire for a child. "Well, there's no reason why you can't still be a mother," my friend assured me. "Singles are now adopting."

I remember how I had smiled at the idea, reminding him that I wasn't young anymore.

"Oh, I don't think it will take that long," he responded, "and anyway, it doesn't hurt to ask."

With that, a seed of hope was planted that I could be a mother. In just six months, I was on my way to Russia to adopt a baby girl named Oksana. Questions flooded my mind. *Would she be there when I arrived at the orphanage? Would she be healthy?*

I continued to pray as I stuffed my baggage in the overhead compartment. I glanced again at the little picture I had of Oksana. "Lord, please lead me to other people going to Russia to adopt."

How I feared traveling alone, but there was no one to go with me.

Before long, in little snippets of conversation, I overheard the words "Russia," "babies" and "orphanage."

"Are you going to Moscow?" I asked the woman to my right.

"Yes, my husband and I are going to adopt two children."

"So am I!" I squealed. "I mean, I'm going to adopt a baby girl."

From then on, we both talked incessantly. I discovered that they were heading to the same orphanage to be met by the same coordinator. We became fast friends. I whispered a prayer of thanks to God for answering my earlier prayer.

When the plane landed in Moscow, it was cold and dreary. I immediately sensed the strangeness of the different culture and my language barrier. But then I met our coordinator, who turned out to be a very friendly Russian woman who spoke no English. Her big, warm hugs were so reassuring.

"Is Oksana there?" I asked, having heard stories of

people getting to the orphanage, only to discover that the child was no longer there.

"Da," she answered with a twinkle in her eyes.

"When can we go to the orphanage?" I inquired, ready to go on the overnight train immediately.

"Soon," the translator said.

"By Christmas? Will I see her by Christmas?"

"Da. Da," she answered with a big grin.

I stayed in a simple apartment of a young couple and their three-month-old daughter, Anastasia. Their generosity was overwhelming. Although their living conditions were simple, they willingly shared what they had.

In just a few days, I left with two other couples to travel eight hours north. When we arrived at Borovitchy, we were tired but so excited. After only a few hours of sleep, we went to the orphanage. Walking inside the large brick building that was home to about 400 children, I whispered another prayer. "Just let her be healthy, Lord."

As I walked the long hall, I met staff members who were warm and friendly. I saw that the facilities were neat and clean. A tall Russian doctor joined us and smiled when he asked if I was ready to see Oksana.

Was I? I thought my heart was going to burst with such a strange combination of excitement, fear, longing, hope.

Together, we walked down the cement steps, through the long, narrow hall to the infants' room. They led me to a small room while they went to get the baby. In only a few moments, they were back.

Oh, I'll never forget that moment for as long as I live! They placed her warm little body in my arms and discreetly stepped out to leave us alone.

"Oh, my," I whispered in awe. "You are beautiful, darling."

I gazed at her big brown eyes and flawless skin. I held her hand in mine, counting each finger. I held her close and sang to her softly, "Jesus loves me." Time stood still.

It was a holy moment, a Christmas moment, a time when the Greatest Giver filled the arms of a hurting single woman with a priceless gift—a baby.

We left the orphanage on Christmas Eve at midnight. My tiny daughter, Noelle Joy Oksana Brani, was wrapped in a soft pink blanket. As I walked out into the night to catch the train back to Moscow, the snow was gently falling. And I thought I could hear the angels singing.

Sharon Beth Brani

Entwined Hearts

*No cord or cable can draw so forcibly, or bind
so fast, as love can do with a single thread.*

Richard E. Burton

After our son was born, my husband, Dick, and I were advised not to have any more children. We had always planned on having two, not wanting our son to be an only child. So we talked with several agencies about adoption, but were given very little encouragement. Someone recommended we become foster parents. Being young and energetic, the idea appealed to us.

We contacted our county agency and completed the necessary background checks, application, and training. We opened our home to any child, any age. Over the course of the next twelve years, we fostered nineteen children, ranging in age from nine months to seventeen years. Some stayed only a few hours. Most stayed a few months.

One day, the agency called to ask if we could accept a thirteen-month-old for a few days. At the time, our son was six, and we were already fostering a five-year-old and an eight-year-old. When asked if we could help out for seventy-two hours, we said, "Sure, we can do anything for seventy-two hours." We hurriedly borrowed a crib, some clothing, a high chair, and a playpen from various families within our church.

The caseworker brought her to the door about 9:00 PM with nothing but the clothes on her back. I stretched my arms out to her, and she came right to me. She reeked of cigarette smoke and sported a very soggy diaper, so I carried her upstairs for a bath. She happily played in the tub, even allowing me to shampoo her hair.

Something happened during those initial moments with her. She captured my heart. Though never connected by an umbilical cord, in the space of a heartbeat, mutual cords of love joined this child and me. Wrapping her in a big, warm towel, I carried her downstairs and excitedly said to my husband, "This is the one."

"What do you mean?"

"This is the one we are going to adopt."

Always practical, he looked at me with incredulity and slowly spoke, "No, Pam, we only have her for seventy-two hours."

I simply responded, "I know that's what the agency said, but she's the one."

Ever protective of me, Dick shook his head and sighed. He gave me a look that said, "Oh, Pam, you're setting yourself up for a big disappointment," and then tried to lighten the moment by playing with Erin.

I dressed her in some borrowed pajamas and fed her a bowl of Cheerios. Then I took her into the living room and rocked her for a while. Contentment and peace flooded my soul. Although she had been with us less than an hour, I felt as though she had always been our daughter and had finally come home.

We did nothing to initiate adopting Erin. We simply treated her as our own from the moment she entered our home. We complied with everything the agency asked of us, and more. We willingly and gladly rearranged and adjusted every area of our lives, including our schedules, our finances, our jobs, and our furniture in order to truly parent this child. We couldn't help ourselves. The love we felt for her was instantaneous, just like parents seeing their newborn baby. The difference was our baby weighed twenty-five pounds and could walk.

What began as a seventy-two-hour emergency placement turned into long-term foster care. Though the rights of Erin's biological parents were terminated after three or four years, appeal followed appeal, dragging the proceedings out for seven long, uncertain years.

The wonderful phone call came one afternoon while my husband was at a class 150 miles away and both kids were in school. Knowing Dick would be stopping to visit his father on his way home, I phoned there and asked that he call me as soon as he arrived. When he answered the phone, he couldn't understand my blubbering and thought something dreadful had happened.

"What's wrong, Pam? Is one of the kids sick? Did the cat get run over?"

At last I was able to draw a deep breath and whisper, "We can adopt Erin!"

"Really?" was all he could squeak out before tears constricted his throat, too.

We sat in awed, thankful silence for several seconds before either of us could speak again.

Thirty days later, Dick and I met in a small county courtroom with our caseworker and a judge to finalize the adoption.

The judge asked, "Why do you want to adopt Erin? Why not just continue to foster her and receive a stipend to provide for her?"

We both answered, "We love her as our own and want her to legally be our daughter forever. We can never lose her. We knew from day one she belonged to us!"

Satisfied, the judge rattled off a proclamation. At last, the little girl we knew from day one belonged to us became our daughter.

Pamela D. Williams

Roots

*A*nd he took the children in his arms, put his
hands on them, and blessed them.

Mark 10:16

"We need to get licensed as foster parents," I said to
my wife on the phone.

One of the things that had brought Beverly and me
together was our mutual desire to care for children who
needed and deserved a chance. Although we felt God
was leading us in this direction, I'd been hesitant and
concerned. What if we tried and failed?

Then I heard John Croyle speak. He was the founder
of Big Oak Ranch, one of the most successful group
homes in the United States, and his real-life stories
pushed me to get started. That's when I called Beverly.

We went through the process, and on July 5, 1987, a
social worker called to say that we had been licensed as
foster parents and would get our first child in about
ninety days.

The very next day, she called again about a "unique
situation." They had two brothers, ages two-and-a-half

and one, needing a long-term placement of a year or more. We went from expecting one child in ninety days to possibly two boys in three days.

Beverly's response was immediate and definite. "If this is what God wants us to do, this is what we should do."

For the next twenty-four hours, we ran around like crazy people. We borrowed a crib and a high chair. Then we went to a store to buy everything we thought we would need—diapers, wet wipes, Desitin, a few toys, some clothing, etc. When we got to the cashier with two full buggies, she asked if we were expecting a baby. My tall, slim, beautiful wife said, "Yes, two of them, tomorrow!"

The day the boys were to arrive, I was speaking two hours away, and I called Beverly every hour to see if she had heard anything. About 4:00 PM, she said the social worker had called and would be there in twenty minutes. I was home in an hour.

And there they were.

Stephen, at two-and-a-half, was a cute fellow with freckles and a one-word vocabulary . . . an angry, strong "No!" to our every question and statement. Randall was a different story. The difference in their dispositions was like night and day. While Randall was with his grandmother since birth, Stephen had been hauled all over the country with his biological mother as she committed armed robberies. He'd been exposed to things that most people could not even conceive.

The boys were with us for about two years when our social worker, who was as close to an angel as you will find on this Earth, called to inform us that the state had decided to terminate parental rights, which would make the boys adoptable. We were thrilled—until she explained that we would probably not be eligible because of a now-outdated law that said that foster parents could not adopt.

"What do you mean, we can't adopt them?" I protested.

I made three trips to see the governor to appeal to him.

"Sir," I pleaded, "if you take a tree up by the roots and transplant it, it has a chance to survive. But if you uproot it a second time, it will probably not make it. These are not trees; they are children, and it really is in their best interest to stay with us. We are really the only parents they know."

On our third visit to the governor, we made a deal. If we would move 100 miles from where we lived, the governor said we could adopt them. The theory was that this way the boys would not, in the future, run into their biological parents, who had been sent to the penitentiary for a long time.

Beverly and I didn't really need to discuss what to do.

We moved.

Of course we did.

We moved out of state with our little saplings, where they had better foster-care laws and a better educational system—where they could stay rooted with us.

It wasn't all peaches and cream. By the time we adopted the boys, Beverly delivered our birth son. We experienced many challenges, as do all parents, adoptive or not. We continued to be foster parents and had the privilege of taking care of fifty children in a period of about ten years. Those children gave us far more than we could ever give them. Some of the older ones are still in touch with us, and our fiftieth child, whom we call "our Golden Girl," still calls us Mom and Dad.

Stephen, now twenty-one, said "yes" to serving our country in the United States Army and has been in Iraq for almost a year now. Randall is twenty and works very hard as a young businessman. He works with a large tree service, and he also cuts and splits firewood to sell as the weather gets colder—quite fitting for transplanted saplings who found their roots and grew.

Dave Gorden

"Do you think he's letting his being
adopted go to his head?"

The Delivery Rooms

A happy family is but an earlier heaven.

Sir John Bowring

Until that night, the idea of a delivery room brought images of bright fluorescent lights, heart and fetal monitors surrounding a sterile white-sheeted metal bed, and a mask-clad medical team at the ready. How was I to know that it wasn't imperative for a mother awaiting the arrival of her children to have a doctor or midwife nearby to experience this rite of passage? I discovered that a well-equipped kitchen and an airport terminal would do just fine.

Our first child, Matthew, was born on a late fall morning after twelve hours of an exhaustive and difficult labor. The pushing, panting, waiting, and pushing-again dance of the final delivery process produced our baby. When the doctor held him up for me to see, red and squalling, I became an instant believer in miracles. Later, my focal point narrowed to the small bundle I cradled at my breast. A nurse wrapped us in heated covers and dimmed the lights. She left my husband,

Gregg, and me together in the delivery room to peer with awe at the new life we had created. Only then did I find the strength to marvel at the pain, the effort, the sheer joy of it all.

Six years later, in the middle of a long-awaited night in May, sleepless and alone, once again I found myself in the midst of the final delivery process. This time, instead of a noisy hospital room, I spent the hours before the delivery of our twins in restless agitation, pacing the rooms of our darkened home. The nesting instinct gripped me. I headed for the kitchen and gathered bowls and utensils from the cupboards.

The clock over the sink read 2:30 in the morning when the oven's timer beeped to announce the first batch of chocolate-chip cookies was baked to perfection. Whiffs of melted fudge and warm nuts scented the air. As I eased the tray from the open oven, the wonderful aroma of freshly baked dough swaddled me like a cozy blanket. A soft kitchen lamp cast a pool of light over the countertops, where the ingredients for my grandmother's recipe were spread out, enveloping me in a cocoon of warmth. Night shadows darkened the rest of the room. Restless and anxious, I crept across the wooden floor in stocking feet, careful not to awaken my sleeping husband or six-year-old son before it was time. While my fingers formed rounded spoonfuls of batter onto another tray, my thoughts flew through the night sky, over the ocean, and into the cabin of the red and white DC-10 that raced toward our home near Los Angeles, carrying our adopted babies from their birthplace halfway around the world to me.

While the last batch of cookies baked, I glanced once again at the clock, the second hand tick, tick, ticking methodically along at a painfully slow pace. I thumbed through my recipe card box, searching for the next culinary creation that would help make the time pass. In a few more hours, the long wait for this special delivery would be over. But it seemed that particular night would never end. I paused to study the latest pictures of Nicholas and Kimberly, which were propped against the teakettle. The social workers from Seoul, Korea, were kind to send us new ones for every month we waited. Staring at their tiny, precious faces, I knew there would be no rest for me until those babies were in my arms.

The jumbo Northwest airliner glistened in the noonday sun as it approached the runway at Los Angeles International Airport. All of the tension and emotions I held bottled up over the past two years through the international adoption process began to melt onto the terminal floor at my feet. I had pictured this scene hundreds of times, dreamed of it nightly, yet I wasn't prepared for the calm that descended over me as the final moments approached. From the restless and busy night I'd spent baking, I expected to be exhausted. Instead, my composure was matched only by my alert and keenly aware senses. With steady, shallow breaths, I pressed my fingertips against the cool, smooth terminal window glass. My world narrowed, moving in slow motion. The chatter and bustle surrounding me dimmed as my focus pinpointed only on the plane as it rolled to the gate.

My family made our way to the entrance where the babies would be carried to us after going through customs. I watched as passengers from Nicholas and Kimberly's flight walked through the tunnel and into the terminal. There were businessmen with briefcases, women with large bags, groups of students in festive moods, and parents holding the hands of their small children. Our babies were nowhere to be seen. My eyes burned from staring intently at so many people. I looked at the ground for a moment, and then blinked to clear the sting. I looked up again, and the social workers holding our children stood before me. Maybe I shouted out in a final release of pent-up tension, or maybe I acknowledged silently the instant relief of finally seeing my babies in person. I can't remember.

The women placed a baby each in Gregg's and my arms. We kissed them and kneeled to give Matthew a better view of his new brother and sister. We switched babies and exchanged a quick look of awe. The same feelings of peaceful contentment that engulfed me as I held Matthew for the first time in the hospital delivery room again swathed me like the warm blanket the nurse used to cover us after delivery. Gregg and I gathered our three children close for the first family picture.

Gregg drove cautiously out of the parking garage and headed for home. I couldn't help but compare the memory of the drive home from the hospital with our first baby, and how nervous and proud he was to get us there safely. I basked in the afterglow of relief and comfort of having our completed family together.

I'm fortunate to have experienced two delivery rooms, each a different process. Now, as a mother of three, the most important long-term job of my life has begun.

The labor was worth it.

Sarah Jo Smith

Reprinted by permission of Martha Campbell. © *2007 Martha Campbell.*

An Unexpected Christmas Gift

The heart of the giver makes the gift dear and precious.

Martin Luther

The sudden jangle of the telephone ringing brought Catherine back to the moment.

It was Saturday morning, December 23, 1939. The windows sparkled and the wooden floors gleamed, though the carpets were worn and the furniture was mismatched in the modest house. The Christmas tree in the living room was decorated with glass bulbs and paper streamers, and gifts wrapped in tissue paper encircled the tree like a festive wreath.

Before the phone interrupted her thoughts, Catherine had been thinking about how, just over a year ago, she had come as a new bride to this small prairie city. Her husband, a widower with one son, was dynamic, self-confident, and gregarious. Catherine was none of these things. She didn't make friends easily, but she did love this man and adored his young son.

She was washing the breakfast dishes when Harry

came into the kitchen and poured himself a cup of coffee from the percolator on the stove. She could tell by looking at him that he was disturbed by the phone conversation.

"A child was brought into the Children's Aid Society this morning. I am the only board member they've been able to contact today. The board has a policy not to place children into a private home at this time of the year as people have the 'Christmas Spirit,' and then don't really want to take on the responsibility of a child later in the year. I am not quite sure what we are going to do; she's only two, and our options are limited."

Catherine shook her head. How desperate and sad would someone have to be to give up a child two days before Christmas? A small child alone at Christmas . . . Catherine's mind swirled on. She felt a little scared of the ideas that were forming in her head. What would Harry think if she suggested they take her? How could she approach the subject? How would Ed feel? She had just started to get to know him. Should they introduce more change into his life?

"I'll go to the office with you," she said.

She was glad Ed was off playing with his cousins.

They bundled into their coats, gloves, boots, and hats, and headed off into the freezing temperatures, neither of them speaking, both caught up in their private thoughts.

Harry turned and surveyed the house they were leaving. Would another child fit in here? Could their family make this work? Could an exception be made to a rule at the Children's Aid Society? They didn't have a lot of money, but he did have a job. The whole world was in an uproar over Europe, and the future seemed dim. But a child alone at Christmas time didn't seem right. A child alone at any time didn't seem right.

They drove to downtown Winnipeg in silence, neither of them quite knowing how to approach the subject of a small child waiting alone in an office on a cold and snowy December morning.

Finally, Catherine began. "What are the rules around taking a child into your home?"

Harry repeated the policy to not place a child in a home during the Christmas season.

"Do you think they would make an exception in our case?" Catherine asked hesitantly.

"I was wondering the same thing," he replied with a smile. "But this is not a baby, Catherine. There is a good chance she may not have anything and may not have been treated well."

The building was cold and silent as they climbed the narrow staircase. Opening the door, Catherine saw the small child sitting ramrod straight and motionless on a chair. She was clothed in a green cotton dress, short mismatched socks, scuffed brown shoes, and a woman's wine-colored sweater with the sleeves rolled up like donuts around her tiny arms. Her black hair was cut unevenly across her brow, and she peered at their arrival with wide grey-blue eyes.

"See what you can do to make this work," Catherine said softly to her husband.

Harry went into the inner office and closed the door.

Catherine wasn't sure where to start. She said "Hello" to the small child as she took a seat two chairs away. She spoke softly as the little girl watched her intently, but did not move or say a word. Catherine started to talk about Christmas, but decided maybe that wasn't such a good idea because who knew where this little waif might be on Christmas morning.

Harry came out of the office fifteen minutes later, and

Catherine could tell by the way he moved that things had gone his way.

Her heart soared as she bent down to the small child and held out her hand. "We would like you to come home with us." The little girl grabbed her hand and hung on tightly. She still had not said a word.

Catherine's mind began to swirl again. How and what would they tell Ed? How should they tell everyone else? What were they going to do about clothes for this little thing? What about Christmas gifts?

"Harry, why don't you go into the butcher and get the turkey. I'll take her with me next door and see about some clothes. I have a little money left over from the groceries."

Catherine took the small child by the hand and walked with her into the store. She emerged shortly with packages and bags, the girl still clinging to her hand.

They headed to Harry's sister's place where Ed was playing. Ed was thrilled to have a sister, and the little girl warmed to his attention. Harry's sister donated a few items her girls had outgrown and a beautiful piece of blue velvet left over from a dress she'd made.

By the time they reached home, the little girl was exhausted. Catherine was pulling a meal together when the child put her head down on the table and fell asleep. Harry carried her to the sofa in the living room. They didn't want to put her upstairs alone when she didn't even know them.

Ed took on fixing up the spare room next to his, complete with soft toys. Harry took over calling his family and letting all of them know they had a new member. Catherine cleared away the kitchen items and went to the sewing machine.

On Christmas Eve, the family took their new daughter in her new dress to church. Harry announced to the congregation that they had adopted a daughter. By the end of the night, there was no room in Catherine and Harry's living room. Neighbors and friends dropped off gifts, food, and money, though the Depression had been hard on many of them and now a war in Europe was taking many of their sons and husbands.

Seventy years later, our children and grandchildren still love to hear the story of the unexpected Christmas gift, my sister's arrival into our family.

Ruth Curran

2

DISCOVERY

Through every rift of discovery some seeming anomaly drops out of the darkness and falls, as a golden link, into the great chain of order.

E. H. Chapin

Adoption of the Perfect Child

Every child born into this world is a new thought of God, an ever-fresh and radiant possibility.

Kate Douglas Wiggin

Could it be him? Counting back, it had been about two decades since I last cuddled him.

A young, blond, blue-eyed man with an ever-so-slight scar on his upper lip browsed through the shirt aisle, unaware of my scrutiny. My heart raced. Yes, it could be Scotty.

"Mom," he said. A middle-aged woman turned and smiled. My heart settled a little. Once I saw her face, I knew this wasn't the mother and son of twenty years before. But I smiled at the memory . . . of the perfect child who was rejected over and over until God sent him the perfect mother.

I was working in the Special Care Nursery as a night-charge nurse. After I scrubbed in, I entered the unit and glanced around. There was only one new baby since the previous day—a good-sized newborn, away from the others, wrapped in a blanket that concealed half his face. The powder-blue knit blanket indicated his gender. There was no name on his isolette.

I peeked into the warmer. What a gorgeous baby. He had thick, wavy blond hair, and his big blue eyes followed my gaze. He seemed more alert and observant than most newborns. His eyelashes were long and his eyes were expressive.

I pulled the blanket away from his face. Then I breathed deeply. Oh, no. Cleft lip. I tilted his head back a little and peered inside his mouth. Cleft palate, too. *Poor babe. There's surgeries ahead for you.* I stroked his cheek and smiled down at him.

In the report room, the day charge was edgy. I could tell she had had a rough shift. She quickly updated us on the babies who were there the night before, then the blond newborn. He was born that morning to a sixteen-year-old unwed mother, who was planning on an open adoption with a thirtyish professional couple. The couple had paid all her medical expenses, had even accompanied her on doctor's visits. They were selected from three couples that the teenager had interviewed. Now the adoptive parents wanted their money back. Their lawyer had pointed out that prenatally all medical tests were negative for aberrations. The ultrasound was read as normal.

"Do they realize it's just superficial?" I interjected.

"Tell me about it," the day charge said tensely. "His brain, vital organs, body, and movements are normal. He's got a dynamite personality—you can tell by those expressive eyes."

"Everybody wants the perfect child," one of my colleagues said with a sigh.

"Did the doctor tell the adoptive parents that his condition is mostly cosmetic? That after a series of operations and possibly speech therapy, these kids are normal, and live healthy and productive lives?"

"Yes, but the couple made it clear they want a perfect child now, not later," the day charge said wearily. "To them, that baby is defective merchandise."

"But that's the adoptive parent's right," another colleague said. "They expected a perfect child, and the perfect child was not delivered."

I groaned. "Geez. Rejected solely because of looks. What is his name?"

The day nurse looked to me with sad eyes. "He hasn't got one. The teenager doesn't want him, never bonded during pregnancy. Poor girl actively detached knowing he was going up for adoption. Says she wishes she had aborted and saved herself and her family a lot of pain and suffering. Now her parents are trying to come up with the money to reimburse the intended adoptive parents so they won't be sued. The baby has no one. To me, he looks like a Scotty."

That's good enough for me. I wrote down his name. "What about the other two couples?"

"They will be visiting tomorrow," the charge nurse said. "But the doctor reported that neither couple is keen on a special-needs child."

I shook my head. "Hardly a special-needs. Surgeons are so good at it now that a cosmetic repair is barely noticeable."

Even though Scotty had a healthy appetite and tried his hardest to suck on a specially designed nipple, he failed. Sloppy sucking endangered him to pulmonary aspiration and choking, so he had to be gavage-fed. A thin, flexible tube was placed from mouth to stomach for formula feedings.

Day two of life, Scotty was moved to a crib. He was also rejected by a second couple. Twenty-four hours later, the third couple decided against adopting Scotty, too.

The day-charge nurse purchased a front-pack infant carrier, and we carried and cuddled Scotty during rounds. Though his time with us would be short, we wanted to convey to this tiny spirit that not everyone rejected him.

On day three of life, his teenage birth mother went home. The next day, Scotty would be going to a foster home. A plastic surgeon visited and suggested that Scotty's lip be closed in a month or so, when he reached ten pounds. The palate would be fused later, between eighteen and thirty-six months of age. He questioned if Scotty had become a ward of the state, and who he should bill for the surgeries.

"I don't know," I said, hugging Scotty against my chest. Then I prayed for this little bundle from God.

About midnight on day three, as I was tube feeding a growing preemie, I heard someone scrubbing in at the sink near the nursery entrance. I turned to see a nurse in a white uniform slipping on a protective gown over her clothes. She didn't look familiar.

"Can I help you?" I asked. No outside personnel are allowed in the nursery without permission or notice. Any nurse knows that. I was on heightened alert.

"I'm looking for—oh, there he is!" she said, walking straight over to Scotty's crib. She picked him up, kissed him on the forehead, and cradled him in her arms. "Here's my boy. I have been waiting so long for you!"

"I'm sorry," I began, "but I haven't been given notice of you coming. I'll have to call security. . . ."

"Please don't," she said with a nasal tone to her voice. Then she looked up at me and smiled a crooked smile. I immediately saw the telltale marks of restorative surgery for a cleft lip. The tone of her speech suggested cleft-palate repair as well. "You see, I dreamed of a blond son with beautiful blue eyes and clefts . . . but my girl and boy were born normal."

"How did you know about Scotty?" I asked.

"The whole hospital knows about Scotty," she said softly. "After I heard yesterday, I went home and had the same dream again. Then, I talked to my husband, and he agreed for me to visit. Now that I hold him, I know . . . we're going to adopt Scotty. And I think we'll keep his name."

I washed my hands in silence.

"Is he able to suck from a bottle?"

I shook my head.

"That's okay," the nurse said, her eyes fixed on Scotty's. "My whole family knows how to tube feed." Speaking to Scotty, she said, "My mom, your grandma, did it to me for months. Just wait until she sees you!"

Then she looked at her watch. "Oh, I have to get back to ICU. I'll be back at the end of the shift. I'll talk to the day-charge nurse and get my husband and lawyer in here. I'm so excited! Molly and Paul will be thrilled to have a baby brother."

I watched as she kissed Scotty once more and then gently placed him back in the crib. She pulled off her protective gown and headed to the nursery door. "God sent him to me," she said with a beaming smile.

"Yes," I said softly in agreement. "And he sent you for Scotty."

Diana M. Amadeo

A Window into Heaven

Children are God's apostles, sent forth day by day to preach of love and hope and peace.

J. R. Lowell

After being married twelve years, we had two healthy, happy boys and were living a very blessed life. Adopting a child or expanding our family were not goals, but as fate would have it, we became aware of a baby girl whose parents were going through a series of struggles. We could not bear to see this beautiful baby go into the foster-care system, so we agreed to take her into our home.

The situation with her family only lasted six weeks before she could return home. However, after she left our home, it awakened a void in us that was very difficult to overcome. Eventually, this void led us to become a licensed foster family to provide a home full of love for children who needed extra help.

While we made this journey to become licensed foster parents, another little soul was making a journey of a different kind at roughly the same time. His mom had many demons she had battled throughout her life. As she traveled her troubled path, obstacles kept her from being the best mom she could be. She entered a hospital and gave birth to a five-pound baby boy four weeks before her due date. And to add yet one more challenge to her already complicated life, he had Down syndrome.

Our paths crossed one Tuesday morning when Michelle was out shopping, and she received a call from our foster placement worker. Melissa asked if we were ready for our first placement. She said she had a Native American newborn boy with Down syndrome who needed an emergency placement for two to three weeks. Michelle wrote down all the details, hung up, and called me to see if I agreed that we could help him. While we had discussed Down syndrome and how to be prepared for it when pregnant with our biological children, we did not receive special-needs training in our foster-parent classes. Nonetheless, we felt we could meet this challenge until an adoptive family was found for him. At 10:30 AM, Michelle called Melissa back to let her know we would love to take him into our home. Melissa gave her the final details, including the fact that he was being discharged at 1:00 PM, and we would need to pick him up at the hospital. That gave us two-and-a-half hours to prepare for what we took nine months to do the last time! Michelle made a quick U-turn from the checkout line and went back to the baby department to load up on all the necessary supplies.

Giving birth to your own child at the hospital and taking him or her home is an amazing experience; going to the hospital to pick up another infant to bring home is surreal. After the journey to find the NICU ward, we were introduced to this little peanut of a baby named Raymond who weighed barely five pounds, and had jet-black hair and the face of an angel. The discharge process seemed to drag on and on, and after ninety minutes of waiting, we finally asked the nurse what else we needed to do to be on our way. She curtly stated, "I will let you take *my* baby when I am ready." We discovered that she had cared for him for three straight days and had formed a deep bond. Already we could see that this baby touched people's lives and hearts at barely five days old.

The next three weeks stretched into months as the state worked through various processes and steps to get Raymond legally prepared for adoption. We did not mind at all. Our entire family adored Raymond from the day he came home with us. As he grew older and became more aware of his surroundings, we noticed that he had a gift. He could sense when people needed special attention. A visit to the grocery store with him in the cart would not go by without at least one or two random hugs for a cashier or other customer. They almost always responded, "I needed a hug today," and frequently teared up. Raymond was a little window into heaven for many people everywhere we went.

The three-week placement turned into seven months before we finally got a call from a new social worker in charge of getting Raymond adopted. After brief introductions, she didn't even ask anything about Raymond, but questioned, "So what is wrong with this baby, anyway?"

Our family had worked really hard to keep some distance in our relationship with Raymond because we knew he would have to leave, and we wanted to minimize our heartbreak. But this type of question seemed uncalled for, and Michelle did not mince any words, "Raymond is perfect, just as God made him!" After Michelle's response, the social worker paused and asked in the kindest voice, "Then why aren't you adopting him?"

I have worked with a lot of good salespeople and sales trainers in my profession, and this was the best sales technique I had ever seen. We had not thought of adoption as an option. We were foster parents; we were taught not to think that way. Our mantra since Raymond had come to live with us was, "God placed him with us for a little while until the right family who needed him was identified."

As it turned out, we needed him.

Michelle and I talked and quickly made a life-changing decision with long-term ramifications for our family. We looked at each other and both realized that our hearts had already made the decision long before it was asked of us today. He was ours. It may have taken this phone call to wake us up to the fact, but the outcome was obvious. He was and had been our little boy all along, and nothing else mattered.

That night at dinner, Michelle and I were so excited to tell our two boys about our decision. When we finally just blurted it out, expecting them to be as excited as we were, their response was, "Well, duh, we already knew that. It just took you two longer to figure it out!"

On National Adoption Day 2003, Raymond became a permanent part of our family. We celebrated with almost a hundred people in our back yard who had supported us through this entire process. Raymond was dressed in a tuxedo and hugged and hammed it up all day long.

And everyone who came will tell you that at some level Raymond has shown them a window into heaven.

Michelle and Stacy Tetschner

A Child Like Me?

With saddened eyes and head bent low,
It's damaged goods most see.
With my unclear past and broken heart,
Who would want a child like me?

I watch her walk into the room.
From a distance I can see.
But dare I take a closer step?
Who would want a child like me?

And then I see her look my way.
She smiles so tenderly.
But do I even dare to dream,
She would want a child like me?

And then, as if I spoke out loud,
She approaches cautiously.
I try so hard to once believe,
She will want a child like me.

But dare I once let down my guard,
And trust that she will see,

Hiding beneath this old stained shirt,
Is a beautiful child like me?

My smile, they say, lights up a room.
I'll be good as good can be.
Oh, please, dear God, let her want
A special child like me.

I feel her hand reach out for mine,
And within her eyes I see,
A single, tiny, shining tear.
Could she want a child like me?

And when she takes me in her arms,
With a warmth so pure and new,
She says the words I've prayed to hear,
"The child I want is *you*."

Lisa J. Schlitt

The Postman

Man proposes, but God disposes.

Thomas à Kempis

"Beep, beep, beep." The sounds the phone made as I pressed the numbers monitored my terrified heart. I tried to breathe and calm my wild pulse. This was the phone call I had waited for all my life.

I always knew I was adopted. The fact never bothered me a bit, though some of my friends seemed distressed. One day in sixth grade, a pesky boy stumbled around at lunch until he finally blurted out, "Were you, uh, formed, or were you adopted?"

I'm sure I gave him a strange look. "Adopted." I started to point out that my parents had chosen me, but I stopped. I didn't want him to wonder if his parents felt stuck with him when he was born, so I kept my mouth shut.

As comfortable as I was in my adopted family, I knew who made my good life possible.

One Thanksgiving, when I was a little girl, my mother, grandmother, and aunts all sat in the kitchen making stuffing while the men watched TV and told jokes. The house pulsed with laughter and the footfalls of running kids. The smell of roasting turkey and pumpkin pie made us all a little drunk. I sent my cousins outside to play tag among the apple trees.

"I'll be out in a minute to write the scavenger hunt," I said.

But first I needed a moment to myself. I crept up the stairs, sat on the landing, and leaned my head on the banister like I did at every holiday. I closed my eyes hard and prayed. "God, please tell my 'real' mother, 'Thank you.'"

I knew that the God who made orchards and grandparents and Christmas could do anything—and that included sending telepathic messages to my mother.

"Thank you," I repeated, and shot a smile heavenward as I ran outside to play.

When I got older, I became fascinated with genetics. I began to wonder where I got my love of books, and if anyone else preferred the woods to Coney Island. I could see that my cousin Robbie looked just like Uncle Dick, and my dad loved music, just like Grandma. I wondered if anyone stuck out her lip like I did when I was thinking, or where I got my crooked middle finger. I felt like Melchizedek, the priest in the Old Testament, who appeared out of nowhere.

On TV, I examined Miss Universe contestants, looking for one who mirrored me. My husband said that my crinkly eyes and Slavic cheekbones made me Manchurian Polish. "Genghis Khan swept through Eastern Europe, you know." I wondered if that mixture was a possibility.

I finally found some faces that looked like mine—in my children. The next many years were full of dinner and soccer and homework, and I thought a bit less often of my birth family. The crazy days of full-time motherhood ended when my youngest child left for her senior year as an exchange student in Germany. Because I planned to visit her at Christmas, I needed a passport. I looked for my birth certificate and realized I had lost it. I phoned the Bureau of Vital Statistics in my home state to apply for a duplicate. The clerk on the phone told me to send a check, but then she said, "It says here you're adopted. You'll have to write to the Capitol."

I wrote down the address.

"By the way," she added, "those records are open now; you can get a copy if you like."

If I liked?

The packet came a couple of weeks later. I looked at the names on the papers and marveled that I belonged to people I didn't even know. I looked up my birth parents' hometowns in an atlas. They were from small adjoining towns in the South. I was stunned that I could have a history I didn't even know about. The papers sat on my dresser for weeks while I considered my options. Fear balanced my eagerness to find them. *What if my parents didn't want me? What if they had moved on and shut the door on the past?* As I wrestled with the decision of whether or not to pursue them, I remembered a concept my kids had learned in the DARE program at school. *When you're afraid to do something, you calculate the risk, and if the potential gain of an action is greater than the potential loss, then the risk is reasonable.* Good advice.

I digested this kid-wisdom until my birthday. I was off work that day, and I finally picked up the dusty adoption papers on my dresser. I called Directory Assistance in my mother's hometown. The operator gave me the listings for people with my mother's maiden name. I was sure that by now she was married, but thought I might find a relative who knew where she was.

Relying on my gift of chatter, I called the first number on the list. I tried to sound bouncy so I wouldn't scare her off. "I know this is a weird phone call," I said to the woman who answered, "but I'm looking for someone who used to be named Mary Jean Walker. She did a favor for my parents a really long time ago, and I just really wanted to thank her."

An ice age crept by before the woman said, "Well, Mary Jean's my daughter, and she's at work. Do you want the number?"

I jotted down the number and thanked her. *My grandmother!*

I handled the paper as if it were nitroglycerin, afraid of what it could do to me. The time had come to compose the most important words of my writer's life. Don't ask for anything, I decided. "No" was too easy to say, and too final. I wrote a couple dozen drafts of my opening sentence and discarded each one. A pile of papers littered the floor by the wastebasket. Finally, I remembered the message I had prayed on the stairs as a child.

I grabbed the phone. "Beep, beep, beep, beep." My heart jumped with each ring.

"Hello, Mary Jean," I said. "Today is my fortieth birthday, and I just want to thank you for that."

I heard a gasp, and then my birth mother said, "I was just thinking about you."

And so it was that God, the Great Postman, saved my messages for all those years and let me deliver them myself.

Kim Toms

Julia

The Lord replied, "I have forgiven them, as you asked."

Numbers 14:20

It was such a long time ago . . . over twenty-five years. But what choice did I have? I was a young college freshman, and I saw no way out. I pretended it was an easy decision and convinced myself there was no other choice.

The people at the clinic presented a detached and impersonal description of the options, but their bias was clear, and at the time, reassuring.

"You've made the right decision," the counselor told me. "You are too young to be a mother, and you have your entire college career and life ahead of you."

I nodded and rubbed my belly, which hid the secret I held close inside.

"Products of conception" was the term they used to refer to the tiny life established in my womb. Not a baby, but products of conception.

"You could also consider adoption," the counselor

continued, almost as an afterthought, reading off a checklist of required information.

I shook my head. "Oh, no, I could never give my baby away." But I could snuff out a life when it was only a clump of cells. The idea of a short procedure to uncomplicate my life and allow me to continue my Ivy League school education was the only option.

At first, I was defiant in justifying my decision. It was the late seventies. Women everywhere told me it was my right to manage my body. But in time, I knew that it hadn't been just my body. The loss of a lost and discarded life started to smolder inside me, burning a hole, a deep abyss of emptiness inside my heart and soul.

Every June, when the baby that never was, whom I named Julia, would have been born, I noticed children who would be her age and asked myself a hundred unanswerable questions. What would she have looked like? Would she have had dark hair like me? Would she have dressed in bows and frills, parading around in party shoes, or would she have been a tomboy, swinging upside down from tree branches and clamoring with abandon on the jungle gym? Would she have loved me? I loved her. . . .

The years passed, and I buried milestones of her unlived life deep inside me. Off to kindergarten . . . a toothless grin . . . elementary school . . . piano recitals . . . junior high . . . the prom . . . graduation . . . college . . . and perhaps by now married and a mother herself. But I was ashamed . . . so ashamed. And the burden of shame grew heavier and heavier. It was like a rock too heavy to carry. And, oh, how I tried to cast it off! I tried to prevent the secret from consuming me, but denial, justification, shame, guilt, and self-condemnation encased me like a cocoon, holding me captive.

I married my college sweetheart, and we settled into

a normal life. We started our family right away and had two sons within three years. The following years were busy. My husband completed medical school, and I worked with expectant families as a childbirth educator.

When my husband finished his medical residency, we knew we wanted another child, and I assumed I would get pregnant right away. But we were dealt a hand of secondary infertility and pregnancy loss. My work as a childbirth educator seemed like a cruel joke. I was certain my miscarriage and infertility were punishment for the abortion I had.

But a greater master plan would unfold. Five years after embarking on the journey of infertility, my husband and I adopted a baby girl from Vietnam. I knew she had been specifically placed in our family; her birthday was the same date as the anniversary of Julia's death.

But forgiveness was elusive. In my heart, I knew God had forgiven me, but a battle continued to rage inside me. Could I forgive myself? I struggled with the difference between forgiving and forgetting. I knew I would never forget, but I also knew I had to forgive myself and discard the cloak of shame I had worn for so many years. I yearned for one more tangible demonstration of forgiveness.

About three years after we brought our daughter home from Vietnam, I received an unexpected phone call from my high-school boyfriend, Julia's father. He periodically traveled to my community on business, and we met for lunch. I yearned to discover if he had any lingering thoughts about that fall afternoon and the life-altering decisions we made.

"Do you remember the date?" I asked.

"No, just that it was the fall of our freshman year." And we both were quiet for an instant, as if lost in a time warp, struggling to separate past emotions and decisions from the lives we now both led.

"I have to tell you," I continued, and I paused, "it's quite remarkable, really. It was November fifteenth, and that's my daughter's birthday."

His eyes locked with mine and he said quietly, "I have a daughter born on the same day."

At that instant, the lingering shame evaporated as I experienced the evidence of grace and forgiveness through the intersection of one date and three unique, yet connected children's lives.

Finally relieved of grief and shame, I fully celebrated the life-giving gift of adoption.

Kathy Pride

A Gentle Morning Mist

After years of unsuccessful adoption attempts, I came upon an ad in an adoption magazine stating that parents were needed for Vietnamese children. I called and said, "I'm old, I'm poor, and I'm Jewish. My husband is even older, has no religion, but he does have four children from a previous marriage, which means he is also divorced. We live at the end of a four-wheel-drive road in Canada. I have an outhouse and a nose ring. Can I adopt?"

The woman at the other end of the line seemed undaunted. None of it mattered as long as we had a valid home study.

Late one Thursday afternoon a year later, another voice at the end of a phone line said, "Congratulations, Ms. Friedman. You'll be going to get your daughter on Saturday."

All the questlike fairy-tale waiting and proving ourselves was over. Now panic set in. I woke, sitting bolt upright that midnight, saying, "Dear God, what have I done? I'll be removing a child from a country that has already had so much taken from it and transplanting her."

Three days later, on December 6, 1998, we arose in
Hanoi at 4:00 AM and drove over potholes for five-and-
a-half jolting hours to Halong Bay, the region of our
daughter's birth.

The next morning, I walked up the stairs of the
orphanage, along with other waiting parents, and saw
my four-month-old daughter sleeping in her nounou's
(foster mother's) arms. "Thuy Yen?" I tentatively asked,
mispronouncing my daughter's Vietnamese name. The
nounou nodded, and with tear-filled eyes—mine happy,
hers sad—we waited for my daughter to wake up.

After an afternoon of paperwork and shifting the
children from the nounous to their new parents, we
began on the long, bumpy road to Hanoi and parenthood. When I got her to smile for the first time, my
heart grew larger than I'd ever known possible.

Once settled back home on our west coast island, I
called my local multicultural association to learn more
about the culture, food, and holidays of Vietnam. We left
home often so Shaina could grow up knowing other Jews,
adoptees, and Vietnamese people. But on our little island,
Shaina remained unique—the only Jewish Vietnamese
rural adoptee. When she began speaking, one of the earli-
est greetings she learned was not, "How are you?" or
"What's your name?" but, "Where are you from?"

When she entered kindergarten, the fairies decorat-
ing all of Shaina's classroom walls were uniformly
Anglo-Saxon and white-skinned. When I pointed this
oversight out to the teacher, she said, "I've never
thought of it before, and no one ever brought the issue
up." This exchange was one of my first inklings that
Shaina would need something more if I wanted her to
have a strong sense of identity. I wondered what she
saw when she looked in the mirror, and the face
reflected back was so unlike any around her. She began

turning to me and saying, "You're just my fake mother, you know. I don't have to obey you."

I'd given her rituals from my Jewish background and exposure to hers. We celebrated Chanukah and Tet. She had an idyllic Canadian setting to grow in, but I felt Shaina required a return to Vietnam where she could absorb the language, culture, mores and morals, sights and smells of her heritage. And where I could allay some of the guilty feelings I had about taking her from her "roots."

When our child was eight years old, we returned to live in Hanoi in a primarily Vietnamese neighborhood where a Western face was rare. Shaina turned to me at one point and said, "Mom, dye your hair black. It's embarrassing to be seen with a westerner."

A translator took us for our visit to Shaina's foster mother. A part of me dreaded seeing her again. She was young and beautiful, and I'd half-convinced myself that my daughter would view her as the fairy god-mother foil to my wicked witch! But I believed it would answer many questions for my daughter, and I was very excited about the reunion.

Not so for my daughter. An excruciating slice of reality TV occurred when her foster mother tearfully knelt and attempted to gather Shaina in her arms. Shaina, terrified, grabbed at me, saying, "Get me away from her!" This behavior only heightened as we all boarded a boat for a day-long tour of Halong Bay. Our visit, while not in vain, was not the happy reunion I had envisaged.

Shaina did grow adept with chopsticks, absolutely loved the food, learned some of the language, mingled in the pandemonium on the streets, and became con-versant with several aspects of cultural behavior. But in a school where she now looked like everyone else, her body language, sense of entitlement, and outgoing behavior bespoke of a life that was not Vietnamese, but Canadian.

My daughter, Shaina Thuy Yen Friedman, looked at me one day and said, pointing to her face, "Mom, this part of me is Vietnamese." She pointed to her heart. "This part of me is Canadian," and as an afterthought, she said, "and part is Jewish." In so doing, she resolved many of my fears that I wasn't providing enough access to all that I'd removed her from or that she wasn't feeling integrated enough in all that I'd placed her in.

Near the end of our stay in Vietnam, I suggested to Shaina that we put an ad in the newspaper searching for her unknown birth mother. This touched off feelings of fear in me, but I was convinced that I had to give her all the opportunities I could to know her past even if it meant her becoming discontent with her present.

"You do that if you want to, but don't involve me," she said.

"But you might be curious to know what your birth family is like."

"Mom, think about it. They would be nothing but strangers to me. You're my mother now."

Consumed with tender and warm feelings, I recalled the meaning I'd been given for her Vietnamese name Thuy Yen—gentle morning mist.

Finally, worries I'd entertained that she was harboring some subterranean desire for or fantasies of her magical perfect birth family were put to rest. Like dew on leaves, they might re-emerge in a new morning, but for now they had evaporated in the strong bright sun of my daughter's love.

Renée Friedman

Matching

Out of the mouths of babes and sucklings hast thou ordained strength.

Psalm 8:2

Our daughter was adopted from China in 2000 at age thirteen months. We have always been open about her story, and that differences—skin color, eye color, language, being a leftie or rightie—make us who we are today.

When she was two-and-a-half years old, we talked while playing on the swing set. She looked at me with her big black eyes and said, "Momma, our faces don't match, but our hearts do."

My eyes welled with tears to think she had gotten the message that love has no color, language, or age differences as long as your hearts match each other's.

Kim McKinney

My Headbangin' Ethiopian Sons

It is in learning music that many youthful hearts learn to love.

Dominique Ricard

On the way home from picking up tapeworm medication at the pharmacy, I discovered that our newly adopted Ethiopian sons were headbangers. I was at a four-way stop trying to figure out whose turn it was to go, when I noticed the back of the van shaking like an uneven load of wash about to abort its cycle.

Looking in the side mirror at the rear of the van, I saw my sons Yakob, then two years old, and Ayalkbet, three, kicking their legs and flailing their arms in the back seat.

They were jamming to Bruce Springsteen's "Born in the U. S. A."

To my amazement, Ayalkbet was singing the song word for word. I pondered the implications of this. He'd only been home for three weeks and had memorized a song in English, with no idea what the words meant.

The thumping in the back seat grew louder. I was afraid they were going to eject from their car seats. When they noticed me looking, they increased their frenzy. From that moment on, music became our bridge.

Ayalkbet has a penchant for John Mellencamp and Pearl Jam. He loves the song, "You Make Me Feel Like a Natural Woman" by Carol King. Yakob loves Janis Joplin and the Rolling Stones, but Marvin Gaye takes him someplace else. The first time I played his CD, Yakob's eyes became two beacons of light, like those cast from lighthouses into a foggy sky, and he started grooving. The boy has soul.

When our sons came home, we spent a lot of time in the car together going to medical appointments, shopping for clothes, and so on. Being frazzled at the time, I didn't rotate the six CDs in the van for months, and those songs became big hits with the boys.

Their first concert was the Temptations. We happened to be on vacation in Sedona, Arizona, and were outdoors watching under a star-filled sky. The boys were on their feet for the whole show and danced with another little boy wearing a cowboy hat.

We caught John Mellencamp at Indiana University's Assembly Hall in Bloomington where we live. During the opening act, the boys chanted, "We want Mellencamp. We want Mellencamp." When he finally took the stage, after a spilled drink and much anticipation, the boys' faces lit up, and they danced vigorously the rest of the evening.

Despite the fun we were having, or perhaps because of it, my inner-censoring parent checked in—the same kind that fifty years ago might have thought listening to Elvis was sinful. So I brought home John Lithgow's children's book, *Marsupial Sue*. I read the story, and it went over okay, but when I played the accompanying

CD of Lithgow singing the story, the boys looked at me like I said it was time for a nap.

Worried that I had created a monster, and also curious about the amazing proficiency of the boys' verbal skills, I met with a professor of linguistics and faculty member in the university's African Studies Program. He was a native of Ghana who has watched his own children become Americanized. He assured me that I was not a bad mom because the boys had traded in their native language, Amharic, for modern rock, and that every individual has his own blueprint for language.

I explained to him that my husband, Rick, and I were torn about seeing the boys' native language dissolve. Anticipating that before they came home, we researched the pronunciations for around forty fundamental words. Some of them include mother—enat; father—abbot; to drink—metatat; to be hungry— merab; toilet—shent bet; bath—gala. Rick and I looked for resources that could help our boys retain and build their native language. We contacted universities and churches, and met people at the local Ethiopian restaurant. We bought some Amharic language software. In the end, however, we decided it wasn't practical to attempt raising the boys as bilingual since my husband and I don't speak Amharic. The professor explained, "If the question is are you doing them a service or a disservice, there is no right answer." He also pointed out that children identify with their peers, and that they want to do what their friends are doing. The key in the end, he said, is to "maintain your identity, and know and recognize other identities."

Two years after the Springsteen incident, I was driving, and we were jamming so hard to the Beastie Boys that people were staring. I didn't care. At that moment, nothing could touch us.

Music is a different experience for me now that Yakob and Ayalkbet have rocked my world. The night of their homecoming, I offered them *Sorene,* a compilation of Ethiopian children's songs, but I quickly discovered that they wanted rock and roll or whatever was growing stale in my CD player.

Music accelerated their learning a foreign language and became a touchstone in our family. When all else fails, we know we can dance.

But now the inevitable is happening. We have a new van with headphones in the back, and Ayalkbet, the oldest, controls the stations while they both listen. I hear them converse about the selections.

"Did you like that one?"

"No."

"Me either."

"I hope they play *'Soak up the Sun.'*"

Colleen Wells

A version of this story appeared in Adopted Families magazine and was first published in NUVO Newsweekly

Lists

The significance of a man is not what he attains, but rather in what he longs to attain.

Kahlil Gibran

When I was in college, I wanted a lot out of life. I wanted to be rich and famous, with a beautiful wife and a really cool motorcycle. But, surprisingly enough, even at that early age, what I wanted most was to be a father. I had recently reconciled with my own dad, and I began to think about the kind of father I would be.

I dated quite a bit in my twenties and spent time with some great women. And while some relationships lasted longer than others, it was all part of the grand audition. My brother Doug called it "trying on hats." While some wondered why I wasn't settling down, Doug knew that I was looking for my future wife and the mother of my children, and that I wasn't going to settle for one who didn't fit.

At some point, most of us begin to compile a mental list of things we want to do, acquire, or be in our lives. Making the list is one thing, but it's quite another thing

to find yourself, years later, checking things off, elimi-
nating items, adding new ones, and ultimately, facing
your own mortality. My list included many of the
typical things a healthy young man is looking for in
regards to attractiveness, and so on, and it also listed
characteristics of the Do Not Date list, including chain
smokers, "psycho chicks," druggies, and the hygieni-
cally challenged.

My list also included some deal-breakers in a relationship. For me, kids were a deal-breaker. I was once
in a relationship with a wonderful woman who didn't
see herself having children. I truly loved her and
wanted to spend my life with her, but I needed to be a
father. While I desperately wanted kids, my Do Not
Date list also included women with kids from some
other guy. I wanted kids of my own. I didn't want the
baggage that came from her previous relationship and
a lifelong connection to the "ex." I could just imagine
the future teenager yelling, "You're not my dad! You
can't tell me what to do!" It was a nightmare in the
making that I just wasn't going to sign up for.

So I thought I had it all mapped out, but I didn't
anticipate falling in love with a certain young lady. She
was smart, funny, and affectionate. We spent hours
together reading, taking walks, and watching TV. She
was everything I'd always wanted, and I couldn't imagine not having her in my life.

Despite my early reservations, we started spending
more and more time together, and she often fell asleep
in my arms. Then something wonderful and unexpected happened. I fell in love with—and married—her
mother.

David Avrin

At the Kitchen Table

Whoever perseveres will be crowned.

Johann Gottfried von Herder

It was silent in the house, except for the clicking of the keyboard. My husband and daughter were sleeping soundly, something that I couldn't seem to do anymore. My body was exhausted, but my mind just couldn't rest, and so many nights I found myself sitting in front of my computer.

I wish I could recall what led me to type in the words "International Adoption" one night while searching the Internet. I didn't know anyone adopting or even having a baby, but that moment seemed to light a fire.

"What would you think about adopting a child from overseas?" I asked my husband one Saturday morning at breakfast.

His pause, raised eyebrows, and smile were all I needed to fan the flames.

I dove back into the Internet, and soon discovered there were so many children needing families. One overwhelming night, I leaned back in my chair and closed my eyes. It was then that I saw them . . . a split-second snapshot of two little children . . . a toddler boy and a preschool-aged girl . . . seated with our daughter at our kitchen table. They were dark-skinned with wavy hair and large eyes. Although I only saw them for a moment, I felt I knew them. The little boy was filled with love . . . so giving and loving. The little girl had amazing determination. She was a fighter and worldly beyond her years. Then, as quickly as they had appeared, they were gone.

Night after night, I searched the Internet for children who had the same physical characteristics, until I eventually stumbled upon Cambodia. I had found the country. Now I needed to find the children.

We immediately filed a request to adopt from Cambodia. Two weeks later, everything came to a screeching halt when allegations of corrupt practices by adoption facilitators in Cambodia surfaced. The U.S. government shut down adoptions to investigate.

I petitioned to let us proceed with our adoption since we were not using a facilitator, but the government refused to consider our case. I was told that there was no foreseeable end to the investigation. It could be years. I was wasting my time. We should find another country.

I did the only thing I could. Against their advice, I boarded a plane bound for Cambodia. With nothing but my faith and an English-speaking taxi driver, I set out to find my children.

After visiting thirteen orphanages, I had not found the little boy or the little girl from my dream.

Then one day, a missionary couple invited me to join them at an orphanage where they were working. There was something different about this place. While there were no toddlers or preschool-age children, there was a nursery of babies.

Knowing that orphanage babies tend to cry when they come face-to-face with foreigners, I tried to keep my eyes averted, but I couldn't help but notice one little boy sitting silently in his crib, looking at me peacefully. I glanced at him quickly, fully expecting a barrage of tears, but instead I found him staring at me. Our eyes locked, and in that instant, I heard in my mind, *You know him . . . you know this child.* The expression on his face seemed to be saying the same thing. I know her.

I was searching for a toddler, but as time and travel continued, I found I could not get this baby boy out of my mind. As my trip came to a close, the thought of leaving him behind in the orphanage, and the fact that I had still not found our daughter, weighed heavily on my heart.

If I was unsettled before my first trip to Cambodia, it doubled in intensity after I returned home. The pull to return to Cambodia was so strong that three months later, I was back on the airplane with plans to visit twenty-three more orphanages, even though adoptions still were not approved. I had to find our daughter. This was no longer a controlled fire . . . it was a raging inferno that could not be contained.

As soon as I arrived in Cambodia, I returned to visit the baby boy. He recognized me immediately and held his arms up for me to pick him up. There was no longer any doubt in my mind that he was our son, but twenty-three orphanages later, there was still no sign of our daughter.

Just days before I was to leave Cambodia, I was visiting our son when a staff worker mentioned a small facility nearby where orphaned children were brought from the provinces to be closer to medical care.

That afternoon I visited the facility and asked about the children living there. I was shown photos of several little girls, but none of them were my daughter. I had just about given up hope when I was shown one last photograph of a little girl they believed to be only eighteen months old due to her size. When they brought her to me, she was expressionless, her eyes encrusted and swollen with infection. I sat her on my lap and she stared into my eyes, never saying a word, but speaking volumes to my heart. I could see a strength in her that was unmistakable, but as she looked pleadingly into my eyes, we both knew that I had found her just in the nick of time.

Sitting on my bed that night, I knew I had found our daughter. I called my husband. "The search is over. I found our children, but it's bittersweet. I have no idea if or when we'll ever be able to bring them home."

With a weary and heavy heart, I arrived back in the United States two days later.

The following day, we received a registered letter informing us that we were to be included in a new special humanitarian initiative that would enable us to complete our adoption!

Thirteen months later, our son and daughter—the exact toddler and preschooler I'd seen in my dream—finally took their places at the kitchen table.

Elizabeth Mallory

"How long have you been circling to land?"

My Mission of Hope

Never doubt that a small group of committed citizens can change the world. Indeed, it is the only thing that ever has.

Margaret Mead

When I was in my late teens, a young priest told me about Mother Teresa, the nun who was working with the "poorest of the poor" in India, and I longed to do something meaningful with my life.

After I married, I began taking evening classes at a local community college. I started with psychology classes, then took a course that was ostensibly sociology but focused very much on the war in Vietnam. I invested a semester of hard work, earning an "A" in that class, as I did in most classes, but I took away far more than a good grade.

I soon became active in antiwar demonstrations and in the presidential campaigns of antiwar candidates. I read everything I could, trying to make some sense of America's involvement in Vietnam—but the more I read, the less I understood it.

By this time, I had two children and was pregnant with my third. Education and motherhood became my equal passions. I continued to enroll in classes and ultimately completed my nursing degree.

Meanwhile, the war in Vietnam dragged on. I felt helpless, fighting for a cause that most people didn't seem to care about. Gradually, the thought struck me that perhaps I could make a single, small contribution by making a difference in the life of one person. Recalling a magazine article I had read about the plight of poor, unwanted children in Vietnam, I asked my husband how he would feel about adopting one of them.

We not only adopted one child, but applied for adoption of a second and third. When the process ground to a halt, it seemed the children would never be released to us. After several frustrating months of waiting, I decided to go to Vietnam and attempt to untangle the paperwork.

Arriving there in November 1973, I was immediately enthralled by this amazingly vibrant country and its people. On my second day, I was invited to work with a nurse at the To Am ("warm nest") Nursery, founded by Rosemary Taylor, an Australian social worker who had been working in Vietnam since 1967. That evening I was greeted warmly by Elaine Norris, a volunteer American nurse.

Elaine was obviously exhausted. The influx of orphaned and abandoned children was increasing daily, and this center was overflowing. They had no more room inside and were accommodating the extra babies wherever they could, even outside on the open porch.

The villa's living room had become a makeshift intensive care unit, filled with very sick babies. Many of them were receiving IV fluids from bottles hanging from nails driven into the walls. Nothing in my training had prepared me for such a sight, and the enormity of the task ahead took me by surprise. Nervously, I confided in Elaine that I wasn't sure I was competent to help with so many babies. Elaine smiled and assured me I would learn quickly. We talked while diapering, feeding, and caring for the babies. At last, bone tired, I crawled into bed. As I drifted off to sleep, I listened to the night's serenade: babies crying, gunfire in the street below, and explosions in the distance.

I woke before dawn to find Elaine working in one of the rooms. Quietly, she pointed to a tiny baby boy and told me she'd been up all night nursing him. The baby was due to travel to a new family soon, but he wasn't going to make it. The sight was traumatic for me. Before that moment, I had never seen a baby die. I stayed with Elaine, and we lovingly comforted the tiny boy until he passed away. By then I was crying so hard, I was sure I couldn't continue to work. The emotion was too much for me. But I couldn't leave the nursery because Elaine was exhausted after a full night's work. She needed me to get back in control.

I urged her to rest and told her I would take over while she slept. Alone, I gazed about the room, frozen by the awesome responsibility I had just agreed to take on. Suddenly, I was in charge of a house full of babies. There was no doctor and no other nurses, only the Vietnamese staff, who spoke little English. There was nobody I could turn to for advice or guidance; it was up to me to make the decisions.

A childcare worker soon approached me with an infant in her arms. She pointed to the child's forehead. I saw his flushed face and felt his forehead; he was burning hot with fever. Together we sponged the baby with cool water, and slowly the fever diminished. When he was sleeping soundly, the woman gently slipped him into a crib.

As I went from child to child, my nursing skills came to the fore, and I knew what had to be done. No sooner had I finished with one child than another would need my attention. The hours blurred into a constant round of nursing each baby. I started recognizing the individuality of each one, and soon could identify them as the unique little people they were.

Finally, I looked up to see Elaine smiling and watching me, looking refreshed and rested. "You're a natural," she told me.

"I have my mission."

At last, I had found the "definite service" for which I had been created. I returned to the United States only long enough to retrieve my children and husband and never returned to America to live again. The work in Vietnam in 1973 was the beginning of my lifetime commitment to children in Vietnam and India. I eventually opened my own organization, International Mission of Hope, which ministered to the desperate children of Vietnam and placed over 1,000 children for adoption.

It's amazing what one can accomplish with a single, small contribution that makes a difference in the life of one person.

Cherie Clark

[EDITORS' NOTE: *Cherie Clark was instrumental in implementing Operation Babylift to help rescue 3,000 orphans from Vietnam in 1975. From there she journeyed to India where she worked with Mother Teresa. She returned to Vietnam in 1988 where she continues to minister to needy children today.*]

3

ON LOVE

The greatest pleasure in life is love.

Sir William Temple

He's Yours

Love is loveliest when embalmed in tears.

Walter Scott

"I will not cry." I repeated my mantra as we drove to the courthouse.

"You will not weep," I admonished myself over and over again as we climbed the gray granite steps to the building.

"I will not shed a single tear," I told my husband as the judge entered the courtroom.

Now, normally I'm not a crier, but you couldn't tell that to anyone who knew me for the past twelve months, for everything about this adoption had made me cry. Absolutely everything. While pictures may say a thousand words, hearing the words, "I've got good news . . . you have a son," was worth a million bucks. I cried as if I'd won the lottery . . . because I just had.

I cried when the plane took off as we headed to Korea to pick him up.

I bawled the first time I saw his beautiful face, and tears of joy and laughter ran down my cheeks when I first glimpsed his "stick 'em up" hair.

I sobbed when I first held him and fed him his bottle.

I cried buckets when it was time to take Karson from his foster mother, and I cried at the airport knowing that I was taking this precious boy from the only family and country he had ever known.

I blubbered the first time he called me "Mama," during his first steps, and when his first tooth appeared, as well as numerous times in between.

In short, the last year had been an endless river of happy tears, but today I vowed I wasn't going to cry.

Not a tear was shed when the bailiff swore me in, nor did they fall as the judge examined the paperwork, making sure that everything was in order. I didn't cry when she asked me to tell her his name, what he liked to do during the day, and what kind of baby he was.

"So far, so good," I concluded. It was then, just when I thought I was in the clear, that the judge sideswiped me.

"Now tell me what it has meant to you to have Karson in your lives," the judge said quietly.

Uh, oh, I thought as I bit my bottom lip to keep the tears in check. The judge had unknowingly just crossed the line. I looked up at her with a look on my face that reflected the fact that there were no words I could ever use that would adequately express what this boy, hopefully our soon-to-be son, meant to me. Yet, we had made it this far, and as far as we were concerned we were already a forever family. I knew I couldn't blow it now.

"The sky is bluer," I said quietly, thoughts swirling in my head. "Since we have Karson, the mockingbird is more melodious, the colors of the rainbow are brighter, and a baby's laugh is sweeter." My voice cracked, and I bit down on my lip just a little harder. Tears were on the horizon, threatening to take me out to sea. "The sunshine is a little sunnier, the grass is greener, snowflakes fluffier, and the wind whispers softer," I stuttered, desperately grasping for the right words that would explain just how precious our son was to us. "Our love is deeper, our hearts are stronger, each minute is more miraculous, our joy more profound . . ."

"You need not say anything more," came the voice from the bench with a tear glistening in the corner of her eye. At that moment, time stopped, and the silence became deafening. And then, finally, the judge looked over her bench, a soft smile gracing her lips and declared, "He's yours."

And with that pronouncement, I did the unthinkable: I smiled.
I laughed.
I jumped up and down.
We posed for pictures.
And later that night . . .
I cried.

Cheryl Dieter

Never Say Never

When I was a young man, I hated kids. They were too noisy, too messy, and asked too many questions. If there were kids playing in the doctor's office while I was waiting, I'd give them the meanest glare I could to let them know to stay away. I used to tell people, "I'm never having kids!" So when I finally got married, I would have been perfectly content if my new wife would have said she never wanted kids either. I figured since kids are so expensive that maybe I'd buy a turbo for my Miata in place of saving for a college fund.

However, my new bride, Barbara May, *did* want children. Six months after getting married, we were pregnant. It didn't faze me a whole lot, though. I knew I had nine months to get ready, and I knew my attitude toward kids would change. But it never had a chance to change. We lost our first child. After genetic testing, we decided not to pursue a biological child, so we applied to adopt a baby girl from China. Still, I was just along for the ride, agreeing to whatever would help ease the pain Barbara was suffering after two traumatic losses.

On October 8, 2003, in Hunan province, China, our

daughter was born. Eleven months later, I held her for the first time. She screamed and wanted nothing to do with me. I asked myself, *What did you get yourself into?* The turbo for my Miata was looking very appealing.

Her adoption certificate was dated September 14th, my birthday. We named her MiKayla Maria Hui.

It has been over two years since that chaotic "Gotcha Day" in China. Now I can't imagine life without her. The love I feel for her is comparable only to the love I have for my wife. Becoming a "dah" has been one of the most unexpected and joyful experiences of my life. I just can't put into words the magnitude of the greatest feeling imaginable. What creates that feeling? It's a compilation of things like . . . taking her out dressed up in a cute pink dress with her hair up in ponytails while people stare at her and exclaim, "That little girl is so adorable!"

It's the speed with which the stress of work dissipates when I hear those Chinese squeaky shoes running down the hall, accompanied by a "Daddy's home!"

It's the feel of her tiny fingers wrapped around my thumb, squeezing tightly.

It's the humor from questions like, "How does Jesus get out of your heart?"

It's the innocent grin underneath spaghetti sauce—which is in her hair, on her elbows, and on the floor.

It's the persistent, "Daddy, come to the sunroom and read to me, pleeeeeeeese" while tugging at my pant leg.

It's that beautiful smile of unconditional love that reminds me that the most important things in life are people and relationships—not Miatas.

Bryan Clark

3 AM Feedings

It was a frail, but sufficient, middle-of-the-night cry. I woke to Brandon's alarm. Three o'clock. *Baby*, I remembered. *Bottle*. My feet took me through the dark to the borrowed crib in the alcove just outside the bedroom door. *He's fine, just hungry.* I hurried downstairs to the kitchen.

Until three months ago, I was a thirty-something, single, urban professional who slept through the night, ate dinner while it was hot, took a shower without treading on plastic toys, and crossed the street without holding anyone's hand. Then, I became a foster parent.

In the kitchen, I flipped on the light. Bright sippy cups and kid-proof bowls overflowed the dish drainer. Ashley and Christopher had come first. They were settling in; but, it hadn't been easy. Christopher was adamant in his terrible-twos way. "You're not my mom; my mom lives over there," he insisted, pointing to wherever "there" was—anywhere, everywhere, just away from me. I don't know why I didn't think of it sooner. One day I said, "You know, Chris, you can have more than one mom. You have mom Hannah; that's your birth mom. You have mom Laura; you lived with her. And now you have mom Shelly. And you can call me whatever you want. But, I just want you to know that it is okay to have more than one mom." His anxiety melted and before long he was calling me Mom.

I laughed, remembering how Ashley had filled a little suitcase with books from the lowest shelf in the living room. It was much too heavy for the three-year-old to carry, so she dragged it everywhere. "She's prepared in case she and her brother have to move, again," I explained to my sister.

Janey corrected my assumption. "No, Shelly. It's her briefcase. She's just doing what you do everyday." *Why hadn't I seen this?*

I also hadn't anticipated Ashley's reaction when I sat her down to tell her the news about her youngest brothers. "Ashley, the little ones are going to come live with us."

"Those are my mommy's babies!" Worry washed over her face. "Are you going to take them?"

"Well, they are going to come and live with us for a while." I hesitated, "and I don't know how long it will be. But, we can take care of them while they're here, right?" *So much of her life is uncertain*, I thought. *Don't make empty promises and don't lie to her.*

Two days ago the Department of Children and Family Services delivered Brandon and Thomas with the clothes on their backs, an extra T-shirt each, half a can of formula, and bad diaper rashes. The old hospital-issue diaper bag reeked of vomit and God knows what else. There were a few hospital bottles and two nipples. I filled one with distilled water and waited for it to warm.

They had never lived together, these four siblings, but played with each other on visits with their birth mom. Now, Thomas, nineteen months, and Brandon, born six weeks ago, needed a place to stay. The few married-with-children people I knew had been dropping things off for three days: bibs, bottles, a few diapers, a diaper Genie, and a bouncy seat. The first night, Janey and a friend came over for moral support. We took turns holding the children, brainstorming about how to make caring for my expanding family more manageable.

Thomas did not really want much to do with me. He was frightened, stood right in front of the refrigerator, and yelled at the top of his lungs. His cherub cheeks flushed red. But, he devoured everything I put in front of him.

I knew the baby would still be crying. *Don't wake up the kids.* I tested the water temperature and popped the lid off the powdered formula. Measuring quickly, I closed the container. Tiny Brandon had been diagnosed failure-to-thrive. *I can see it in his eyes: just lifeless.*

Shaking his bottle, I ran upstairs. I glanced into the kids' room. Thomas was quiet in the second borrowed crib, Ashley and Christopher, still asleep. They all wanted to be together. Of course, they couldn't sleep in my room; it was against DCFS regulations. Not even Brandon. We had to put his crib in the hall where I had my desk at the top of the stairs. From my bed, I could see him and hear him breathing. It just didn't seem close enough.

I scooped him up, "Sshh," and slid onto my bed to feed him. His cry thinned. The vanity lamp cast a halo of soft light over his head. I put the nipple in his mouth. *I love this time alone.* As a new parent, I still had a lot to learn about children. But, somehow—when there's a baby in our arms, even novices know exactly what to do. I started cooing my little string of sweet nothings. Brandon stopped sucking. He looked into my eyes and smiled for the first time. Then he went back to his bottle. "Failure-to-thrive my behind!" I whispered, indignantly. Reassuring him, I added, "You'll be fine my little angel."

That smile was the only motivation I needed to feed Brandon every three hours, night and day, day and night for the next ten months. It didn't take long for me to discover that cold dinner is not so bad, rubber ducks don't take up that much room in the tub, and there is something very comforting about holding tightly to four children while crossing the street.

Two years later, I adopted Ashley, Christopher, Thomas, and Brandon. Together we thrive.

Elizabeth Watkins with Rhonda Richards-Cohen

Adopting Amy

In the man whose childhood has known caresses, there is always a fiber of memory that can be touched to gentle issues.

George Eliot

When I worked in the Community Mental Health sector in Scotland, I came across many people with surprising stories. I was attending a seminar one day on the rights of adopted children when I first met Amy.

I was sitting next to her at lunch and mentioned I had little experience with people who were adopted. I was there mainly to listen.

"Well, I have experience," she said with a smile, and then began her story.

Many years ago, when she was only nineteen, her parents were both killed in a car crash. Being an only child, she was absolutely devastated. She stayed for a year with relatives, but finally found the courage to return to their family home.

By that time, a new family had moved in next door.

Amy was standing on the front porch crying when a little girl's voice asked, "Why are you crying? Are you very sad?"

The pretty little girl with long, dark, curly hair and huge brown eyes looked about four years old. Amy sniffed a lot and managed to say in a broken voice, "My mum and dad both died a year ago, and I just came back to the house."

The child, named Lois, asked a number of very direct questions that Amy found herself answering. The conversation drew the attention of Lois's little brother, Gary, who came to find out what was happening.

They asked if she would be moving into the house, and Amy explained that it was too full of sad memories.

Lois studied her and asked, "Weren't you happy here with your mummy and daddy? Don't you have happy memories then?"

Amy stared at her in silence for a few moments and then said, "Well, yes, I do. We were all very happy here indeed. It's just that being here alone, without them, makes me sad."

"But you could come and visit with us all the time, and we could come over and visit with you, then you wouldn't be on your own anymore!" Lois pointed out as Gary nodded in agreement.

Amy smiled at that as a man's voice called, "Lois, Gary, where are you?"

Their father, Mark, introduced himself. He knew Amy's story. Everyone in the neighborhood did. He sympathetically cautioned Amy not to part with the house or its contents too soon and regret it later.

Amy stayed in the house for a while, and over the next week or so, the children called round a lot. She learned from another neighbor that their mum had run off with some man for whom she had been working.

Their dad was still very hurt and quite bitter. He, Lois and Gary, along with their grandmother, had moved to the area to make a new start and try to leave the sad memories behind them.

These lovely children had their sadness, too. They had been told that their mother had gone off to live a new life, and it seemed to hurt Gary a great deal more than Lois. Before long, it became apparent that Lois saw Amy as a replacement for their missing mother. Grandma was fine, but she didn't play silly games, and she couldn't make their dad smile. Amy could.

Amy settled down in her old home, got a job back in town, and spent many happy days with Lois and Gary. It took Mark some time to put his pain behind him, but during those years he and Amy grew closer. She went to school opening days and sports days with Mark. She cried at prize-giving when Lois came first in her class.

After five years, Mark confessed, "I cannot envisage my life without you, Amy."

"Me neither," she admitted with a kiss. "Lois made sure of that."

The adoption seminar lectures were about to begin, and Amy smiled at me as we glanced at our watches.

"At least you have the experience of adopting children," I commented.

Amy laughed, "No, you see it wasn't that way. They adopted me."

Joyce Stark

A Real Little Orphan Annie

*M*usic resembles poetry; in each are numerous
graces which no methods can teach, and which
a master hand alone can reach.

Alexander Pope

"Put your coat on," I suggested to my daughter as we
hurried out the door with the rest of the family.

"I don't waaaaaant to wear a coat!" The way my
daughter whines, you'd think she was eight years old
instead of fourteen.

"Whatever, let's just go." Mark me down for Mother
of the Year.

We headed to meet my parents, their friends, and
more family at the high school to see the musical, *Annie*.
I was highly anticipating this evening, not only because
it was my first time to attend a musical since I became
involved with productions not too long ago, but also
because this was the year my husband and I adopted
our own little orphan Annie. I imagined my daughter
and me bonding over "Tomorrow," the tears streaming
down our faces as she realized the wonder of theater

that I discovered at her age, and the sentiment of this one's message.

But as soon as we arrived, she found a friend, and promptly told me she was going to go "run around the school." I had to respectfully deny her request, which she did not take well.

"You treat me like a baby!"

I mentally rolled my eyes as I realized this evening was not going to be what I'd imagined. "Come on, Ali, they're seating."

The eight of us traipsed to our seats. I very thoughtfully put a seat between my husband and myself for my daughter . . . but she chose to sit at the very far end of the row with her friend. Internally, I sighed. My husband and I had brought Ali into our home last year and made the adoption final this year. It had been a tumultuous journey, to say the very least.

Oh, well, at least I could enjoy the musical with *my* mother, who had come with me.

The curtain opened, and the adorable orphans began to sing about parents they knew were out there somewhere in "Maybe." I sang along in my head as we saw the orphans and their "Hard Knock Life" come to life in the orphanage the high-school scene shop had artfully created. The awful headmistress, Ms. Hannagin, made me want to laugh and boo as she sang about how the "Little Girls" drove her mad.

I'd been there, trust me.

I cheered with the audience as Annie finally got Sandy the dog to come to her in that famous scene, and I didn't even notice that my daughter, on the other end of the row, was enjoying the musical almost as much as I was.

When intermission was called, I was almost startled when she came up and gave me a tight hug. "I love you, Mom."

"I love you, too," I said, tears in my eyes. "Can we sit together for the second act?"

Ali nodded.

As Daddy Warbucks sang to Little Orphan Annie about who would need him, who would dream he'd find one little girl, I hugged my daughter close and kissed the top of her head.

There are some moments in life that only music or drama can really express.

Amanda Cole

Shower of Love for Rosita

It is the will, and not the gift, that makes the giver.

Bruno Lessing

"Mama, Mama." Rosita shook me.

I turned over, moaned, and looked at the clock. 5:00 AM. *What is she thinking?*

She chattered in Spanish. I smiled in spite of my reluctance to wake up so early. What fourteen-year-old girl wouldn't be excited about a party planned in her honor?

Later, we bustled around the kitchen as we made final preparations. Rosita came over to the stove and gave me a playful grin. "Mama, why for me?"

I looked at her rosy cheeks. Joy filled my heart as I delighted in my new daughter. "We always have showers for new babies."

"Me, baby?" she asked in her limited English.

I chuckled. "No, but it is like that because we just adopted you."

Stan, my husband, met Rosita on a business trip in an orphanage in Bogota, Colombia. After a childhood of neglect and severe abuse, at eleven years of age, she had fled to the streets. She ate out of garbage cans to survive and slept in doorways under newspapers to fight off the chill at night.

Eventually, she found refuge in an orphanage run by a Christian ministry. When she saw Stan, she ran to her room and gave him a little needlepoint she had made. When he looked in her eyes, something touched his heart. He sensed God saying, "Adopt her."

Stan came home and shared Rosita's story with me. I prayed about it and sensed God's purpose in it, so I agreed. After fighting two years of red tape, we finalized the adoption in November and brought her to be with us in the United States before Christmas.

Now, Christmas decorations graced our house, filling it with cheer, making the shower all the more festive. Spicy apple cider, cinnamon buns, and a variety of cookies filled the air with their delicious aromas. Upbeat music danced in the air, lifting our spirits.

As the guests arrived, colorful gifts piled up under the Christmas tree. The chatter of friends greeting each other and catching up on news created a sense of energy and excitement.

Rosita kept running to the tree to gaze at the most recent deposits. As they accumulated, she unclasped and clasped her hands. Her voice had a nervous edge, "Mama, *mucho, mucho regalos* (many, many gifts)."

Twenty women crowded around in eager anticipation to see her reaction to their shower presents for her. First, I shared with them a delicate colored poster Rosita made to express her appreciation. A rough translation from Spanish shared her heart: *For all of you with much affection. I love you very much. Thank you for all you have done for me. May God bless you and give you much blessings. I will carry all of you in my heart wherever I go. Thank you. Smile.*

Then, Rosita opened the presents. She seemed confused by the abundance of gifts, so I handed them to her one at a time. She smiled with joy and expressed genuine gratitude for each gift. Clothes, a necklace, perfumed shower gel, lotion, gift certificates, and much more delighted her young heart.

Three-fourths of the way through opening the gifts, she stopped, plunged her head into her lap, and started sobbing. I panicked. I had no idea what had upset her. I put my arms around her and tried to calm her. I fumbled in my mind to try to find the few Spanish words I knew. My heart beat faster. *What can I do?*

I sensed a nervous concern from the other women. I held Rosita for several minutes until she composed herself. Finally, one of the women who had been a missionary said, "I know Spanish. Maybe I can help."

She questioned Rosita in Spanish and translated.

Through her tears, Rosita said, "I have never had so many gifts ever in my whole life. I am so grateful to you for giving me these things." She paused and wiped the tears from her eyes. "When I was home and then on the streets, no one ever gave me a gift, and now I have so many. I love you all, and I will never forget you. I will never forget this day. Now I have my mama, my papa, and my brother, and I love them so much. You are all special to me, and I have you in my heart. I will never forget you. Thank you so much."

I glanced around the room at my friends. Some of the women dabbed their eyes with tissue, and others smiled at her with tears in their eyes.

On Christmas Day, more gifts delighted her young heart. Later in the day, she came into the kitchen to find my husband and me. "Mama and Papa, I really love all the gifts. It is first time I had gifts for Christmas, but the thing I love most is having family."

Sharon Gibson

Love Is Enough

*O, memory, though bittersweet, both a joy and a
scourge.*

Madame de Stael

My favorite story as a child was one I didn't completely understand, yet made me feel special. "We
chose you out of all the babies in the world," my
mother told me from as far back as I could remember. It
wasn't until I was ten years old that I finally understood what she meant; I was adopted. I was nearly
thirty years old when I understood how my biological
mother felt when she gave me up.

My son, Jaime, was a laughing child with strawberry
blond curls, sapphire blue eyes, and an inquisitive
nature. He wasn't so much mischievous as curious, and
as he got older he climbed bookcases and furniture and
cabinets to look inside and drag out whatever he
found. One morning before six, he woke me up.
Through sleep-blurred eyes, Jaime looked odd.
Blinking and rubbing away the sand and grit, I looked
again. He smiled a lopsided smile, his teeth white in his

mask of smeared makeup. His chubby hands pulled at my arm. "Look, Mommy." Little handprints in mingled shades of green and blue and violet and pink covered my arms.

I got out of bed and followed him into the bathroom, every surface a smeared Jackson Pollack in every shade of eye shadow, blush, and lipstick I owned. His variegated body parts decorated the inside of the claw-foot porcelain tub as I bathed him. Jaime looked up at me, his eyes bright with excitement, and he giggled. I couldn't help myself. In spite of how much work it would take, I laughed, swung him up into my arms, and kissed his painted cheek.

Each day was a struggle, working two full-time jobs and seeing my son only before work and on alternate weekends when I had a day off. I felt like I was cheating him, and myself, but I was trapped. I couldn't quit one of my jobs. I couldn't afford the babysitter and a place to live. We had nowhere else to go and no one to help.

When Jaime was nearly two years old, just two weeks before Christmas, I made a decision. I had changed my mind when he was born because I believed love was enough. The attorney hired to protect my rights and the doctor who delivered my son talked me into keeping him. It wasn't a hard sell; I wanted to keep him, but wasn't sure how, since I was barely making it without a child.

I wasn't supposed to see the baby after he was born, but somehow the nursery slipped up and brought him to me. The moment they put him in my arms, I was lost. The parents were hurt. The attorney was angry. But they both sent me flowers, and Jaime and I went home.

Sitting in the judge's chambers the morning I met with him and Jaime's new parents, I swallowed back the tears as I answered his questions. "Yes, I understand what I'm doing. Yes, I am giving up my son of my own free will. No, the parents have not paid me or given me any money. No one is coercing me. No one is threatening me. No one has made me any promises of financial gain or any kind. Yes, I want to give up my son."

No, I didn't want to give up my son. I still don't want to give him up, even though I haven't seen him since he was nearly two years old. No, I don't want to surrender the memory of his laughter the morning he woke me covered in eye shadow, blush, and lipstick, or the way he looked when he led me to the bathroom and showed me he was a rare and special artist.

No one forced me to give up my son. But the voice inside me said love was not enough, and I had to choose between working eighteen hours a day for enough food and clothing (and makeup) and seeing the mischief and laughter in my son's eyes every morning.

Jaime has a different name now, and he is twenty-five years old. I don't know where he is or what he does, if he went to college or got married and has children of his own. I have no idea how to find him or if he would welcome me if I did. He belongs to someone else now. All I kept are the memories of a little boy who woke up laughing every morning.

It has taken me a long time to understand the meaning behind the story I loved to hear as a child. "We chose you out of all the babies in the world."

I met my biological mother when I was eleven, and she was a nice woman who seemed a little sad. When she talked to me, she wouldn't look me in the eyes. She talked about my biological father and showed me a small picture from a high-school yearbook. He played basketball, and he wasn't very tall; neither was she. I wanted to know where I came from, why I'm so much taller than my parents. Why was my hair brown when she had strawberry blonde curls and my father's hair was blond? Why wasn't I thin? Where did my grey eyes come from?

"Why did you give me up?" I asked.

"I didn't finish high school, and I didn't have a good job. I couldn't give you what you needed or what you deserved."

"Didn't you love me?" Afraid of the answer, I still wanted to know.

She finally looked me in the eyes. Her eyes were blue like sapphires. "Yes, I love you. Your parents could give you everything I couldn't."

"Even love?"

"No one loves you more than I do."

I can still hear the words, but I didn't believe them then. How could someone love their child and give her up to strangers? *Love is all you need,* I thought. I was a child. I didn't understand.

Love sometimes is not enough, not when you have to see your child crying from hunger or forced to live in a shelter or small apartment in a bad part of town because it's all you can afford.

Working two jobs was not enough. My love was not enough. I held on to my love the day I answered the judge's questions and signed the papers that made another woman Jaime's mother. I did what I had to do to take care of my son. Now, love and memories of Jaime are all I have.

I know what my mother went through. I understand what she meant, and love is finally enough.

J. M. Cornwell

I Am His Mom

Shortly after his thirty-ninth birthday, Billy, our adopted son, called me the day after Thanksgiving. "Mom, I gotta talk to you."

"Sure, son, what is it?" In stunned disbelief, I listened as he told me his birth mother had telephoned him the day before Thanksgiving. He waited to tell me so he wouldn't spoil my holiday. This woman had paid someone fifty dollars to search the Internet for him. They took a number off the original birth certificate and traced my son's birth records to us. The courts had told me it could never happen, but it did.

Trying to say all the right things, I told him I didn't mind that he meet with her.

This was the only time I ever lied to one of my children. I did mind. I didn't blame him, but I did mind.

He was *my* son. I sat up with him when he was sick. I sewed the rips and tears on his jeans. Why should I share him now? He has two children. My grandchildren—not hers.

As Billy was growing up, we had talked openly about his birth mother. He was only ten when he first came into our lives, yet he held a faint memory of her. Although I knew he loved me, I was aware of the remembrance of her lingering in the background of his mind. Trying to encourage him not to be angry, I told him she probably had a very good reason for not keeping him more than the two years he lived with her. I promised, when he was older, if he wanted to find his birth mother, I would help him. And I would have, but he chose not to.

Not even in my dreams did I expect she'd find him.

I tucked my skepticism away so as not to mar his excitement. I knew, because the social workers had told me, that his mother had given him away when she was young and recently divorced. She had remarried and had other children. After thirty-seven years, I didn't understand why she wanted him now.

Billy has now met his other mother and accepted the explanation she gave for not being able to keep him. I couldn't be with them at their first meeting, the day before Christmas Eve. I wanted to give them space and was quite sure both she and I would have felt very awkward. Truthfully, there was another reason I didn't go. I was quite intimidated and not at all sure where I would fit in this new picture.

But the next day, while I was preparing dinner for our family Christmas Eve, Billy arrived early. He stepped up behind me and kissed me on the cheek. "I love you, Mom," was all he said. But that was enough.

Billy wants his two families to meet. I've agreed. He believes I am gracious enough to share him, so I'll try. He was without a mother for so many years. Surely, he deserves to have two now.

All I want is for my son to be happy and find peace within himself. His thirty-nine-year enigma is solved. I'm here to share his joy, or I'm here just if he needs me.

I am his mom.

Jean Kinsey

I Could Not Conceive

They told me I could not conceive, and tests showed
  they were right;
They considered but the physical, forgetting our
  Father's might.
True, my child, I did not conceive you within the limits
  of my womb;
But still you grew within my heart—a heart with
  boundless room.

They told me I could not conceive, and in one way they
  were right;
Now I know they are the barren ones, comprehension
  out of sight.
For they cannot conceive, my son, of how it feels to see
The face of a child, not of my flesh, but of my destiny.

They cannot conceive, my child, of what it means to
  love
Another woman, another man, who prayed to God
  above
And then decided to love enough, to give to me their
  son

To love, and raise, and call my own, until my life is
  done.

They cannot conceive, dear one, of bonds beyond the
  ties
Of if you have your daddy's nose or if you have my
  eyes.
They cannot conceive, my child, of all the Lord still has
  in store
For this family he created, not of my flesh and bone, but
  more.

They told me I could not conceive, and in part their
  words were true . . .
For I cannot conceive, dear son, of never loving you.

Valerie Kay Gwin

A Grandma's Love

If becoming a grandmother was only a matter of choice, I should advise every one of you straight away to become one. There is no fun for old people like it!

Hannah Whithall Smith

What if I can't love her? What if I don't even like her? I was so excited to finally be in Hanoi, Vietnam, but I was also ashamed. Why couldn't I keep these doubts from creeping into my mind, sometimes thundering like a flash flood through the canyons of my terrified brain? My twenty-nine-year-old daughter Loren was about to become a single mom.

Two years earlier when she had told me about her dream to adopt a daughter, I was the one who had encouraged her. With the exception of my husband, all our family and friends thought we were nuts! I'd been behind the idea from the beginning.

Why was I so scared now?

"The babies are here! The babies are here!" Tam from the Claudia Hotel announced breathlessly as she burst into the room. Loren and I lunged for our cameras and raced to the lobby. Other adoptive families were already gathered, all in various states of disarray and hysteria. Caregivers stood, each with an infant in her arms.

"Mom, where is she?" Loren asked, panic edging into her voice. "These are all infants—none look big enough to be Mindy."

I glanced at each tiny, precious face. "Wait, there's one over there in the corner who looks bigger than the others."

Loren pressed through the crowd of weeping parents and made her way to the caregiver. "Thuy?" she asked tentatively, pointing to the child the woman was cradling. The caregiver smiled and nodded. Loren reached out and gently stroked her daughter's face for the first time. "She's so tiny! I can't believe she's twenty-three months old! She's so beautiful!"

I was crying hard now; in fact, I was sobbing rather sloppily. I somehow managed to extract my brand-new camcorder from its case and press the record button. *Why, oh why*, I silently cursed myself, *had I not practiced with this contraption?*

The caregiver gently passed Mindy to Loren, and in that single moment our lives changed forever.

"Oh, Mom, she looks so scared," Loren said as her miniature daughter rested her head against her new mom's chest.

"She's beautiful, Loren! Her features are just perfect." Already the proud new grandma was looking past the butchered short haircut, the smell of dried urine, and the grief-stricken look on that small face.

We took Mindy to our room, and in the next few moments I saw that my daughter would be the most loving and wonderful of mothers as she gently maneuvered through her first diaper change, her first wrestling of legs and arms into a fuzzy sleeper, her first bottle feed, the first of many, many nights of singing lullabies and walking the floor with a traumatized child.

"Gosh, Mom. She's swimming in the twelve-month sizes! Most of the clothes we brought are way too big." Then she smiled, "Do you remember those dreams we both had?"

"How could I forget?" I had been living in the tiny kingdom of Eritrea in northeast Africa with my husband while I waited for "the call" to come from Loren in California. "We were both pretty stunned when we discovered that on separate continents we had simultaneously dreamed that seventeen-pound Mindy was absolutely gigantic with hair falling to her waist."

I chuckled. "Another night, at the same time, we both dreamed that when they handed you your child, she turned out to be a cat!"

Two days later at the Giving and Receiving Ceremony, my doubts were but a distant memory. I had fallen head over heels, insanely in love! When the official asked Loren, "Don't you think you're too young to be adopting a child?" I knew then that I would slay fire-eating dragons to keep him or anyone else from taking Mindy away. My heart raced in fear, and then I breathed a sigh of relief when Loren replied, "My mother was only twenty-two when she had me. I love the idea of being young enough to play with her and chase after her."

We had two magical weeks in Hanoi, a special bonding time for all three of us. We watched as the little girl who hadn't had the strength to press a button on a musical toy, or make a fist, or give a kiss, whizzed through the pages of her own child-development manual with lightning speed—walking, running, clapping, laughing, eating huge bowls of noodle soup, adult-sized platters of chicken, veggies, and rice. We doted on her every word, her every action—suddenly, she was our everything!

Back home at last, Mindy met her grandpa for the first time. As her big brown eyes gazed up at my six-foot-tall, 280-pound husband, she deftly wrapped him around her little finger where he has remained firmly entrenched for the last nine years.

At nearly eleven years old, Mindy was beautiful, smart, strong, with a keen wit.

Only one thing was missing . . . a sister. Loren decided to adopt again.

"Lor," I said one day, "I had a dream."

"Oh, no!"

"There were two girls. One had brown hair. The other was small and a bit scruffy. I didn't know which one was yours."

Loren had requested a five-year-old girl, but several months later she felt a tug—a very strong tug of the famous red thread. A nine-year-old girl was calling her from Vietnam.

Loren had heard about this girl and how badly she wanted a home and a family. She was described as a bit shy, a bit mischievous, very sweet, and very smart. They might have been describing Mindy. "Why were we so set on a five-year-old?" we asked ourselves. "Wouldn't a nine-year-old be just perfect?"

At long last, the referral photo arrived—oh, my, that lovely face, those huge eyes fringed by impossibly long lashes! And in the sunlight, her hair looked brown just like the girl in my dream!

But this time I'm not as afraid. I can hardly wait to bring my second granddaughter home. This time I *know* that I will love her.

Nancy O'Neill

"This is our newly adopted daughter, Corina,
and this is our son from a previous adoption."

4

DIVINE INTERVENTION

*M*an's ultimate destiny is to become one
  with the Divine Power which governs and
  sustains the creation and its creatures.

Alfred A. Montapert

Our New Family Picture

Nature is too thin a screen; the glory of the omnipresent God bursts through everywhere.

Ralph Waldo Emerson

"I know it's here! I know it is!" Olya said, sounding more frustrated by the minute.

Olya, our nine-year-old daughter, adopted from Russia two years earlier, was hastily thumbing through photos in photo boxes in our living room. I was determined to finally start putting pictures in photo albums this year.

After our son Liam was born twelve years ago, I didn't have time to continue with my photo albums. Riley followed two years later, and the pictures continued to pile up. I finally decided I would not get to them anytime soon and started simply plopping them into photo boxes. I told myself, *Once the boys start school, I'll get around to that.* That was followed by, *Once we finish remodeling the new house,* then, *Once I finish my degree,* then, *Maybe after we get back from Russia, after the adoption.*

Lately, Olya had been fascinated with looking at all the pictures in those boxes. She wanted to know everything we had done before she joined our family. She wanted to see what the boys looked like as they had grown. She wanted to see what her grandmas and grandpas and her aunts and uncles looked like when they were younger.

I had been hesitant to let her see these pictures. Usually, she would ask, "How old was I when you took this picture? What was I doing in Russia back then?" After learning her traumatic history, I was not sure how beneficial it was for her to know how much joy we had experienced over the years, when, simultaneously, on the other side of the globe, Olya's young life had been unbearable. She had seen her father's murder. Her mother committed suicide. She had watched her sister be attacked and nearly raped. Olya begged strangers on the street for money and food. The tragic events went on and on.

But tonight, she was on a mission. "I want to find the picture of when I first saw you guys," Olya said. "The first picture of all of us together."

"Sweetie, the picture of us meeting you in the orphanage is in the frame in the dining room," my husband Will said.

"No, not that one," Olya sighed.

Her brother Liam offered, "There is one right here on the window sill from when you first got here."

"No, no, no," Olya insisted. "The one where we are *all* in the picture."

I shot a worried look to Will. We had yet to take a family portrait. There actually was no picture of all of us together. What was she talking about?

"I'm getting close," Olya said. "I know it's in this box right here."

Liam glanced at the lid, marked 1996. "Olya," he said, "you've never even seen these pictures before. Besides, these are from 1996. You weren't born until 1997!" He rolled his eyes in annoyance.

"Here it is!" Olya squealed. "I found it! I found it! Look, here it is!" She waved a photo over her head. Our curiosity piqued, we scrambled around her, but quickly became more confused.

"Olya," Riley exclaimed, "I wasn't even born yet in this picture! Look, I was still in Mommy's tummy."

"I know!" Olya said, beaming. I looked at the picture, which my parents had taken of us a month before Riley was born. We had been vacationing at the beach. Will had one arm around me, the other holding Liam. I was holding my pregnant belly as we stood in the sand, the blue sky and white fluffy clouds behind us.

We all stared at each other, not knowing what to say to Olya.

"Where exactly are you in this picture, honey?" I asked slowly.

"Right here!" Olya said, pointing to one of the clouds. "I was up in heaven, and this was the first time I saw my family. I smiled when God showed me. He told me I was just going to have to wait awhile before we could all be together."

A chill ran down my spine. I remembered that day so clearly. My father had remarked on the clouds in the background. I precisely remembered him getting ready to snap the picture. He had paused and said, "Look at those beautiful clouds. It's as if they are smiling right down on us!"

Now, we finally knew. It was our first family photo, long before we knew who was going to be in it.

Sharon M. Yager

Greatest Father's Day Gift

The manner of giving shows the character of the giver.

John Casper Lavater

It was a beautiful Sunday morning in 1998, and it was a special day at my house. My two teenaged kids were going to treat Dad to breakfast for Father's Day.

Then the phone rang. Once again my family was asked to sacrifice their day and put their plans on hold while Dad, the detective, responded to the needs of another.

I was advised that there was a fifteen-year-old female rape victim at the hospital in a nearby city. I assured my family that I would be home quickly and that this should not take too long. My wife and teenaged daughter just gave me the "Yeah, right" smile that I had seen so many times before and sent me on my way.

Once at the hospital, I met with the staff and another officer who was present. When I began to attempt to interview the victim, I found that she was developmentally delayed and slow mentally. After about an hour with the victim, I finally began to gain her trust and learn what took place on the previous night. While I was explaining to the victim's guardian, her aunt, what I knew thus far, we were interrupted by the nurse. She explained that, although the victim had told all of us that this was her first sexual encounter, a routine test indicated she was five to seven weeks pregnant. *Wow,* I thought, *another can of worms just opened. I might as well kiss this Father's Day good-bye.*

After a couple more hours with the victim and no good description of any suspect or explanation as to who got her pregnant, I finally went home late that afternoon.

Over the next several weeks, I worked leads on the rape, trying to develop a suspect. None surfaced. During one of my calls to the victim, her guardian told me that the victim was not mentally and physically able to care for herself, let alone any new baby. Then she dropped the hammer on me. The aunt bluntly asked, "Would you like to adopt the baby once it is born?"

The guardian kept telling me that she felt as if I was meant to adopt the baby. She told me to think about it and to tell her later.

My wife and I had two children already, both of whom were in the middle to late teens, and for the past several years, I had been pestering her for another baby. The answer was always the same. It was not that she did not want another baby; it was just that we were approaching forty and were just getting comfortable in our lives. The kids were now old enough to help themselves, and we had time for ourselves. Any time I broached the subject, I got the same answer. "If you find someone who will give you one, then you can have it." She knew people did not just give babies away like puppies, so she had nothing to worry about.

I went home that night and again began to talk about how I would really like to have another baby, and again I got her same answer back. "Find someone to give you one, and you can have it."

Then, pow! I hit her with it! "Done deal," I said. I then told her of the situation and the offer to adopt the child. She was stunned.

Over the next several days, we analyzed our lives, and she pretty much convinced me that we should not take on any more responsibilities than we already had. Besides, we did not know anything about adoption, the health of the still-unborn baby, and a variety of other things. Besides, we wanted what would be best for the child. We had some married friends who could not have children, so we introduced them to the birth mom and her guardian.

Months passed, and I thought everything was settled. Then three weeks before the baby was to be born, I heard it was a girl. I had always wanted a girl. I was sad I missed this chance.

One afternoon, I got another call from the aunt, who was very distraught. After several months of the birth mother making arrangements with the other couple, they backed out of the plan. Now the baby would be given up to the county when born. Auntie pleaded again, "Please, will you take the baby?" She then went on, "Although the plans were made with the other family, me and my niece always wanted your family to take the child. Somehow it feels like you are supposed to raise her." She pleaded with me to please reconsider.

Well, it was not me she needed to convince. When I heard this and realized that I now had the chance not only for a baby, but a baby girl to boot, I flew out of the office with a plan.

I called my wife and told her we were going to dinner

at our favorite romantic restaurant. That evening, I told her of the latest phone conversation with the aunt. She interrupted me as she smiled and said, "For the past few months, I've prayed about this. Although I felt like it was God's will that we adopt this child, I wanted proof, so I asked that if it was his plan, then to reassure me by making it amazingly easy and with no worries or hurdles to jump."

I sat stunned, loving her more than ever.

"Call the aunt and birth mother. Tell them we would be more than happy to adopt the baby."

With shaking hands, I made the call. Three weeks later, we awoke at 3:00 AM to a phone call saying we were having a baby!

Being in the room during the birth at the request of the birth mother was incredible and something that we had never discussed or expected. We all spent the night with the newest addition to our family, and as I walked out the doors of the hospital the next day with that little warm bundle in my arms, I was ten feet tall!

Later that night, as my wife and I lay in bed staring at our little angel, she said, "You, of all people in this world, should never be able to doubt that there is a God and that he truly gives us the desires of our hearts."

She kissed our daughter, then me. "This belated Father's Day present was worth the wait."

Clifton Bush

Adoption from the Soul

God is a circle whose center is everywhere, and circumference nowhere.

Empedocles

When God put the desire in my heart to adopt, I was ten years old. My parents and I were driving in our maroon Mercury when an announcement came on the radio. Thousands of orphans from Vietnam were being flown to the United States, and they were seeking families to adopt these children.

"Can we adopt one?" I asked.

My mom looked at my dad. "What do you think?"

My heart raced; perhaps my prayers for a younger brother or sister were about to be answered. I didn't dare breathe . . . until I heard my parents say, "No."

I sat back in my seat and vowed that I would adopt a child myself when I grew up.

Twenty years later, I was shopping with my daughter, Rachel, when I noticed a flyer for an adoption agency called Holt International. On the front was a picture of a beautiful baby. I took it out to the car to show it to my husband Len.

Len and I are strong believers in miracles. We had seen and experienced God doing many things over the years, not the least of which was giving us our daughter, Rachel. We had been told numerous times by numerous doctors that we would never be able to conceive a baby.

When Len read the flyer, he immediately responded with an enthusiastic, "I think this is from God, and we should pursue it!"

We filled out the simple form on the flyer and mailed it right away. It wasn't long before we got a letter from Holt saying they had children from Korea immediately available for Colorado families. Thus began the overwhelming yet exciting process of adoption.

I had nightmares about the woman who would do our home study. In my dreams, I would open the door to look upon a matronly Gestapo-looking woman with white gloves. She'd go through my home checking for dust on the top of my refrigerator and in any nook and cranny she could find.

I was a bundle of nerves when the day arrived for us to meet our real, live, home-study lady. There was a knock on the door, and I opened it with sweaty palms. To my delight, there stood a sporty young woman, about my age, wearing a big smile. Jody from Colorado Adoption Agency and I became fast friends and even prayed for one another, since she had adopted children, too.

The day finally came when we received a call saying they had a little boy for us to consider. I was on pins and needles as I called Len at the church where he was the youth pastor, telling him to be on the lookout for a fax from Holt. When he came home with the fax, the baby in the picture looked like a little black blob in white pajamas. We didn't care what he looked like, so we eagerly read the written information. He was born two months premature, had a heart murmur and . . . might be blind from excess oxygen given to him at birth.

I wasn't concerned about the premature birth or the heart murmur. But blindness? I didn't know anyone who was blind, so I wasn't sure what we would be facing.

Len and I asked people for their counsel on making this decision. Most responded with, "There are thousands of children who need to be adopted. Pick another one." This didn't sit well with us. We realized that prayer was the only way for us to make this decision.

That night, we prayed about this baby boy. I couldn't sleep, and I went to the couch so I wouldn't keep Len awake. I prayed and cried out to God until I finally fell asleep in the wee hours of the morning. At 4:00 AM, I woke up as I heard God say to me, "Adopt that baby." I jumped up from the couch and ran to Len, shaking him from a deep sleep. "We need to adopt that baby!" He sleepily said, "Okay," and immediately fell back to sleep.

After months of waiting, it was finally time to go to Korea and pick up nine-month-old Colin Josef. We decided my mom and I would go, and Len would stay home and take care of Rachel.

My mom and I set off for the adventure of our lives! After our seventeen-hour flight, we arrived in Korea and made our way through customs. The adoption agency had given me several instructions ahead of time on where to go, how to exchange money, and what to expect while in Korea. Mom and I walked arm-in-arm to a line for a cab. The reluctant driver took us all over Seoul, stopping to ask people for directions. One group would point east, the next west. We went four-wheeling cross-country in this yellow taxi cab, down alleys and countless neon-lit streets, at breakneck speed. After hours of screeching, horn blowing, swerving to the left and then to the right with reckless abandon, our frustrated driver deposited us and our frazzled nerves at the gate of our destination. We were exhausted and unimaginably grateful to find our home for the night.

The next morning was our scheduled time to meet Colin. We waited in the office for him to come with his foster mother. It was more than exciting and a little scary. Would he be healthy? Would he be blind?

Then she walked through the door and handed Colin to me. I took him in my arms. He seemed to look up at me with dark eyes. Could he see? He took his tiny hands, each on one side of my face, and gently stroked my cheeks.

The foster mother said, through the interpreter, "That is his way of saying 'I love you.'"

"Mom!" I cried. "I think he can see!"

I handed him to his grandmother who had traveled with me halfway around the world. He put his hands on her face and said, "I love you."

This fifteen-pound, nine-month-old baby knew he was meeting . . . and seeing . . . his family for the first time. Perhaps God had woken him up at 4:00 AM, gently whispering in his heart, too.

Coni Billings

Front-Page News

God is the poet of the world, with tender patience leading it by his vision of truth, beauty, and goodness.

Alfred North Whitehead

In late February 2000, my sister watched a television program that featured children, somewhere in a foreign country, living under a bridge because they had nowhere else to go. This was not the first time she had seen a program of this nature, but for some reason on this particular day she felt moved to do more than just watch. She went to bed that night and prayed that if this was something that she and her husband were to pursue, that God would give her a sign . . . not just any sign, but front-page news, something she could not misinterpret.

The following day, she told me about all this. I was stunned because that same night I'd had a dream that she and I had both adopted baby girls from China. But she didn't believe that this was the sign she had asked for; it wasn't front-page news.

The next morning, she got up and raced to get the local paper. Nothing. No sign.

Around midday, my mail arrived, and I nearly fainted. On the very front page of a little local weekly paper was an article about a family who had adopted a child. I ran to the phone to call my sister, but she wasn't home. I thought I was going to burst. Not more than thirty minutes later, she called me crying, saying that she had seen the paper and knew what had to be done. God had answered her prayer and had done so with a sign, in just the manner she had asked.

Six months later, after mountains of paperwork and processing, our family caravan of three vehicles arrived at the airport. My sister couldn't stop shaking or crying, but these were tears of joy, soon to be tears of relief.

As the passengers filed off the plane, I thought for a moment that my sister might collapse, but her husband held tightly to her as a tear ran down his face, too.

Then there he was. The last passenger was a woman with a baby strapped to her chest, his wide eyes looking around. My sister quickly composed herself and wrapped her son in her arms, and then we all took turns holding the newest addition to our already close-knit family . . . our front-page news.

Virginia Chaney

Christmas Providence

Ask and you shall receive, seek and you shall find, knock and the door shall be open unto you.

Matthew 7:7

After exhausting all other avenues first, our attention turned to adoption. Soon, by word of mouth, we had located a birth mother due to deliver in the fall. We excitedly made plans for our new little baby. All was well until the day of the baby's birth. We'd had warning signs from the family, but the birth mother assured us that she would hold firm to her commitment to us. Then the day we were to take the baby home from the hospital, the family decided to keep the baby and "try" to raise it on their own. I cannot find the words to describe the loss, disappointment, and anger that consumed us.

After the agony we had endured throughout the year, we decided to spend Christmas alone together. A rented cabin in the mountains of Tennessee seemed to be the ideal getaway. The day before we were to leave, I awoke before Jennifer and began to recall what we

had been through the previous twelve months. My
heart ached as I thought of the pain she had endured
and how much she deserved to have a baby of her own.
I started to pray, reminding God of the kind, loving,
motherly heart he had given Jennifer. I had asked God
to bring a baby into our lives many times before, but
this time I begged, "Please, God, give us a baby for
Christmas." It would be a fitting end to an otherwise
dismal year.

We really enjoyed our time away at the cabin in a
beautiful part of the country. Our Christmas was very
nice, and as we lay down for an afternoon nap, I was a
bit saddened as I recalled my prayer. The day was half
over, and nothing had happened, so I went upstairs to
pray. I reminded God of my prayer for a Christmas
baby. I didn't care how; I was ready to turn it over to
God. I prayed that he would blow us away when his
plan was revealed to us. Little did I know that his plan
was already a gale-force wind.

The rest of our Christmas day was spent with the
usual calls to and from family. Then I did something for
the first time ever on Christmas . . . I called my brother
Willard in Houston. During our conversation of "what
did you get," he received another call.

When he resumed our conversation, he said, "Eric,
you're not going to believe this but that call was from a
friend saying her niece had a baby this morning. She
was placing the baby for adoption, but the adoptive
parents backed out because the baby is unexpectedly
biracial." Willard went on to explain that their friend
remembered we were trying to adopt. "She wants to
know, are you interested?"

My mind immediately raced to my prayer. "Of course!"

After several calls to family, our attorney, and the
birth mother, it appeared that this was going to hap-

pen. Knowing we would not sleep, we loaded up at midnight and headed back home to Alabama. The following morning, we flew to Houston and picked up our precious Christmas baby at the hospital.

I always believed that God had a plan, a big plan, to bring a baby into our lives, but I never expected a Christmas miracle!

Eric Myers

Hope on the Line

*T*rust the Lord with all your heart, and do not rely on your own understanding.

Proverbs 3:5

A telephone call can be life-changing.

The first telephone call in a series of life-changing telephone calls for me was from my obstetrician. After some pressure from my medical doctor, he had finally agreed to induce my nine-month pregnancy. It was a week before my due date, but at my last visit with the doctor, he couldn't find a fetal heartbeat. An inducement was scheduled. Unfortunately, my worst fears were realized when I delivered a ten-pound, two-ounce stillborn son.

The following years were filled with hurtful memories, a deluge of baby-product advertisements, and adoption applications. My husband and I had always talked about adopting, even if we had biological children, so we filled out the forms and waited.

To take our minds off the loss, we decided to move from our two-bedroom home to a four-bedroom one in a neighboring county. We kept believing that someday God was going to fill those rooms.

Then another phone call almost derailed our hopes. I had called the adoption agencies to give them our new address, and several of them gave us the devastating news that due to the fact we had moved to a different county, we could no longer remain on their list. Our step of faith was starting to look like a huge mistake.

We had been in the new house about one week when my husband asked if I wanted to go to a special church service that night. I told him no. To be perfectly honest, I didn't really feel like going and hearing someone tell me how much God loved me when at the time I didn't feel like he did. I couldn't understand why we were having to go through so much pain. My first pregnancy had ended in a twelve-week miscarriage, followed by the stillbirth. None of this was making any sense.

We decided to stay home that night to unpack and arrange at least one of the rooms in the new house. We chose the nursery. We worked on the room until around midnight when my husband, who had to work the next morning, went to bed. I stayed up to finish, but mainly just had a pity party. I cried out to God, "This is so unfair! I don't understand! You know how much I want a baby! Please, help me trust in your plan."

Finally, I gave up. I told God that I didn't understand why all of the loss had happened, but I was going to trust him in spite of it. I knew he had an overall plan for my life. At two o'clock in the morning, I collapsed into bed.

At six o'clock, another life-changing phone call came. One of the adoption-agency women said, "We have a three-week-old baby boy waiting for you."

Needless to say, I was on the next flight to pick him up!

Not long after, we got another phone call about another baby available. He wasn't born yet, but we agreed to adopt him and anxiously awaited his birth.

When that day came and we received the phone call of his birth, I was in my second trimester of another pregnancy!

Three boys in two years! That's proof positive that God has a sense of humor! And that phone calls can be life-changing . . . when you trust his plan.

Martha Bolton

"You'd better be the adoption agency."

My Sister's Story

Faith makes the discords of the present, the harmonies of the future.

Robert Collyer

The year was 1942. It was a horrendous time in England during the Second World War. Bombs devastated our cities and disrupted our lives. My sister was a teenager, and because many of our young men were overseas defending our country, she was drafted into the Land Army. She and other teenage girls worked at the farms, brought in the crops, and took care of the animals until the war ended and life became, hopefully, normal again.

My sister loved being in the Land Army, though everything was not happy in her life. Our mother died, Father was transferred to London to help with the war, and our own home was bombed and destroyed.

Then, into her life came a love story. She became engaged to a Royal Air Force Spitfire fighter pilot. It was a perfect love match. Tragedy struck, however, and her fiancé was killed. She was pregnant with his baby. My sister was in an emotional turmoil. After much soul-searching, she decided to give up her baby for adoption. She held him briefly after birth, and then he was whisked away.

Months followed months. She fell in love and married a G.I. They came to America where she and her husband had three children. Sadly, her husband died at an early age, and she was left to raise the children by herself.

But she never forgot her firstborn son. There was a constant ache in her heart, and when St. Patrick's Day, his birthday, came around, she would wonder what sort of a life he had.

Time went on. Incredibly, her son was able to trace her. And so it was that, on her eightieth birthday, he came to America to meet her. He brought with him his son, and now she had additional grandchildren.

It was a fantastic and joyful meeting. During the course of the weekend, my sister was asked by her son whether she would mind telling him where his father's grave was. She happily gave him directions.

On his return to England, he went to the grave. To his amazement, he found the grass surrounding it beautifully manicured. An old gentleman stood there by the grave so my nephew introduced himself. The old man said he had been tending it for more than sixty years.

"Your dad was my buddy," he said. "We flew together. He was a great guy. In fact," he continued, "I have his flying jacket at home if you would like it."

Thus, you have the end of the story. My sister's dream came true; she was reunited with her son again and knew that he was having a happy life. My nephew found his mother and happily connected to his newfound family. And now he has his father's flying jacket as tangible proof that God does indeed work in mysterious ways.

Diana M. Millikan

A Miracle

We sat in church, my husband, Carey, and I, listening to our friend Herb share stories of the hard conditions of the orphanages in China: too many abandoned children and too few workers and resources. He had wept as he witnessed firsthand little babies, alone and unloved, weak, and some dying. Herb met a woman named Joy who was pulling sickly babies out of the orphanage and nursing them back to health, then returning them and taking others. He was so moved by the plight of these little ones and the precious heart of this courageous woman that he had come back to the States, committed to raising both awareness and funds to help Joy in her labors. My husband's tender heart was moved to give a substantial donation to the Home of Joy, and I thought the matter was closed.

Several months later, Herb returned to our church, selling scrolls painted with scripture in Chinese character for donations for the Home of Joy. As Herb showed us these scrolls, a thought popped into my head: *Adopt a toddler girl from China with a cleft lip and palate.* I knew Carey would never go for this because after our first two biological children were born, a girl and a boy, he had been quite content. We had the ideal American family. Then I convinced Carey to have a third child, and we were "complete." Because we had started our family later in life, Carey being eight years my senior, I knew he was way beyond ready to move on from the baby stage of life. No more diapers and car seats! So I put the thought in the back of my mind.

I was flabbergasted when Carey told me that while we were looking at the scrolls, he had a vision. "It was the hand of God picking up a little girl from China and putting her into our home," he said with amazement. "She was a toddler with a cleft lip and palate."

Carey is someone who has always believed that God can do miracles like visions and healings, but that he doesn't do them today. He was so scared and skeptical that he went to ask a friend for advice about how to know when God is speaking to you. He couldn't deny that he had experienced something supernatural.

When Carey and I both realized that God was directing us to adopt our daughter, it was a very emotional process, with lots of tears and fears. In fact, our first thought of adopting happened in November 1997, and we did nothing about it until March 1998, when we finally stopped wrestling with God.

We called an adoption agency and shared with them our desire to adopt.

"China has very strict rules now, so let me ask you a few questions," the man explained. "How old are both of you?"

When I told him our ages, he replied, "Because of your ages, you will not be able to adopt an infant. China requires that there be a maximum of forty-five years between parent and child so you will only be allowed to adopt a toddler."

Perfect! No diapers or bottles!

"Do you want to adopt a boy or girl?"

"A girl," I replied promptly.

"Good, because it is literally impossible to adopt a boy from China."

"Do you have any biological children in the home?"

"We have three."

"Well, this is where we run into difficulties because China has a strange policy that if you have biological children in the home, you must adopt a child with a fixable disability such as a cleft lip or palate or missing limb."

Where others might have been shocked and discouraged, I laughed and cried. God had spoken to us again. I shared with this Christian man what we had experienced. I thought he might think we were crazy, but he, too, rejoiced with us, and we started the paperwork immediately.

Seventy documents, thousands of dollars, and fourteen months later, we were on a plane to bring our precious little girl home.

We had decided to name her Johanna Allegra Xiaoru Gromis, Johanna meaning "Yahweh is gracious," and Allegra after her grandmother, meaning "Joy."

Because we had an "unusual request" child, they had to search at least five different orphanages to find a child with a cleft lip and palate. Typically, children with cleft palates do not survive in orphanages because they require special care that cannot be spared for one child. But since March 1998, we had prayed that the Lord would help Johanna find favor with the workers, and that they would love and care for her. God clearly honored our request.

Unlike the other babies, Johanna had three women from her orphanage accompany her on her journey to us. They wept when they handed her over to us. We embraced her and all of our dreams—but she reached out and cried for them. The director of the orphanage came to the hotel the next day to check on her. Our adoption group leader told us that that had never happened before in all his years of leading groups through the process.

When we got to our hotel, we discovered that, at eighteen months, Johanna already knew how to hold a pencil and draw little circles, and eat with a spoon. The workers at the orphanage had taken the time to love her and teach her. God had answered yet another prayer.

We landed back in the United States to a reception of our three children, our extended family, and loads of friends. Johanna entertained everyone with her bubbly personality the first day. Our family is very lively and funny, so everyone agreed that Johanna was simply born in the wrong country, and God fixed the mistake.

Three months later, we realized that all the money we had spent on adopting her was back in our savings account—$2,000 was from gifts; the rest was from a retroactive check, a life-insurance policy, and a tax benefit for adopting. God was showing us that in our obedience, he would bless us beyond our wildest imagination, and it wouldn't cost us a cent.

Today, eight-year-old Johanna continues to be a joy to others and especially to us. Through her surgeries, speech therapy, and painful dental work, she exhibits the strength God gave her to survive those first eighteen months of life and to gain the affection of others.

God blessed our home with a fourth blessed child.

My husband now firmly agrees that God does do miracles today.

Cheryl Gromis

5

LESSONS

Life is a succession of lessons which must be lived to be understood.

Helen Keller

Mother's Day Blessing

I sat at church on Mother's Day, anticipating . . . again . . . the annual ceremony where all the moms are called to the altar to stand while the entire congregation raises their hands and blesses them. I reminisced about all of those years where my brother, sister, dad, and I watched Mom go up.

I recalled the past four years when I had longed to go up but instead sat in my seat, trying not to think about another year gone by.

Though admittedly sometimes strained, our faith had seen my husband Dave and me through the many disappointments.

And there had been so many disappointments.

Four years of infertility. A failed adoption.

My brother was adopted and I had heard and truly believed all my life that every child is created and assigned to his or her parents. So when the call had come, we said "yes" to the baby we assumed was assigned to us. The agency said it was the only time in their fifteen-year history that the birth mother had changed her mind. As we clung to each other after they took him away, Dave and I sobbed with the reality, "He was not our baby." Though we were privileged to love and care for him for three days, the grief of traveling home with empty arms had overwhelmed us both.

Undaunted and faith-filled, we began the wait . . . again.

Then, three months later, four days before my birthday, on a Sunday morning I thought, *I better turn my cell phone on. I have a feeling the call is going to come.*

"The call" didn't come that Sunday.

Or Monday.

Or Tuesday.

As I anticipated my birthday in two days, I confided to a friend, "I have a hunch I will share my birthday with a daughter for the rest of my life."

I repeated this strong intuitive feeling to another friend as we shared lunch on a patio café at 2:00 PM on Tuesday. A bee landed on my arm. Before I could brush it away, I cried out in pain! I had never been stung by a bee before.

"The call" didn't come the next day, Wednesday, either.

On Thursday, my birthday, my cell phone rang. It was our adoption agency. "This will be a happy day," she said.

They are the kindest, most thoughtful people, I thought. "You got my birthday from our records. How sweet of you to remember."

"It's your birthday?" she squealed. "I had no idea! A baby girl was born at two o'clock on Tuesday . . . "

"Will all the mothers please come forward," I heard the priest say.

As I approached the altar with Mom at my side I could see we were both trying not to cry. I stood with the women of my parish who had watched me grow up, holding our tiny three-week-old baby against my chest.

"Who's this?" Father Don exclaimed in a whisper.

"She is our baby daughter, Dagny Grace." I could hardly keep from shouting.

With my little girl in one hand, and my mother's hand in the other, I bowed my head, accepting the blessing bestowed by our faith community.

Mom and I then took our seats and did our best to focus on the rest of the mass.

As it ended and Father was about to say the final prayer, he nearly leapt from the altar and raced down the aisle. I couldn't imagine what was the matter. He approached our row, took his microphone from his lapel, and put it before my lips.

"Tell us, Christie, what does this day mean to you."

Normally I'm one of those people who is terrified to speak in public. But this time I stood and faced the hundreds of smiling faces. "Everything."

Father beamed and nodded to our baby. "Who is this?"

"This is our newborn daughter, Dagny Grace," I said, hardly believing my own words.

Father simply said, "Tell us."

"For years I prayed to have a baby and I longed for the day when I could stand before this congregation on Mother's Day and receive the blessing. And today I stand here with our baby girl. This is the child God created and assigned to us. We know, now, that adoption is not Plan B. It just took us a while to realize that it was God's Plan A all along."

Christie Rogers

Do You Love Me as Much?

Before you were conceived, I wanted you. Before you were born, I loved you. Before you were here an hour, I would die for you. This is the miracle of love.

Maureen Hawkins

"Mom, do you love me as much as you would love a real kid?"

I asked that question at least once a week when I was ten.

I don't know why her first answer didn't satisfy me; maybe I was looking for inconsistencies. Her answer was always the same, though. "What makes you think you aren't real, Nancy?" That was followed by a long talk about how much she wanted me, how she had seven premature babies who did not live, and that prior to the time they learned I was available for adoption, she was so depressed that they had tried drastic measures to help her smile again. She assured me that her life began, in many ways, the day they brought me home. She let me know, once again, that I was truly wanted, loved, cared about, and that I grew in her heart while I grew in my birth mom's tummy. She gave me constant assurance I was "real and wanted."

Yet, I always wondered.

It's not that I thought my mom was lying, exactly. But since she didn't have any living children of "her own," maybe she just didn't know how much she would love one of them compared to stinky old me.

I would like to say that my childhood was perfect. That it was a fairy tale of toys and love and no punishments. That I was perfect. The reality is not tragic, just normal. Yes, my parents made mistakes, and, of course, I was not perfect. I am sure there were days they wondered what on earth they had gotten themselves into. I know there were certainly times I fantasized about the perfect birth parents, as many adopted kids do. I often pretended that the Captain and Tennille were my first parents and invited me to sing on their show and tour with them.

I was especially close to my mom, yet somewhere in the back of my mind I always wondered if I was loved as much as birth children were loved by their parents. Was I somehow missing out?

On a cold, rainy, horrible day in 1980, my mom crossed the street for the last time. Somehow, she did not see the car headed toward her. At only sixteen, I didn't know if I would ever recover. Gone were all the things a young woman needs a mother for, the insight from someone who has been where she will be going.

Seventeen years later, I, too, gave birth to a premature baby and, like my mother, lost him a short time after birth. I had buried my mother . . . wasn't that enough, God? How could I survive the death of my son?

It was finally determined that I would probably never get pregnant again, let alone carry a baby to term. The same condition that prevented my mother from having children plagued me. My grief overwhelmed me. I wanted to talk to Mom and I did, but I longed for her replies. In the midst of this, we, like my parents, applied for adoption.

I almost didn't pick up the phone that day. I was depressed because it was almost the anniversary of my son's due date. I was hiding. The call was normal until the woman at our agency asked, "Why would I call you on a Saturday?"

It took a few moments to dawn on me that Saturday calls about adoption were rare . . . unless . . . "Oh, dear God!" I screamed into the receiver. "There's a baby, isn't there?" I jumped up and down, yelling my joy and crying at the same time. I called my elated husband and all of our friends and family before it dawned on me that I hadn't found out if the baby was a boy or girl.

Sunday, the twenty-seventh of April, was nippy and bright. An eternal cab ride to South Chicago brought us, nervously, to our destination. The birth mom looked at me shyly as she placed her . . . my . . . our . . . baby boy into my arms. I did not know how to react. I didn't want to show my elation in the face of her obvious pain. My heart bled for her, but soared for me. "He's so soft" was all I could say. I wanted everything out of my mouth to be perfect, to tell her how much I would love him, how we were naming him after my husband, that we would cherish him. That moment was the most precious of my life. It changed us forever. When she placed Gene-Gene into my arms, she opened the entire universe for us. She made all of our dreams come true.

I am the mother of four boys now—two adopted children and two miracle birth children, born as early as some of my brothers and sisters. Forty years of technology gave my babies the chance that my siblings did

not have. I know a lot now. I know that little boys like
jokes about all sorts of disgusting things. I know I have
more patience than I dreamed, and I know what pure
love is.

Most of all, I knew the answer the day my oldest son
came to me and asked, "Do you love me as much as you
love my brothers? The ones who grew in your
tummy?"

"Yes, sweetheart, I do. I love you just as much as my
mommy loved me."

Nancy Liedel

He Is Mine

I tiptoed into your room one night.
I watched you sleeping there.
Your tiny body looked so snug
Wrapped in peaceful slumber's care.

I thought of how you came to be
The child we'd longed to know.
I wondered at the sight of you:
"How could she let you go?"

Tears streamed down my cheeks as I
Felt the pain she must have known.
For I will have to let you go
Some day when you are grown.

A mother I might never meet
Had given me her son.
Yet, surely as you've filled my heart,
A piece of hers you'd won.

"How could she let you go?"
The question kept returning.

And in the depths of my own heart
A question kept on burning.

"How can *I* ever let you go
When years have come and gone?"
I stood there by your crib until
The nighttime turned to dawn.

And as the sun peeked through the shades,
The voice of God broke through.
"I trusted her to give him life
And now I'm trusting you.

"To show him what is right and wrong,
To love him and to be
The one who teaches him the way
To come back home to me.

"He wasn't hers to give, you know.
And he's not yours to own.
I've placed him in your life to love
But he is mine . . . on loan."

Valerie Kay Gwin

Adoption Means . . .

Mother is the name of God in the lips and hearts of little children.

William Makepeace Thackery

"Mommy, what's 'adopted'?" I sit in the bathtub and rub the washrag over my round tummy, watching the soap bubbles make frothy swirls on my skin.

Even at four years old, I know what she will answer. I only ask because I love to hear her say it.

It was never a secret in our family that my sister and I had been adopted. The word was familiar to me before I had any notion of what it meant. Years later, as a teenager, I would wonder at sensationalized television movies that portrayed shocking revelations of adoption: adult children thrown into the depths of despair, appalled at having been betrayed by their parents—or, no, they weren't their parents at all, were they? Identity crises. Rage. Anger. Depression. Psychotherapy.

But none of these dramas made any sense to me. Adoption is not something my family talks about; it's simply not that dramatic, that important. My sister and

I are not "adopted daughters"; we're just daughters.

After each of my own children was born, my entire family was struck with temporary amnesia: we marveled at how each baby looked exactly like my father. Eventually, someone would snap out of it and realize that was just a coincidence—or maybe a function of the fact that my dad's head is huge and round, so pretty much every baby looks a little like him.

As pedestrian and routine as it may be to my family and to me, it is certainly a dramatic revelation when my adoption comes up in mixed company.

"Oh . . . I had no idea you were adopted." (I have yet to craft a response to this one: was I obliged to disclose that at some earlier point in our relationship?)

"Is your sister your real sister?" (We may not share the same hair and eye color, but she's real enough to have called me "Four Eyes" and "Brace Face" and to have been maid of honor at my wedding.)

I've heard people refer to my lack of ancestors, as if I had hatched from an egg or a pea pod. There are the concerned questions about medical mysteries carrying with them the apparent assumption that I'm perhaps more likely to get breast cancer simply because I don't know if my biological mother, aunts, or grandmothers ever had it.

And, of course, there is the grand prize winner: "When did you find out?"

And that's the thing. I didn't find out, because I always knew. There's no need for secrecy when there's no scandal, so my mother told us early and often, and she said it well.

Mommy pours a cupful of cool water over my head and smiles.

"'Adopted' means you were loved enough to be given up, and loved enough to be taken in. 'Adopted' means twice-loved."

Mandy Houk

Dear Son

Dear Son,

It has been more than thirty years since that long, lonely night when you entered the world. Yet, I can still recall almost everything that happened. I can still see the kind face of the compassionate young nurse who helped me get through it. I can still hear the unique noises of the busy maternity ward. I still remember going into shock, being covered with hot blankets, and lying for hours in a hallway near the nurses' station so they could closely monitor my condition. But, most of all, I remember every detail of the healthy, beautiful baby boy I delivered that night.

The little boy I would never hold and would never see again. The little boy I had opted to carry, under my heart, for nine months rather than abort. The little boy I was not emotionally or financially equipped to care for. The little boy whose fate I had agonized over for weeks. The little boy who I had finally decided needed to be turned over to another mother.

I remember the incredible, indescribable emptiness I felt as I walked out of the hospital without you in my arms, wondering if the feeling would last forever. I remember sobbing uncontrollably that day, six weeks later, when I signed my name to the papers that forever terminated my rights to call you my son. I remember the debilitating depression that set in shortly afterward and lasted for months.

For years, I looked into the eyes of little boys and wondered if any of them were you. Although I did not personally handpick your new family, it had been an open adoption. I knew who they were and the name they gave you, but I also knew that it was in the best interest of us both that I refrain from contacting you.

Sometimes, motherhood requires us to make difficult choices. It forces us to think with our hearts as often as we do with our heads. It compels us to make every decision on the basis of what is best for our child, regardless of the personal cost to ourselves.

I did not give you away because I did not love you. I was not eager to get rid of you because you reminded me of someone or something I wished to forget. On the contrary, I wanted you very much. I have not and I will not ever forget you, the circumstances surrounding your conception, your gestation, or your birth. I made the choice that all of my maternal instincts told me was the most beneficial one for you.

I was the woman who gave birth to you, but the woman who carried you out of that hospital and took you into her home is your mother. She is the one who rocked you to sleep and got up at 2:00 AM to feed you. She is the one who held you in her arms and walked with you all night when you were unable to sleep. She is the one who took you to well-baby checkups and sat with you in emergency rooms.

She is the one who read you stories, gave you baths, taught you to brush your teeth and comb your hair. She is the one who made sure you knew how to write your name and count to one hundred. She is the one who consoled you when you were hurt, encouraged you when you were insecure, and reassured you when you were afraid of monsters under your bed. She is the one who believed in you and tried to convince you that you could do anything. She is the one who was always there to laugh with you and to cry with you.

She is the one who stayed up all night worrying that first time you drove the car alone. She is the one who checked out every girl you dated and worried about one of them breaking your heart. She is the one who guided you in making college and career choices. If you are married, she had to release you into the care of another woman, praying all the while that she would love you as much as she herself did, just as I had done all those years before when I entrusted you to her.

The woman who became your mother *chose* to take you. She accepted you as you were. She was willing to take on whatever challenges you came with. I believed that she would love you as unconditionally as I myself did. She was in a better position to meet your needs than I was, so I made the choice to entrust you to her. It was a very hard choice, but I believed with all of my heart that it was the best choice for both of us. I hope that you have been able to forgive me for making it.

I may not ever have an opportunity to see what kind of a man you turned out to be. I will probably never know if you have a daughter with my eyes. It is likely that I will not hold you this side of heaven. But that does not mean that I do not love you. You are a part of me, and I have never forgotten you. You were never unwanted.

Love, Mother

Bridget Colern

Expecting Again

*A sweet, new blossom of humanity, fresh fallen
from God's own home to flower on Earth.*

Gerald Massey

I rode an emotional roller coaster for months each
time my husband, David, and I were expecting. I cried
at the drop of a hat, worried about any and everything,
second-guessed my parenting ability, and became such
a daydreamer. I wasn't safe operating a motor vehicle.
It was the same each time—with Haley, Molly,
Hewson, and just two years ago, with Jonah. The difference is that the first three times I was pregnant. The
last time, we were waiting to adopt.

The closer our adoption came, the more I experienced the symptoms of pregnancy. Instead of watching
my belly expand, we watched the mountain of paperwork accumulate on our dining-room table. Instead of
reading *What to Expect When You're Expecting* for the fourth
time, we attended a ten-week class for adoptive parents. Instead of registering for my baby shower, I
wandered through thrift stores trying to replace all the

baby items we'd given away when we finally gave up on having a fourth child.

Those were the differences, but the similarities were far greater.

Just like the first three times, I was an emotional yo-yo, falling apart over the sappiest TV commercials and magazine ads, or sometimes for no reason at all. One glimpse of a baby on the street, and I turned to mush.

The feelings of helplessness were back, too. When I was pregnant, I'd stand by the side of the road waiting to cross and hold my breath for fear I'd inhale car exhaust and harm my developing child. I worried that, unbeknownst to me, asbestos was wafting through the heating vents in my office. I swore off alcohol, coffee, and artificial sweetener, but worried there was something I'd forgotten to eliminate. This time, I felt even more helpless as I wondered if my son was already born or if his mama was still pregnant with him. Was she eating right, taking prenatal vitamins, wearing her seatbelt? I couldn't allow myself to contemplate the harmful things she might be doing.

I have to admit it was kind of cool keeping my figure this time (or what's left of it). But other things were the same, like the overwhelming doubts. Could I love this baby like I loved the others? How will the family dynamics change with another one? How would my oldest adjust to no longer being the only boy? I worried about birth defects and whether I'd be a good enough mother to parent a special-needs child. Plus, this time I had new concerns. Will he want to find his birth parents some day, and how will I deal with it if he does? How much do we tell him about his life before us, and when do we begin?

The nesting instincts were the same, though. The closer the time came for our much-anticipated call, the more my thoughts turned toward home, not just getting his little room ready, but the entire house. I wanted it to be an oasis of love and acceptance, the way a home should be. I wanted to offer him a chocolate-chip cookie, a speckle-tailed dog, *Runaway Bunny*, a fire in the fireplace, bunk beds in the boys' room, soup on the stove—a Mama-and-Daddy-love-each-other kind of home, and achieving it for him was nothing short of an obsession.

I kept telling myself this was all crazy. I wasn't pregnant. There was nothing going on hormonally inside of me to bring on this deluge of emotions. My body wasn't nurturing a little life and going through the changes that naturally come with it.

When our David Jonah arrived, though, I realized something. My body may not have been nurturing a new little life, but my heart most certainly was.

Mimi Greenwood Knight

Whose Stomach Was It?

Truth is beautiful and divine, no matter how humble its origin.

Michael Idvorsky Pupin

When my adopted son, Tyler, was about three years old, he saw his first pregnant woman. In bed, at prayer time, he asked, "What was wrong with that lady's belly?"

I described God's miraculous plan that allows a baby to live in the womb.

Tyler asked, "Was I in your tummy, Mommy?"

"No," I replied softly, "in someone else's."

"Was it Daddy's?"

"No."

"Was it Poppy's?"

"No."

"Was it Chuckie's (our cocker spaniel)?"

With my chuckles under control, I said, "You were in your birth mother's tummy, and her name was Mary."

Tyler said, "Oh, like Jesus' mother," and rolled over and went to sleep!

Debra J. Haralam

Real

They always talk, who never think.

Matthew Prior

We happily introduced our brand-new, eighteen-month-old son, Aaron, to one of our church elders and his wife. Both had stooped to say hello and embrace our child. Then the woman looked up at me and nodded, "Someday, you'll have real children."

I froze. *Did I hear that right? Real children? Is this bubbling child beside us a figment of our imaginations?*

"I beg your pardon?"

The lady beamed. "I said that maybe someday you'll have real children. You know, not an adopted one."

Lord, give me restraint! "Our son is as real as it gets, thank you."

I was steaming with indignation. How dare anyone consider this child to be not real to us! It was a very real child who woke us with cheerful playing noises in the morning and scrambled into our bed to cuddle. His very real hands became really sticky after eating a banana or squishing spaghetti on his plate. His very real feet wiggled when we applied socks and were ticklish when we played This Little Piggy. Very real tears were kissed away, and very real chubby arms hugged us back, to say nothing of the very real brown eyes that watched our every move and copied it with real alacrity. Did they not realize the very foundation of Christianity involves spiritual adoption? Grrr.

That was my first encounter with that type of prejudice, but not my last by any means.

Five years later, I was one of the fortunate who became pregnant after adopting. The intensity of awe in becoming pregnant after being told you can't is indescribable. But even more amazing was what happened after my second son's birth.

The nurse walked into the room and just gave him to me. "Here's your baby boy!"

Yep. She just handed him to me without one questionnaire being completed, one medical exam, one fingerprint, one home inspection, or one peek into my psychological profile. I could have been an axe murderer for all she knew of me, yet because I gave birth, I was an instant, trusted, authentic "mom."

"Is that it?" I asked in disbelief.

Confused, the nurse asked what I meant.

"Well, my oldest son is six, and is ours through adoption. We went through hell and high water, under microscopic scrutiny, fingerprinting, fire-department inspection, and they even looked in my refrigerator before I was deemed worthy of being a mom. Because this baby came from my womb you assume I'm going to be a good mom. How does that make sense?"

She laughed the laugh of a woman who hasn't the foggiest notion of what I'm talking about and wants to hurry up and leave the room. "Oh, yeah, some people just aren't good parents, but now you're a real mom!

Ha-ha-ha! Do you want a breastfeeding coach?"

Well, I had, but as my blood boiled, my milk let down, and a coach wasn't needed. "I was a real mom before," I growled as the nurse shrugged and left.

Since when was the act of giving birth the only condition for being a real mom? I groused as I nursed my newborn, amazed at his tiny size even though everyone else called him hefty at eight pounds, two ounces.

What makes a mom real? I wondered. *She has to be more than just someone giving birth or adopting. She has to have a desire deep within, and be able to translate love, guidance, and nurturing through words and action. She has to be soft and squeezable and pliable. She also has to be fairly rock solid, with thick skin and a hard shell for the teenage years. She has to make decisions based on the best interests of someone else, and even sacrifice her time, energy, possessions, dreams, desires, and person on occasion. She has to be able to say yes, no, maybe, later, never, and always at the right times. Okay, she even has to bake cookies at least once, but more than anything, she has to want to be a mother to a child.*

My husband walked in with our wide-eyed six-year-old, and I patted the bed for Aaron to join me. Mike lifted him onto the bed, and Aaron peered at the baby curiously.

"Mommy, is that Sam?"

Aaron's dark, wavy hair bent low over the baby, and I tousled it. "That's Sam. Say 'Hi' to your brother."

"Hi, Sam. We've been waiting for you."

He was right. We, all three of us, a very real little family, had been waiting for the addition of another.

"You want to hold him?"

Aaron nodded, and Mike situated him with pillows under his arms before handing Sam to his older brother.

A Polaroid captured the very real expression of awe and wonder of Aaron and Sam together for the very first time. And though some may say it was gas, I'm sure the smile on Sam's tiny face was a real one. I know ours was.

It isn't who you are born to, who you give birth to, or even who you share DNA with that makes a family. It's deeper than that, and much, much more real.

Patti Wade Zint

"One is our birth child and two are adopted.
We love them the same, so we never
remember which is which!"

Some Children Are Special

Those lives are indeed narrow and confined which are not blessed with several children.

John Burroughs

A blur of wings, two hummingbirds dart among the honeysuckle vines curled around the lattice on the right side of the two-story Victorian home. Vera and I sit on the creaky old porch swing, swaying to and fro, creating a slight breeze. I close my eyes and take in a deep breath of fresh air laced with the sweet scent of honeysuckle and summer.

The sound of a child crying snaps me out of my quiet reverie. I hear her running footsteps and wails.

"That's Karen!" Vera exclaims, throwing down her needlepoint. She rushes to meet Karen in an embrace. Karen buries her face in her mother's bosom and sobs.

"Calm down, Karen. Calm down. It's okay. Mommy's here." Wide, round strokes of her mother's hand on her back soothes her. "Are you all right? Are you hurt?"

Karen calms noticeably. They climb the sun-bleached wooden porch steps hand in hand. Vera sits on the swing next to me and stations the girl in front of us. "Now tell Mommy what has you so upset."

The tears return, and she sputters, "Th-th-the other k-k-k-kids w-w-w-were p-p-picking on m-me." Vera takes her in a mother's hug and strokes her long ebony-black hair until the tension and tears subside. She pulls a ragged tissue from the pocket of her housedress, and with a little mama spit rubs tear streaks from the freckled cheeks. "Tell me about it."

Karen's eyes, swollen from crying, fill again. "Malcolm and his bratty friends got mad at me for no reason. We were on the playground. I wanted a turn on the swings and he said . . ." Tears threaten to swallow her words. "He said . . ."

"What did he say, baby?"

"He said, 'Go home. Nobody wants you here. Your own mother didn't even want you.' He told everyone I was adopted."

Vera doesn't miss a beat. "He's just jealous."

"What? Why would he be jealous of me?"

Karen's confusion mirrors my own.

Vera explains, "He's just jealous 'cause his parents got stuck with him. We picked you out special."

Jessica Kennedy

The Note

Temperate anger well becomes wise.

Philemon

I was angry in Korea. I had been angry all of my life because I was an odd construction of a person: a Korean-looking girl on the outside, a Caucasian-sounding girl on the inside. I didn't know who I was, and I was having a hard time accepting the parts I did know about myself. My background read like that of a hundred thousand other Korean adoptees: I was abandoned as a young child and found in what my mom always called a "police box." Doctors estimated my age like I was a stray dog at an animal shelter. I was given a new generic name and a new generic birthday. I wasn't always accepted as a "white girl" in my little Midwestern town because of how I looked, and for the past few weeks in Korea, I realized that I was having a hard time being accepted as a Korean girl because I couldn't properly speak the language.

"How much longer?" I whispered to my fellow traveler. "I'm starting to feel sick." I was on a bus with around twenty other Korean adult adoptees on what was called a "motherland tour" of Korea. The idea of the trip was for us to get in touch with the land that had given us birth . . . and also rejected us.

The bus shuddered, having to carry us up yet another winding and dangerously narrow road somewhere in Seoul. We were not given the secret location, and instead we were told we were going to a "hospital" where young and unmarried women went to give birth and face the certainty of giving their babies up for adoption. We were about to meet women who symbolized our own birth mothers who had abandoned us, and allowed our fates to be met in a far-off land called America.

We entered what appeared to be a small reception room that was dimly lit and uncomfortably hot. There were no windows to let in the July sun, and cold lines of folding chairs and tables awaited our arrival. My travel companions and I nervously glanced at each other with looks on our faces that said the same thing, "What are we doing here?"

The manager of the hospital entered the room and warmly greeted us. She was a short woman, with permed hair in tight ringlets around her head. Her eyes were small, but as she spoke, her eyes appeared to get larger with each word. "The women want to express their gratitude that you have come to visit them. Please understand that for these women, their journey is hard, because for some of them, not even their families know they are here. The shame of being an unmarried pregnant woman in Korea is still great."

Two main doors opened and, one by one, pregnant Korean women filed in, their faces drawn down to the floor, and each belly appeared to be rounder and fuller than the last. The girls silently sat down opposite each of us. A tiny woman sat across the table from me. She appeared to be no older than twenty, just three years younger than me. She had a short pixie haircut and wore a light pink maternity shirt that barely contained her bulging belly. I knew she had to be close to her due date. She was the first young Korean woman I had seen who didn't wear makeup. She tried to keep her eyes on the floor, but every now and then she would glance at me with pretty, pitiful eyes.

"Anyonghasaeyo!" I tried to say cheerfully, but she barely nodded at me.

I looked down the table and saw my companions also trying unsuccessfully to speak to the women sitting across from them. I stared at the faces of these anonymous women and noticed how desperate and miserable they looked.

The woman sitting across from me passed me an origami-folded crane made out of a bright pink paper. How strange and cheerful the crane seemed in this damp and lonely room.

Suddenly, one pregnant woman touched her belly and began to cry, deep sorrowful wails. Her friends hugged her and also began crying, and my own tears stung my eyes. I realized why these poor women were crying . . . because they saw us, and they realized who their babies would become. Their babies, much like us, would never be able to talk to them, and they would never be able to understand who they were.

As the tears continued to drown my eyes, I could feel the bitterness in my heart seep out because for the first time, I got it. When I saw how much it tormented these women to be pregnant with babies they had to give up, I realized the deep cost of what my birth mother went through. Knowing that she didn't give me up because she was selfish and uncaring lifted a great burden from my heart, and for the first time in my life, I forgave my birth mother for placing me for adoption. I started to heal.

I reached across the table, and taking the pregnant woman's hand, I smiled at her. I placed a crumpled note, previously translated into Korean, gently into her palm. The note told this birth mother, any birth mother, not to worry about her unborn baby. Her baby would grow up to be a good person in America. I continued to hold her hand, and I hoped she could see the sincerity in my eyes. Because in that moment, for me, I held the hand of my birth mother, and she held mine.

Kimberly Hee Stock

6

DEFINING
MOMENTS

*Life becomes harder for us when we live for
others, but it also becomes richer and
happier.*

Albert Schweitzer

A Box of Nothing, a Box of Everything

If God has taught us all truth in teaching us to love, then he has given us an interpretation of our whole duty to our households.

Henry Ward Beecher

When my husband and I made the decision to adopt a child from China, we were hesitant to tell anyone. How would our families feel? Would they support us? Would they ask too many questions or try to change our minds?

Indeed, we got the usual questions. Why adoption? Why China? Isn't there another way? We answered the best way we knew and continued on our paper-chasing way.

Were they really happy for us? In my heart I knew there were lingering doubts, but my heart also knew that in a village across the world there was a little one we loved already, patiently waiting for us.

On our family Christmas, after we opened the gifts, we ate too much, laughed too hard, and prepared for our annual game-time. At every family gathering, a board game becomes the center of attention for both young and old. This time my sister introduced a different type of game. In the center of the living room she placed a box with the words "Box of Everything" written on it. Everything? My curiosity was tweaked.

Everyone was handed a brown lunch bag, taped closed. We were instructed to pass the bag whenever we heard the words "left" or "right." My sister then began to read a story aloud, and every time we heard those words, the bags were passed in that direction. It reminded me of "musical chairs." We passed, dropped, picked up, and passed those bags again, and all the while the children giggled. At the end, my sister informed us we could now open our paper bags.

"There will be one winner," she stated with a smile. I opened my paper bag to discover that I had won! As I started to gloat to my brothers, I heard my husband shout, "I won, too!" My sister just shook her head in confusion and said, ""Well, I guess I made a mistake; you'll just have to share."

We opened the Box of Everything together. First, I took out a can of soup, then a granola bar, Tootsie Rolls, and a dog toy. We don't own a dog, so I was laughing hysterically. I continued and discovered a plastic fork, spoon, and knife. Just when I thought I had found everything, I reached down to the bottom and saw an envelope with my name on it . . . and my husband's name, too. How could that be? I thought this was a game.

I opened the envelope and saw a baby card . . . no, an expectant-parent card, and then it started . . . I couldn't stop . . . the tears formed and rolled down my face. I couldn't . . . I couldn't read through the tears. I made out the words . . . "A gift to help you get to China." The tears dropped on the card . . . on my hands. I was frozen . . . speechless . . . but I continued. And in the box were more envelopes . . . heartfelt wishes . . . "We are so happy for you. We love you. We can't wait to meet your baby." My heart was so full it felt as if it would burst!

Every lingering doubt faded away.

In that one moment, my life changed forever.

In that one moment, a box of nothing became the "Box of Everything."

In that one moment, I couldn't wait for our child to meet my wonderful, welcoming, loving family.

Kim Gaudiosi

Whose Plan?

We must be willing to get rid of the life we've planned, so as to have the life that is waiting for us.

Joseph Campbell

I never thought I'd consider adoption. My mother gave birth to six of us, and my sisters delivered twelve babies. All my life I'd known I wanted children, and I wasn't worried about my ability to have a baby, even when I married at the age of forty-two.

As I expected, I became pregnant immediately. I did not expect, however, to have numerous miscarriages and subsequent infertility.

My husband wanted to explore adoption, but I did not. Long ago I had worked as a secretary for an adoption agency and knew of two cases where adoptive parents had to "return" their children to birth parents. I also knew my age excluded us from a domestic adoption from the agency.

I was talking to a fellow teacher one day about how we wanted children so badly. She handed me an announcement about an informational meeting at a local adoption agency that specialized in international adoptions.

For some reason, unknown even to me, I took the announcement home and showed it to my husband. I didn't really want to go, but he said, in his sensible way, "What do we have to lose?"

At the beginning of the adoption meeting, I felt extreme doubt, but as the presentation went on, I started having an overpowering feeling that this was what we were supposed to do. I got goose bumps. I felt that God was directing our lives at that very moment; this was our destiny.

We put in our adoption application for a little girl from China, but a month later, before we even began our home study, we received a call asking if we'd be interested in a little boy, a special-needs child, with an open bilateral cleft palate.

We collected information about this anomaly. I have to admit that, once again, I felt extreme doubt. When we received a picture of the little guy, we immediately fell in love with him. We both knew this was our son.

We hurried through the rest of our paperwork and traveled to China four months later. When we first saw Keelan, he looked so small and scared. At twenty-one months, he had been through several foster homes and had two cleft-lip surgeries. Gaining his trust took awhile, but we were soon tightly bonded, and he became the joy of our lives.

Today, Kee is five years old and in kindergarten. His palate was repaired long ago, and he has been dismissed from several years of speech therapy. He is affectionate, confident, funny, and brilliant, often wise beyond his years.

My pregnant niece Amber's growing belly opened

up a myriad of questions for Keelan about his birth mother and why we didn't have natural children. I told Kee, "Well, your father and I tried to have children like Amber, but it just wasn't the plan. God had a plan that we were supposed to get this wonderful little boy from China." I then launched into his adoption story and got teary-eyed as I always do. Keelan hugged me tight, looked up at me with his beautiful dark eyes, and said, "I was born for you!"

All along, God had a plan, and when I finally let go of mine, I was able to receive the child who was born for us.

Melody Davis

Life's Little Lessons

God is great, and therefore he will be sought.
He is good, and therefore he will be found.

John Jay

Susan was only eight months old when she and her older sister, Jasmine, first came to stay with my family as foster children five years ago. Jasmine was a quiet, shy little girl of two, with a frizz of curly black hair and long eyelashes that framed beautiful brown eyes. Susan, with a crop of tangled black hair and big brown eyes, had pudgy lips we couldn't resist kissing.

For three years, Susan and Jasmine lived with my family, and we waited for the chance to call them our own. At last, that wonderful day came, and I was finally able to call Susan and Jasmine my real sisters.

Remembering the troubled, terrible background they came from was hard to take, even humbling. Yet at times that background helped them to see things I often forgot. Most people consider adoption as taking someone into your family, accepting them, and teaching them. But adoption is mostly about us learning.

I had just bought a brand-new iPod Nano, and was sitting on our couch listening to it with Sue-bee, as I sometimes called her. Even though she was only five, she loved my music. She was scrunched next to me, as usual, with one of the headphones in her ear while the other was in mine. It was a time we often shared, just listening to the music we loved together.

Normally we didn't do much talking during this time. We were nodding to the beat of the song "Defying Gravity" from the *Wicked: The Musical* soundtrack when suddenly Susan pulled the headphone from her ear and held it up.

"What are you doing?" I asked.

With a serious look on her face, she replied, "God is here. God is right here, next to me."

I smiled. "Are you letting God listen to the music?"

"Yes," she replied solemnly, continuing to hold the headphone up for some time.

We often think of adoption as helping someone, as instructing them. But I can say with all honesty that, oftentimes, we learn more than we could ever teach.

Maresa Aughenbaugh

Pet Connections

*I love these little people, and it is not a slight thing
when they, who are so fresh from God, love us.*

Charles Dickens

My son Dmitry was six years old when we adopted
him, after he'd spent his entire life in a children's home
in Russia. It was love at first sight for us. But the first
few months here were difficult and stressful for Dmitry,
who had to adjust to an entirely new life and a new language. The predictable tantrums and the phrases, "No,
I won't and you can't make me!" or, "I didn't did it!"
punctuated his initial time here. To complicate matters
further, just as life was settling down and Dmitry was
beginning to understand that he was truly loved and
appreciated, my nine-year-old stepson, Frank, suddenly and unexpectedly came to live with us. Dmitry
became distraught at this turn of events. It was only
later that we discovered, to our horror, that his immediate worry had been that there was, perhaps, a plan to
exchange an unruly child for a better-behaved one.
It was in the midst of all this change and confusion

that we decided to add a puppy to the mix. We talked with the boys about how the new puppy would become part of our family and about how we should treat and take care of it. My husband and I had always had dogs in our lives and never even remotely considered the possibility that this would present any problems we couldn't easily transcend.

When the big day came, all four of us went to Save-a-Stray. We chose an adorable eight-week-old wriggly black and tan puppy that had just been brought in with its litter mates.

The woman at the shelter gave the dog a bath, wrapped her in a towel, and handed her to Dmitry. She sat between the boys in the car on the way home. Our first clue that this dog was not going to be easy came when she shredded the towel by the time we got her home.

The boys named her Maverick, and the name turned out to be appropriate. Maverick had a wild streak and a mind of her own, but she was ours, for better or worse. Unfortunately, in that early time, it turned out mostly to be for worse.

Past experience told me that it was within the normal range of puppy behavior to chew socks and shoes. But when I put the dog in the bedroom for ten minutes so I could talk to someone at the door, I returned to discover she'd chewed my down blanket and had begun stripping the wallpaper off the walls and gnawing at the edges of the carpet! Maverick wasn't malicious, just anxious and high-strung beyond words. She was also affectionate and would, unbidden, sit on your lap and lick your ear all evening. She was, as Dmitry put it, a good dog with bad behavior.

There came a point in time, I shudder to admit, when in desperation, I considered, momentarily, trying to find her a new home. She seemed unmanageable. She jumped on elderly visitors; she ran wildly around the house; she destroyed anything that could be chewed. We tried crate training, but despite our best efforts, she was claustrophobic and shook uncontrollably and howled. We tried doggie obedience school, private training sessions, and discussions with the vet who prescribed anti-anxiety meds short-term (for her, not me).

But Maverick remained a terror. I was at wits' end. I was trying to manage the needs of two displaced kids, and I thought the fact that the dog received the lion's share of my time a little odd.

"You can't give her away," my husband said flatly. "The kids will think they're next. They think of her as a member of the family. They have to know we keep members of our family, even when they don't behave." He had a point. In my heart I believed he was right, but I was just totally exhausted.

I hung in there, though. I kept my patience, threw away the destroyed items, and reassured the dog every chance I got. Gradually, her behavior began to calm down.

One day, after things had settled down, when Dmitry and I were folding laundry together, Dmitry said, "Well, I guess no matter what Maverick does, she will always stay with us."

"Yes, she will. After all, she's ours."

Then he furrowed his brow. "So you mean there's nothing Maverick could do that would make us have to send her somewhere else?"

I thought about this for a minute. "Well, if she bit people we would have to do something different. We couldn't allow her to hurt anyone," I said, cautiously.

He nodded in agreement. "Oh, she would never do that. She has a good heart. She doesn't want to hurt us."

"That's true," I said.

It was a short time after that conversation that a friend came to visit Dmitry. As he was showing the other child how to pat Maverick, the dog began running wildly around, grabbing things, and generally misbehaving.

Before I could get a chance to intervene, Dmitry looked at the other child and said, "You know, you don't have to be perfect to be in our family. You just have to not bite."

Ellie Porte Parker, Ph.D.

Almost Adopted

Train up a child the way he should go, and when he is old he will not depart from it.

Proverbs 22:6

Until we returned from mass that Sunday, there was no indication that anything would be different, that our relatives were about to shuffle our lives again. Sister said we had visitors, or "Parlor," as they called it at St. Agatha Home for Children.

Five of the nine kids in our family lived at St. Agatha because my father had died ten years earlier, and my mother never got over the depression that followed. She died after we were in the Home for two years. My three older siblings were squeezed into relatives' homes, and one was in the Air Force.

Dad died because the hospital gave him the wrong type of blood. A lawsuit followed, and money was put in trust funds to support us. That and any other family resources had to be used before welfare or other social-service money could be applied.

Helen and I walked down the path on the girls' side,

while our brothers, Jack, Tom, and David, meandered down the boys' side, and headed to the Gothic red brick admin building, the same place Uncle Eddie and Aunt Rita Mary dropped us off three years earlier for a weekend, "to see if we liked it" here.

We went in together. Uncle Eddie, one of our court-appointed guardians, and his wife, Aunt Rita Mary, were there. With them were my older sister, Ginger, our brothers Jerry and Billy, who'd come on the bus from New York, and our social worker, Sr. Jane, dressed in her customary black habit. They introduced us to a couple with them, Mr. and Mrs. Smith. Uncle Eddie, a chief of detectives at NYPD, did the talking as usual. He explained that these people were considering giving us a home with them, and that we would be going for a visit there today "to see how we liked it."

It felt like the blood drained from my body, and I went cold with dread. There was no point in saying, "I don't want to go. I'm used to it here now. I'll graduate next year."

Numbly, we followed the adults. We folded into cars for the drive to Scarsdale, in Westchester County, where the Smiths lived.

Scarsdale! Jack and I exchanged looks. Everyone knew that was a posh neighborhood. But the Smiths could have had their own circus on the lawn and fountains running with chocolate, and it would not have released the fear I felt gripping my stomach. I clasped our youngest brother, ten-year-old David's hands the whole time.

The Smiths' home was a mansion. We curiously searched the main rooms, the many bedrooms, even a recreation room. Best of all, they had a boat dock right on the Hudson River. We piled into their cabin cruiser and went for a jubilant ride. It was easy to forget all else as we sped through the water, our hair flying back, exhilarant. After a couple of hours, we returned to the house for dinner. A lady in a housekeeper's uniform served us, and I knew I was truly among the rich. I hate to admit that, for just a moment, I kind of liked the idea of being waited on.

We thanked the Smiths at the end of the afternoon and piled into our uncle's car again. Ginger, Jerry, and Billy took the bus back to New York City. On the ride back to St. Agatha, Uncle Eddie and Aunt Rita Mary asked us how we liked it there. The two younger boys loved the boat and couldn't say enough about it. David loved the big house and all its amenities. Helen and Jack were silent, as usual. I, to be polite, said I liked the boat and the house, but kept my reservations about the people to myself. I thought they were nice, but I'd learned that people were often nice when everything went their way. I needed to know them more.

Uncle Eddie said, "Would you like to live with these people? They want to adopt you."

An electric shock went through me. *Adopt us? No one ever said anything about being adopted. Why would we ever want a part of our family adopted into another?* I realized I should feel grateful. Some of the other kids at St. Agatha spent their entire childhood in the Home. They secretly longed for someone to adopt and love them. And here was this amazing offer.

"I don't want to go," I blurted out. "They're nice people, but I'm used to the Home." My voice cracked. "I changed schools eight times before I came to St. Agatha, and again after I got here. I don't want to change for my senior year." The last sentence came out almost hysterically, so out of character for me. I was surprised my uncle didn't pull over. He and his wife merely exchanged glances. I knew that what I wanted would not count, and that they would do what they thought was best. But why? Why move us?

A week passed before I learned our fate, a week of almost asthma-like panic while waiting to hear. The following Sunday, we went to Parlor at two o'clock, dressed in our Sunday clothes, and met the same assembly of relatives. My uncle, as usual, took command.

"We've considered this opportunity for you kids to go and live with the Smiths and discussed it with Judge McGrath." This was the judge in charge of our case over the years. "The reason we've been talking about moving you is that your trust fund will run out before Helen and David, and maybe even Tommy, graduate. The rest of you will be gone, but they will have no funds left, so they could be sent anywhere in the next few years, and we would have no say."

I held my breath.

"We have decided not to have you go live with the Smiths. It's just not a good fit."

I was so relieved and jubilant, I barely heard what came next.

"Judge McGrath has an alternative plan," Uncle Eddie was saying, "which we've been working on all week, and which will solve your financial problems."

Huh? My attention drifted back. *What was he saying?*

"He knows of an elderly woman who lives in a big empty house in the Bronx and would be willing to take you all as foster kids."

Lightning struck again.

Hastily, he proceeded as we mounted our protests. "You'll be near your other brothers and sister. Ginger even wants to come and live with you. And Jack may come if he wants. Your grandparents, aunts, uncles, and cousins will be just a bus ride away. Best of all, you will all be together in one house, a family again."

He let this sink in. I'd have to move again! I'd have to change schools! Reason fought back. We would be together, something that had not happened in over three years. Oh, we saw each other piecemeal, at chapel, or at school, but we were only together at Parlor. The steel rod of fear that had held me rigid began to bend.

No mansion. No boat. No continuity for my senior year could compare.

We would be together again as a family.

That's all that mattered in the world.

Nancy Canfield

Two Little Girls

Of all the joys that lighten suffering earth, what joy is welcomed like a newborn child?

Dorothy L. Nolte

"Who does she look like?" my mom asked me with a look of love only a mother could have.

As a five-year-old boy, I had no idea; my newborn sister just looked like a baby. I was suddenly aware of what it meant to be adopted. There were similarities between people in my family. My older sister looked like my brother, and they both looked like Mom and Dad. My little sister looked like my older sister, and they both looked like my grandmother.

I never looked like anyone.

I didn't know what I was missing until I looked at my family without me in it. Things became clear.

I was different.

The birth of my sister was a defining moment in my life.

Everyone around me had an idea what they might have looked like when they were infants and how they might look when they were older. I had none of that. All I had was me. What I was like when I was born was a mystery. What I would become was anyone's guess.

As my sister got older and got her first teeth, ate her first solid food, and said her first words, I began to feel a part of my life was missing. For her, there were people who could recount all of the days of her life, from in the womb, to the day she was born, continuing for the rest of her life. I, on the other hand, did not have this. No one could tell me how much I moved when I was inside my mother or if I cried a lot when I was an infant. No one knew what my first meal was or when I caught my first cold. The first memories of me were at a court-house. My desire to know the whens and wheres of my early life may seem trivial to some, but for me it was as if the first two years of my life did not exist.

The weight of these issues was great, but as people often do, I got used to the discomfort. Eventually, I forgot about it entirely. For nearly twenty-five years, I went on with my life. It wasn't until I was about to become a father that these memories started to stir in me again. Besides the normal questions a new parent asks, I longed to know what it felt like to have a blood relative with a face I could see myself in. I wanted to know about every moment of my child's life, and tell her stories and memories that I'd never heard about myself.

When my daughter was born, the magic of holding her and finally looking into a face that reflected my own was indescribable. I felt a peace roll over me, and with a rush of emotion I began to cry. I cried out of the pure joy of fatherhood, and I finally understood how much my parents loved me.

When I told my father and mother that they were grandparents for the first time, I heard the same joy in their voices that I had. It didn't matter that they weren't there, that they didn't see my daughter's first breaths or hear her first cries. They loved her instantly.

Suddenly, it didn't matter what I didn't know, what I didn't hear, or what I didn't feel. I was holding a new life in my arms . . . my daughter's . . . and mine.

Anthony S. Tessandori

"It's not about the gene pool, honey.
It's about being bathed in love."

Open-Door Policy

Welcome as happy tidings after fears.

Thomas Otway

What do you say to the people who have just given you their child?

When it came time for us to send our first "update letter" to our son Ben's birth parents, my husband and I searched long and hard for words to express our appreciation for them, our compassion for the sorrow we knew they were feeling, and our delight in the six-pound wiggle-worm who anointed us with upchucked formula every few minutes. After drafting multiple versions of our letter, we carefully selected photos showcasing Ben at his cutest and popped the packet in the mail.

For two years, we deluged Ben's birth mother with a running commentary of his life. In return, Jen allowed us into her life. Her ten-page letters—printed on fluorescent pink paper—detailed her breakup with Ben's birth father, her problems with her family, and her senior year of high school.

I mentioned the rapid-fire exchange of letters to

someone in my extended family, who inquired, "Doesn't keeping in such close contact with Jen prevent her from moving on with her life? Wouldn't it be better for her if you decreased contact or cut it off altogether?"

I hadn't thought of that. I'd assumed the communication had been healthy for Jen. Horrified at my naiveté, I wrote Jen and asked whether our ongoing exchange of letters, photos, and videos was helping or hurting.

Jen replied, "I *love* the contact. Knowing my son is healthy and happy helps me move on with my life."

Reassured by Jen's response, Robert and I discussed the possibility of opening the adoption further, to include visits with Jen. "What are we afraid of?" we asked each other. "Jen's the nicest person in the world. In fact, it feels like she is one of our closest friends."

The three of us agreed to meet for dinner at a restaurant near Jen's office. During dinner, when Robert and I asked Jen if she wanted to see her son again, she stared thoughtfully at us for several seconds before replying softly, "I'm not sure."

Jen shared her fantasy in which Ben, at age eighteen, would run toward her in slow motion through a field of daisies, arms outstretched, the orchestral rendition of "Born Free" swelling in the background. He'd announce, "Hi, I'm your son," and they'd embrace.

Jen admitted she hadn't begun to process the possibility of seeing Ben when he was only two years old.

A few weeks after our dinner with Jen, our family visited Robert's parents, who live in the city where Jen worked. My goal was to can dill pickles with my mother-in-law and sisters-in-law. Robert and I planned to meet Jen at her office at five o'clock and dine with her at a local restaurant.

The pickling process took longer than expected, and suddenly it was time to meet Jen. My husband was nowhere to be found, so I enlisted my sister-in-law's help. We buckled Ben into his car seat, jumped in the car, and drove to Jen's workplace.

Leaving Ben in the car with my sister-in-law, I zipped into Jen's office, where I explained the pickle dilemma. Then I casually added, "By the way, Ben's out in the car. Would you like to see him?"

Jen's olive skin turned grey. She heaved a few deep breaths and stammered, "Yes, I think I'm ready to see him."

Forgetting we were supposed to be running in slow motion through a field of daisies, Jen and I hurried to the parking lot. With a flourish, I yanked open the back door. There were no orchestral crescendos, only the sound of the radio blaring the traffic report. Ben, still strapped in his car seat, looked up and chirped, "Hi!" while Jen hyperventilated.

"This is so weird," she gasped. "Here he is! He's right here!"

Then I said something I've never regretted. "Would you like to come to my in-laws' house and have dinner there instead of at a restaurant? I'll warn you, there are a bunch of us. We're canning pickles and the kitchen's a wreck, but we'll be having a picnic in the back yard."

Jen took another deep breath and said, "Yes, I'll come."

Minutes later, we pulled into my in-laws' driveway and climbed out of the car, observing the typical family drama of screaming cousins chasing each other all over the yard. As the adults became aware of Jen's presence, they drifted over to meet her. That day, Jen was welcomed—not just as an acquaintance or as the birth mother of our son—but as a family member. She's been with us ever since.

Laura Christianson

Appropriately Impolite

Politeness is not always a sign of wisdom, but want of it always leaves room for suspicion of folly.

Walter Savage Landor

"Oh, my gosh! What a cute little baby!" The bubbly waitress squealed with delight at the sight of our newborn. "His hair is so dark and curly," she added.

She took our order and then gave a second glance at our two older blond boys before giving another long, hard stare at Ian, reclining peacefully in his portable car seat.

"Hmm, your little one is a bit darker than your other boys. It's amazing how different his coloring is . . ."

"Well, he's . . ." my husband began.

I cut his sentence short with a swift kick under the table. "Yep, he's a bit darker," I said matter-of-factly, looking her straight in the eye.

Our waitress was Dorothy from *The Wizard of Oz.* Like all the other servers at the restaurant, she was in costume, but even in her adorable blue and white gingham dress and ruby slippers, she could not pry out of me the details of our new addition to the family. I simply didn't feel like I wanted to tell her. Dorothy reluctantly backed away from our table and retreated to the kitchen to post our order and, I'm sure, gossip to the cook that the lady at the far corner table had another man's baby and her poor husband hadn't a clue!

"What's up with you?" my husband asked the minute the waitress was out of earshot. "She is obviously curious about him. What's the big secret?"

There was no secret. I was proud and thankful to have adopted our beautiful, biracial son. Ian was, and still is, an answer to our prayers, and I loved showing him off. I even loved telling others of the miraculous way in which he came into our lives. It was just that suddenly I became sick to death of the prying nosiness of strangers. Something snapped in me, and I chose that moment at that restaurant to exercise my right to privacy. I decided sometime between, "Let me show you to your table" and "Are you ready to order?" that I'd had enough.

This "not talking" empowered me. I finally felt in control of the situation. After having given birth to two babies prior, I felt quite prepared to care for a newborn again. What I wasn't prepared for, however, was all the curious glances and invasive questions I would be bombarded with when we were out in public. So, after over a month of obliging every curious stranger I came in contact with, I decided to rebel. The barrage of comments and questions amongst strangers had, in my opinion, gotten out of hand.

Take, for example, what had happened earlier that afternoon. I was stopped by a woman at the golf course as I watched our oldest son, Erik, who was seven at the time, on the driving range. She followed me down the stairs, asked if that cute baby-boo in my arms was adopted, and then held me in captivity as she gave a long, drawn-out dissertation about her sister's friend who's a very sweet woman and has wanted to adopt a newborn simply forever. The woman cooed and petted Ian's head and then, in the same way you might admire someone's shoes, asked, "So, where'd ya get him and how much did he cost?"

If I had been better at thinking on my feet, I would have admired her breasts, questioned her on whether or not they were really hers, and then inquired where she got them and how much she paid! But I couldn't think that quickly, and besides, I am way too polite.

Days before, I was alone pushing Ian in the stroller on the bike path near my home when a stranger jogging in the opposite direction literally did an about-face and began jogging beside me.

"Is that your baby?" she inquired out-of-the-blue.

"Yep, he sure is!" I said, smiling. Ian was an exceptionally happy and cute baby, and I loved being able to say, after two years of trying to adopt, that this bundle of joy belonged to me.

"He's really yours?" She questioned me again.

"Yes, he's all mine!" My smile faded a bit. I was beginning to wonder if this was an interrogation.

"Did you adopt him or is your husband black?" she asked, eyes scrunched together as she inspected him more closely.

At that, my smile disappeared completely. "We adopted him," I said bluntly. I was shocked at the nerve of this stranger.

"Where does his real mother live?"

"I am his real mother, but his biological mother lives . . ." I stopped myself. Why was I telling her all this? I veered the stroller off the path and away from

Nosy Nellie, kicking myself for sticking around and answering her questions for as long as I had.

Any politeness I had left ended when I encountered Dorothy at the restaurant.

At the end of the meal, she summoned a quirky waiter in a jungle explorer costume to take my birthday photo as she placed in front of me a miniature birthday cake. (She added six dollars to the bill for this "complimentary" gift.) The two of them sang the restaurant's original rendition of "Happy Birthday" before Dorothy began quizzing Dr. Livingstone, I presume, on whether or not he, too, thought our baby was the cutest thing and, "Doesn't he look different from the other boys?" The jungle explorer confirmed her opinion and looked to us, in vain, for the answer. *Dorothy*, I thought, *click your heels and go home to Aunty Em. I'm not talking.*

As we walked out to the car, my husband and the boys teased me for being stubborn and not giving the waitress the information she was so desperately fishing for. We had a good laugh at the frustration I obviously caused her, and I felt appropriately impolite. I'm sure Dorothy didn't mean any harm, but it felt good to stick to my resolution that no matter how thrilled I was with our new son, I did not owe an explanation of his situation to every inquisitive stranger who begged to know. And on that night, I enjoyed the fact that flying monkeys couldn't have driven it out of me.

Cathy McIlvoy

Tummy of an Angel

Even a child is known by his doings.

Proverbs 20:11

As an adoptive parent, I had rehearsed in my head all of the insightful answers I was going to provide when my son, Nathan, asked me questions about his adoption.

One night while preparing for bed, when he was only three-and-a-half years old, he asked to see his baby pictures. The first pictures in the album were of a baby shower for him before he was born. He wanted to know why he was not in the pictures. I carefully explained that he grew inside another woman's tummy and that she wanted us to be his mommy and daddy. I emphasized how very special she was. I also shared with him how much we wanted him and had waited for him for fifteen years. When his questions ceased and he seemed satisfied, I tucked him in.

As I lay in bed, I prayed and hoped I had said all of the right things. I wanted so desperately for him to understand what I was trying to convey.

The next morning, which happened to be my birth-day, he ran up to me excitedly. He was extremely artis-tic and could not wait to show me the picture he had drawn.

My eyes filled with tears. He had drawn himself as a baby inside the tummy of an angel, with hearts and flowers all around her.

I knew that moment he understood.

Nancy Morse

"I think babies grow in a mommy's tummy
and adopted babies grow in a mommy's heart."

Love's Language

When Jesus saw this, he was indignant. He said to them, "Let the little children come to me, and do not hinder them, for the kingdom of God belongs to such as these."

Mark 10:14

My baby is much like any other—cute, precious, obstinate, beautiful. But if I had to describe her in one word, it would be mysterious. She puzzles me daily. She has this book, for instance, passed down from her older brother. It's a rhyming one with wonderful illustrations—tremendous dinosaurs squeezed into tiny bedrooms, pleading, demanding, whining to their human parents about having to go to bed. At fifteen months, Miranda is quite taken with it. I try to point out what's in the pictures, but she usually shoves my hand away and pulls at the page, eager for what's coming next.

On one page, a dinosaur kisses his mother good night. "Kiss, Miranda, see?" I always say. And I kiss her, for what is probably the three-hundredth time that day, on the cheek, the head, the back of her chubby neck.

I don't understand how her mind works. She is adopted, has only been in our home for seven months, and is often a serious, quiet child. Though seemingly content, she's not what you would call bubbly or overtly joyful. Today, I followed her around the house with my camera for nearly an hour trying to get one picture of her smiling. I didn't succeed. She played, toddled, laid on the dog, climbed up and down and up and down the stairs, all the while pleasantly entertaining herself, stoically, laughing only at her brother's antics or a finger wiggled under her chin.

And, most puzzling of all, she doesn't talk. She can say "uh-oh" when she drops something. But that's it. Nothing else. Not even "da-da" or "ma-ma." I often wonder if it's the language thing, having heard only Spanish in Guatemala for the first eight months of her life. How strange it must be to suddenly hear all new words—nothing familiar. It has to delay a child's speech in some way, *doesn't it?*

"She's not delayed!" my friend exclaimed when I mentioned this. I shook my head. No, no, I didn't mean delayed in that way (although, I admit, I breathed a half-sigh of relief when she finally mastered walking— and the remainder of that breath will be withheld until our first conversation takes place). I only meant that an early language switch must have some effect on speech skills, *doesn't it?*

There are so many speculations, questions, doubts, and concerns that go along with any child, but an adopted child comes with so many more unknowns. Still, it is all just parenting—that crawl across a tattered bridge spanning a vast cavern. Getting to the other side is part endurance, part determination, much luck, but mostly blind faith.

Will my daughter talk? Most surely she will. For now I have to remain content with the small bonds we make. The way she picks up a book and backs into me when I'm sitting on the floor, so that she winds up in my lap. The way she'll wave good-bye—sometimes— usually when whoever is leaving is already gone.

A few hours after we read the dinosaur book, I was in my room getting ready to go out. She was very quiet, and when I went looking for her, I found her on the floor of her room with the dinosaur book opened on her lap. I smiled at the delicate way she turned the pages, then I ducked back out the door, not wanting to disturb her. But something made me turn around again. I peeked back through the doorway and saw she was looking at the "kissing" page. And then I watched in amazement as she leaned forward and planted her trademark open-mouthed, wet gem of a kiss right on the picture of the mother.

I went back to my room, sat at my makeup table, and reapplied my wet, smeared mascara.

She loves. She *loves*. For now, that's all I need to understand.

Cathy Cruise

7

OVERCOMING OBSTACLES

Courage and perseverance have a magical talisman, before which difficulties disappear and obstacles vanish into air.

John Quincy Adams

Parker's Story

Miracles are the swaddling clothes of infant churches.

Thomas Fuller

The birth of a child is always a miracle, but occasionally one child puts the meaning of "miracle" in a whole new light.

Parker's birth mother was in a single-vehicle car accident that would ultimately leave her brain dead. When the paramedics brought her to the hospital, tests showed she was eight weeks pregnant. Though the accident deprived her brain of oxygen for an extended period of time, her brain stem still allowed her to breathe on her own. Her sister asked the doctors to keep her alive to sustain the pregnancy. As she lay there in a coma, a child growing inside her, there was no way of knowing what damage might have been done to the fetus as a result of the accident. It would be a waiting game.

That game ended on December twenty-first, after only twenty-eight weeks of gestation. The mother coded, and Parker came into this world by emergency C-section, weighing in at three pounds, seven ounces and seventeen inches long. He would be in for the fight of his life, literally.

Immediately placed on a respirator and other medically necessary equipment, Parker laid in an incubator in the Neonatal Intensive Care Unit (NICU), waiting. With his mother gone and no father to be found, his aunt became his only connection to this world. Only time would tell if he would have the strength to survive. Luckily, as the days turned into weeks, he was still fighting, but his prognosis was poor. Knowing that she would be unable to care for a newborn, his aunt began looking for someone to adopt Parker. That's where we came in.

Our first concern, naturally, was his health. After meeting with his doctors, our greatest fears were realized. We were told that he would never breathe on his own, that he had severe lung disease, metabolic bone disease, liver problems, and his retinas were starting to detach. This would require surgery and might leave him visually impaired or even blind. Not knowing what to do next, we put our faith in God and prayed for a miracle.

Sometime around 7:30 that very same night, after sixty-one days on a respirator, Parker pulled out the tube and began breathing on his own. Our hearts were filled with an indescribable joy, but we knew that was only the beginning. And so, we waited.

By the end of the next week, Parker was moved out of the NICU and into the step-down nursery, and we were able to hold him for the first time. What a thrill!

As the days turned into weeks, the news only kept getting better. The medications for his liver function were working, and he was putting on weight. Though he would require three eye surgeries, his retinas didn't fully detach and most likely never would. His MRIs and CT scans showed a normal, healthy brain, and he was beginning to show normal reactions to sound and light. His lungs, however, would remain his greatest challenge. Severely underdeveloped, his lungs still required oxygen to help him breathe and maintain his oxygen levels. By now he had been in the hospital for a grueling three months and tipped the scales at seven pounds, eight ounces.

As the fourth month rolled around, there was talk of Parker finally being allowed to go home. He would need to remain on oxygen and a monitor to check his oxygen saturation level, and also an apnea monitor that would sound an alarm should his breathing fail. The nursery we had always dreamed of looked more like a hospital room, but we were finally ready. With his aunt carrying him out, Parker Bryan left the hospital on April 8, 2002, weighing eight pounds, five ounces.

The year that followed was filled with amazing things. Weekly physical therapy sessions loosened his stiff joints and tight muscles. His exercises and care became a full-time job. Parker was indeed visually impaired and required his first pair of glasses in July, but then a whole new world opened up to him. Once he could see, he made tremendous improvement.

By then he only required the apnea and pulse-ox monitors at night, which made our lives a whole lot easier. Carrying only the oxygen tank around seemed like a walk in the park. In the fall, cold and flu season was upon us, and his little lungs just weren't strong enough to combat even the common cold. He started to develop a wheeze, and we were introduced to yet another piece of medical equipment—a nebulizer— twice daily. We disinfected everything, and we waited.

In late August, he only required oxygen at night. He continued to meet the goals set for him by his physical therapist at his weekly sessions. By October, he was off the oxygen completely, though it remained in our home in case of emergency.

That emergency came the week before Thanksgiving. He woke up in the early-morning hours, gasping for air. We took him to his pediatrician who immediately called for an ambulance, and he was admitted to the hospital in respiratory distress. His oxygen level, respirations, and heart rate were critically abnormal. We had averted an infant heart attack, but were told to expect at least a week in the hospital. We looked at each other and said, "They don't know Parker." We prayed for another miracle, and after only four days, Parker came back home.

On his first birthday, he was taken off all monitors, a gift from his pediatrician. In January, he was finally able to sit on his own, and he got a new pair of glasses. We discovered he had a "lazy eye," so we patched his "good" eye for three hours a day to strengthen the weaker one, and by February there was already a huge improvement.

Parker is now fifteen months old and has been crawling for two weeks. He loves being able to get around, especially in the kitchen where he can pull up on the cabinets and drawers. Needless to say, his therapist is proud, not to mention his mom and dad. He has an amazing smile that fills any room and a laugh that you just can't contain.

We have so much to be thankful for: the ultimate sacrifice of his mother, the love of his aunt, the gift of so many talented physicians and therapists, friends and family who have helped us, and for the countless prayers that have made this all possible.

Every time we look at our son, we know we are looking at a miracle and await the future that holds many more.

Brent and Linda Wood

The Whole Family

And whoever receives one little child like this in My name receives Me.

Matthew 18:5

Glancing at the winter sky, which was settling into ever darkening shades of gray, I was excited that Robert would be home soon to take me to the firm Christmas party. It was one of our first outings since our three-year-old daughter Mykah's open-heart surgery seven months earlier. Hearing giggling, I glanced at seven-year-old Jesse, dangling upside down over the couch while Mykah offered him a pretend cup of tea.

The phone rang. Billie Shotz, our caseworker and friend from Buckner Adoption Agency, had a request. Would we participate in the Rocking Moms and Dads Program for a baby in the hospital? Due to the severity of his heart problem, he had been removed from the adoption roster. When I called Robert, there wasn't a second of hesitation before he said, "I think we should go."

"Yeah, I agree. But what about your party?"

"There will always be parties."

Leaning over the three-week-old baby, there were no bells. No whistles. No voice from heaven. It was the baby himself. He looked into our souls—first one, then the other. Maybe it was because of the serious life challenges we had already met together, but we knew. It only took a look, a smile, and a nod. This was our son.

The next day, wheels were set in motion to bring our baby home—but not without resistance. The adoption agency and the baby's cardiologist understood what we could not—he only had six months to live. We could only smile.

I said, "God prepared us for this baby. Two years after we adopted Jesse, I became pregnant. At the sonogram, we learned that the baby would die at birth. It was unbelievably hard, but Psalm 116:15 is true: 'His loved ones are very precious to him and he does not lightly let them die.' A few months later, we walked into grief. When we adopted Mykah, she needed heart surgery. Both of those events were to prepare us for this little one."

Robert interjected, "We have always been ready for this. Shoot, we were even CPR-trained before Mykah was born."

Quite naively, on Christmas Eve, we embraced life with a medically fragile child we carefully named Zachary, which means "Jehovah hath remembered." Life wasn't going to be just bottles and diapers—it was a serious crash course practically resulting in a medical degree. We needed organization. It was Robert who simplified the confusing doses and times that meds had to be given by creating a log.

We did not walk into these challenges alone. Nurses and staff brought clothing, toys, and a precious baby

Bible. Visiting clowns gave perfect gifts for sneaking under the tree. Still, we arrived home to a sad-looking travel bed as just the month before we had given our baby items away. Then the doorbell began to ring. Church friends, neighbors, a babysitting co-op, and Bible study members brought one thing after another. One group committed to bring a meal each week for months. Blessedly, furniture was hauled in. The best gift was the Bible on tape since we no longer had time to read!

Our little one responded to his massive changes. He was at peace. That holiday was magical as our family had been given the best Christmas gift ever. We not only had a Christmas baby, but we had burden bearers.

The day after Christmas, the reality of living with a medically fragile child became real; Zach started fibrillating. This was to be the first of many extended trips to the hospital. Each time, the support system adopted their role. They became prayer warriors, cared for the two older kids, or ministered to us. When he grew older, one even became CPR-trained so Zach could be in a preschool co-op. It became evident that Zach was adopted by a village.

Still, some days were beyond intense. On one hospital stay, his EEG went flat, and his kidneys stopped. If he lived, he would be blind, deaf, and a "vegetable." His adopted team prayed life into him, and he became known instead as the smiling, miracle child. We started "Challenge Zach." He sang beautifully in a musical, swam in the ocean, and skied between his daddy's legs. He lived life pressed down—shaken together and overflowing. His sister and brother adored him. He was joy, and we and his adopted community loved every moment.

As his heart struggled to beat, ours melted. Ultimately, we realized that because Zach had a broken heart, he was able to give a piece to us all. We did not deserve to have Zach-man in our lives for four-and-a-half years. God let us. Zach lived 1,717 amazing days. Numerology tells us that "one" means God and "seven" means completeness. Zach brought completeness to our and his adopted community's lives. He made us whole.

At his going-to-heaven celebration, we did something Zach loved—released balloons. Something unexpected happened. The balloons clustered together and floated up as one into the clear blue sky. It seemed to confirm we had been in this together—a whole family. Each of us in the village is grateful we adopted Zach-man.

Truly, he is with Jesus, and Jesus is with us, so Zach isn't far away.

Sandy Wright

Unstoppable Love

Where there is Great Love, there are always miracles.

Willa Cather

One afternoon in February 2003, I attended a prayer meeting for a mission trip going to Haiti. As I sat there, I knew in my heart I was to go on this trip. I do not travel often to other countries, nor do I travel very far on a whim. I suffered a spinal-cord injury seventeen years ago, leaving me paralyzed from the mid-chest to my toes, unable to walk or control anything except my arms, my head, and my mind. I live on my own and drive, but how would I manage in a third-world country?

Still, I knew I was to take this trip.

Four months later, I sat on a soccer field in a country that I barely knew existed. Several children sat around me, staring. I don't know if it was the wheelchair, my white skin, or merely a supernatural lure that children always seem to have for me. The Haitian people speak French. Since I was unable to speak with the children, I made up my own games. I had them write their names on a piece of paper. I had a picture of myself with me, and I took it out just to show them. One boy, Alex, took the picture into his hand, held it close to his heart, and motioned that he wanted it. *Hmm*, I thought, *why does he want my picture?* I gave it to him and forgot about it.

The next evening, part of our team went back to the crusade. They told me the kids had asked for me, but Alex wanted me to have his picture and phone number. It was sweet, but I still didn't think much of it.

A few days later I found someone who could speak to Alex in his language. I called to invite him to the crusade that we were having. Alex's mother got on the phone, and my friend interpreted her question. "Will you adopt Alex?"

"What?" How strange. I asked my interpreter if this was a frequent occurrence, and he said no. Again, I did not think much of it.

The very next morning, God spoke to my heart with a vision. He showed me Alex at my wedding! God has a great sense of humor. I had come to Haiti with the only money I had to my name, and so far there was no sign of a husband. But I vowed, "This is truly a testimony, Lord. I can barely feed myself, but I will adopt, feed, clothe, and take care of a child one day."

I learned that Alex's mother had eight children and no husband or job. An orphan is defined as a child who has no parents or only one parent who is unable to provide for him.

I knew that I would be seeing Alex in a few days at the crusade, and I looked forward to it with both anticipation and also a bit of denial. I had not been there two minutes when I felt the small, tender hand of a child in my hand and heard a soft voice say, "Mama Diana." I looked up into the eyes of the most beautiful child I had ever seen in my life. Alex. I was speechless, thinking, *Mama, who?*

For the next four days, Alex sat with me during the crusades, just like a child sits with his mother. The first night, he took my Bible, drew a heart in it, and wrote, *I love you, Diana.* Hearts have a very significant meaning to me. When I see them, I always feel they are from God, and he is telling me how much he loves me.

A few days later, Alex's mother gave me a letter. In it, she used hearts in place of O's in her words. She also put three hearts on the envelope. I prayed, "God, is Alex the reason you have given me hearts in special ways all these years?" The next morning, I found a large, sequined object on the ground. I picked it up and received my answer from the Lord. In my hand was a pink sequined heart. I admitted then that Alex had my heart, and I had his.

The day before we left Haiti, I arranged to meet with Alex. I asked him why he liked me. He said it shouldn't matter what color our skin is but what is in our hearts. I told him if I could take him home in my suitcase, I would. I jokingly told him that he picked the wrong American as I was not financially able to adopt him. I told him he must pray and ask God to make everything happen. I told him to pray for my husband to come because he needed a father.

I returned home, but talked to Alex on his neighbor's phone every week. I did not care if he couldn't speak English; I longed to hear his voice, to hear him laugh. And just maybe he would call me Mama Diana again.

I scraped up money to send him to school for the next year.

I compiled all the necessary information to adopt a child, only to find out that I didn't qualify. The only thing I had was love. If only that was all adoption required.

I trusted and waited, not knowing how or when this

would be possible. Then, in February, to my surprise I knew I was supposed to sell everything I owned and go to Haiti to live indefinitely.

I have been here with Alex for three months now. I stay at an orphanage where there is also a school. I am teaching English here where Alex comes to school.

I'm still trying to adopt him legally, but the adoption took place in our hearts the day we met.

Now, every day I look at him without end, and he says in his limited English, "Why you look at me big?"

I say every day, "Because I love you so much."

Hopefully, by the time this story reaches your heart, Alex, Mama Diana, and Papa will all be together as a family.

As I unpacked my suitcase from my trip I came across the paper I'd had the children write their names on; Alex was the first one who had signed his name.

Diana Green

Koala Bear

A babe in the house is a wellspring of pleasure, a messenger of peace and love, a resting place for innocence on Earth, a link between angels and men.

Martin Farquhar Tupper

We were a gazillion stinky diapers, a bajillion bottles, and three colicky babies past infancy. Zigzagging through toddler country was a bit tricky. Completely content with life as it was and preparing for the journey into teensville, we had no intentions of upsetting the apple cart.

On Independence Day, our family gathered at my brother's house, as usual. My husband, John, our three daughters, and I brought a menu of time-honored festive foods, consisting of hamburgers, hot dogs, potato salad, and dessert. My brother Sam and his family provided the explosive-style fireworks, and after dark we would all sit back and shout out the *oohs* and *aahs* that Sam expected for his efforts.

When we arrived at Sam and his wife, Janice's, house,

I went to help prepare the food and put the finishing touches on my American flag sheetcake loaded with strawberries, blueberries, and whipped cream, pilfered straight out of the latest issue of *Family Circle* magazine.

Sam walked into the kitchen holding the most beautiful blue-eyed baby boy with rosy, chapped cheeks and disheveled blond hair. Judging by the way he rested his face against Sam's chest with a half-cocked smile, he looked like he had just woken up from dreamland. I instantly handed the blueberries over to Janice so I could get my "baby fix."

"Who is this sweet-looking little baby?" I asked, as I hugged my brother merely to get a whiff of the baby smell that all mothers commit to memory.

"This is Cole, and he's hungry," Sam said, in a gruff storybook voice.

The aroma of baby powder flooded my senses, and instantly the nostalgia whisked me off to an unforgotten place.

"He belongs to a former coworker of Janice's who is having trouble caring for him," said Sam.

Sam handed me the baby and bottle as I took a seat in the rocking chair. As Cole nestled into my arms, he began to drink heartily and take comfort in twirling my hair around his small, clammy hands.

"He's been with us for about six weeks now. If we hadn't agreed to become his guardians, he would have been placed in foster care. We just couldn't let him be bounced around from place to place, so until there is a permanent place for him, he'll have a home right here with us," stated Sam.

He went on to explain that there were no family members willing to take care of Cole because they were all saddled with his other siblings. His mother had already lost them in the court system, so it wasn't looking good for this little boy. John and I spent the rest of the day holding and rocking this sweet, unfortunate little boy. Cole would lay his head against my chest and wrap his arms and legs about me like a baby koala clinging for life to his mother. I knew from a mother's perspective that this child hadn't been held, touched, or even acknowledged for the majority of his six-month life.

After the last of the fireworks went up in a blaze of glory, it was time to say our good-byes. Peeling this beautiful baby from my chest and handing him back to Sam shook my inner core.

The ride home was quiet. My heart was aching. John reached over, clutched my hand, and said, "You're thinking about Cole, aren't you?"

As I looked over at my husband, my eyes welled up with tears. With a half-hearted smile, I said, "You know me so well." I added, "What do you think about us adopting him?"

John's answer was a huge surprise, "I think . . ." he said, after a lengthy pause, "yes. Absolutely. I haven't felt fate like this since the first time I laid eyes on you, and that little guy needs us."

We spent the next month talking to social workers, guardians ad litem, and attorneys. We were approved to have visits with Cole and started the adoption process. Every weekend, our entire family drove from Jacksonville to Daytona to spend time bonding with Cole so this would be as easy as possible for him. When November came, we would be able to officially adopt Cole and bring him home.

On October thirtieth, I received a phone call from the social worker. "Cole's grandmother has decided to take him, and family members take precedence in considerations for placement of a child."

I couldn't grasp what I was hearing. Unable to speak, my gaze became fixed, and all I could see was sorrow and devastation colliding.

"How can this be? All of a sudden, two weeks before the adoption, she can just show up and say, 'I think I'll take him now'?" I cried. "Please don't do this to him!"

"I'm sorry, but we have to follow procedure," explained the social worker sympathetically.

"When is he going to her?" I asked.

"In the morning."

In desperation, I asked, "Is there anything we can do?"

"You can try, but I've seen this happen so many times, and unfortunately the odds aren't in your favor," the social worker replied.

After speaking with our attorney and getting the same story from him, I felt lifeless. Later that day, I placed a call to the social worker to make arrangements to see Cole at his grandmother's home to say good-bye. The next day, we drove to Daytona to see the child who was, in our minds, our son, for the last time.

Cole was sitting on an oriental rug in the middle of the living room dressed in a white diaper, looking like a lonely little Buddha when we arrived. As soon as he saw me, he gave me the biggest deep-dimpled grin and lunged forward over a mountain of toys to get to me. I met him halfway across the floor and scooped him up into my arms. I held him and spoke to his grandmother for over an hour. I needed to feel he was safe so that I didn't bolt out of there with baby in tow. My emotional treading became more than I could bear, and any shred of hope that I had completely abandoned me.

I gave Cole a big kiss, and in the happiest tone that I could manage, I said, "I will always love you."

As I handed him to his grandmother, the last thing I said to her, speaking through the tears that peacefully rolled down my face, was, "He likes to be held close, arms and legs wrapped around you, like a baby koala."

Stefanie Johansson

Meant to Be

We are but instruments of heaven; our work is not design, but destiny.

Owen Meredith

I'll never forget the first time I laid eyes on a photo of Xu (pronounced *Shoe*). A colleague and I were attending a regional meeting of the Lutheran Adoption Network in New York City where speakers were sharing information about "waiting children." Xu, in China was one who, in the world of international adoption, meant that special efforts were needed to find a family because the child had some kind of special need. Xu was an adorable two-year-old Chinese boy with white-blond hair, very fair skin, and blue eyes.

"Albinism," the speaker said, "a condition affecting pigmentation and often vision."

I was drawn to his picture. I whispered to my colleague, "Oh, my goodness, I'll have to adopt this little guy because he looks like my own son."

The description of him drew me to him even more. The orphanage staff wrote that Xu "has a smile for everyone he sees," and he is "very smart and likes to be helpful." Most impressive, his name meant "hoping to scale the heights of science in the future."

I brought the photo and description home with me, and showed it to my husband and two children. They were not as enthusiastic as I, but they didn't say "no" either. As much as I liked the idea of making Xu part of our family, I was sure that lots of other people would find him as irresistible as I did, and I was confident he would be placed in another home soon.

When the Lutheran Adoption Network had its annual meeting a year later, I couldn't believe Xu was still a "waiting child." Now I knew I had to do something . . . either convince my husband and children that Xu was to be the newest member of our family, or find another family for him. I told Lutheran Social Services right then and there that I would find a family for him.

I started talking about Xu to everyone I knew. Past and current adoptive families were most interested in hearing about him. One of my former clients suggested that we e-mail his information to different groups. A month later, I received a telephone call from an attorney who knew of a couple who might be interested.

Admittedly, my heart sank a little because I was still trying to figure out a way to make Xu ours. However, what I learned about this family made me feel a divine hand was at work in the efforts to find Xu a home. The couple was young, healthy, successful, childless . . . and the prospective adoptive mother had albinism.

Pam had grown up with serious vision impairments and made numerous adaptations throughout her life. When I sat with the couple to do their home study, I was truly inspired by her achievements and her never-give-up attitude. At thirty-eight, Pam was an elite-level runner for the United States Paralympic team and had represented the United States in four Paralympics. She was an ardent advocate for blind athletes and very active with the disabled sports movement. She served on the board of the United States Association for the Blind and was one of ten athletes in the United States named as an Ambassador for the United States Anti-Doping Agency. She was a motivational speaker at youth programs to promote acceptance of differences, and she frequently consulted with parents of children with disabilities. Standing beside her, supporting her, and eagerly anticipating his new role as "daddy" was her husband, John, a staff attorney for the Montgomery County courts.

I knew this was the best family for Xu, and I was excited for the process to be completed. After the documents were submitted to China, the family sent photos to their waiting son. Tears came to my eyes when I saw a photo of Xu at his orphanage looking at the photo of his adoptive parents. Although he was not yet four years old, he seemed to recognize that he and his mother shared the same condition.

It's ironic that in training prospective parents, we always include information about what it is like to adopt a child who looks different from them. In this case, a little boy in China found a mother on the other side of the world who looked like him.

Kelli Myers-Gottemoller

Susan, the Prophet

Of all animals, the boy is the most unmanageable.

Plato

A thought occurred to me the other day, just as I was wiping juice drops off the wall and cookie crumbs off the cat, right after pulling an ornery little boy out of the dishwasher. I was reflecting on how I'd been forewarned that this final child—this sturdy, handsomely blond boy adopted in my midlife—might be the straw that breaks the parental camel's back.

While completing our adoptive home study, "Susan," the social worker, came to check out the surroundings this new little fellow would be moving into. She scrutinized the kitchen, bedrooms, bathrooms, and living space, expertly averting her eyes from dusty corners, cobwebbed ceilings, and ringed bathtubs. Then she sat down to interview the three siblings who would be welcoming this new brother.

Thankfully, the children's interview was incident-free and smooth.

Almost *too* smooth.

These seldomly soft-spoken siblings barely said a word.

"My, they sure are quiet," Susan commented. "Are they always like this?"

I mentally panned back to page 172 in my adoption handbook, trying to remember if truths—or good impressions—were more advantageous.

"Uh, well, they're pretty shy," I said, crossing two fingers and four toes. Confronted by six raised eyebrows, I added, "but they tend to liven up after you get to know them."

"Well, we'll just have to do that then, won't we?" she smiled.

The eyebrows lowered skeptically.

Forty minutes later, still not much had been said, except that one sibling was really excited about the baby, one preferred a leashed ferret, and the third just wanted some assurance that his room would be upwind of the diaper pail.

As she turned to go, Susan looked at me and predicted, "Well, as quiet as these three are, you're bound to get a wild one *this* time!"

We both thought she was being funny.

She, however, laughed longer than I did.

Apparently, extrasensory perception is a prerequisite for social-work training.

Susan, it seems, hit the nail on the head.

At the orphanage when we visited him, our son's primary caregiver said in Russian (which was translated for us), "He is a busy boy."

"Busy"—a simple, nonthreatening word—must have lost some vigor in the translation. For, as scales occupy fish, "busy" occupies Alec.

If there's a drawer in his reach, there are clothes being tossed helter-skelter. Right hand over left shoulder;

left hand over right. This one's empty; it's on to the next.

If the pantry's left open (rendering the protective doorknob cover useless), the lower shelf is his domain. The chips come out, the pretzel bag's a bust, and heaven help the peanut-butter jar that gets in the way.

Yet, this whirling dervish has a method to his mayhem. He problem-solves with acute perception.

He studies everything he sees with unwavering intensity.

We are constantly amazed at his resolve, his mental recall, his willfulness . . . his energy.

Which brings me back to Susan's prediction.

I really shouldn't be upset with her, just because she saw the Russian handwriting on the wall. Alec's "busyness" certainly isn't her fault—yet, did she have to predict it so smugly?

There are, I admit, times when I'm struggling to tape his diaper on at night (if you have to ask why, don't ask) that I, myself, want to yell, "Why, Susan? Why couldn't you have forecast a calm, little Muscovite who sits in his car seat on command and never stands on the open dishwasher door? What would have been wrong with anticipating submissive cooperation, rather than impish stubbornness? Why did you predict the coming of Dennis the Moscow-Menace?"

Yet, what goes around comes around. Even for social workers.

Eight months after Alec arrived at our home, hearts, and the kitty litter box, Susan, the Prophet, gave birth. And, Lord help her, she had twins.

I predict they'll *both* be hell on wheels.

Cindy Kauffman

A Unique Bond of Family

Grandmothers are a special gift to children.

George William Curtis

"Hello, you don't know me, but I have your grand-daughter. Your daughter gave her to me last night, with your number in case of an emergency. I'm her apartment manager, and my husband and I want to adopt her baby, but we thought family should have the first opportunity to keep her."

Three hours later, I drove to meet this stranger at a gasoline station just off the interstate. This petite bundle of energy talked as she rocked Brianna in her arms and relayed to me how she was given my granddaughter. Not understanding why someone who wanted to keep a baby would be motivated to call me, I asked her, "Are you an angel?"

She handed me my newborn granddaughter with the hospital-issued diaper bag filled with formula and her birth certificate. The following day, I spoke to her by telephone, and again she expressed her interest in adopting the baby. Then, I never heard from her again.

I still wonder if she was of this realm.

Only a few days before, I had been sitting in the neonatal unit, cradling my first grandchild, knowing that she wouldn't be mine for long. This fragile, innocent, three-pound little life was born six weeks early, by Caesarean—"failure to thrive" in the womb of my reckless teenage daughter, Leah, who chose to live on the streets. She and her boyfriend of two weeks planned to keep the baby, a decision as well thought-out as two children wanting to keep a puppy.

I was embarrassed that the nurses and other visitors to this sterile environment might think I was anything like the two kids who only showed up after sleeping for most of the day. My heart was sickened as I observed them treat her like an object of show and tell. The revealing clothing my daughter wore was far from maternal. Their stench reeked from partying the night before. Food, diapers, shelter, and the emotional needs of another life were far from their thoughts, but very close to my broken heart.

I sat rocking and holding this precious life through an entire hospital shift, praying for God's intervention. I shuddered at the thought of what her future could be. I prayed that my daughter would relinquish Brianna to a loving home, and I knew that once she was released from the hospital, I would never see her again.

Time was on Brianna's side since it would be several weeks before her release. The hospital social worker and eventually Child Protective Services (CPS) and other agencies became my allies. They witnessed the lack of maturity and desire by my daughter to provide a home for Brianna. CPS urged me to encourage Leah to allow me to take the baby indefinitely, but I knew my home would only become a power struggle between my daughter and me, and that she would ultimately have all of the legal rights. I could foresee the day she would stop by with her latest boyfriend, demanding her child as they headed off into the sunset to start a new life. Taking this baby into my home would only mean heartache and trouble for my family. My husband and well-meaning friends and family advised against it.

I prayed for God's revelation of what was best for Brianna. I prayed for a burning bush or a flashing sign on a billboard. I prayed and prayed, and still no clear answer appeared except the ones echoing from my family . . . "Don't, don't, don't."

I attended a meeting at the hospital among the social workers from various agencies and CPS. Leah was to attend, but she overslept and missed the 1:00 PM meeting. I was stunned to hear the CPS worker report that Leah would be allowed to take the baby upon her release. A safety plan was established. One of the agencies would check on my daughter daily, offering assistance with formula, transportation needs, and other services to keep a close watch.

At six weeks, Brianna was released from the hospital, and on her first day out, Leah had her in an apartment swimming pool. "She was only getting her feet wet." Three days later, CPS discovered the boyfriend's criminal record. By court order, he could not be around young children. Leah had to choose between her baby and her boyfriend.

She gave her baby to a complete stranger.

It wasn't a burning bush or a billboard, but an angel at a gasoline station who was the sign from God that I was to take this baby home. Yet we knew that we could not keep Brianna as our own. Later, I pondered the odd twist of fate that I would soon be relinquishing parental rights of Brianna, when seventeen years earlier, I was the one adopting a baby—her mother. I'd wanted a baby so badly, and now I was giving one up.

God led us to a couple several weeks later. They adopted Brianna and changed her name to Sara, not knowing it is my mother's name. Luckily, they wanted Sara to have us in her life, with the exception of her birth mother, who is still a prodigal.

Within nine months, Leah was pregnant again. My husband and I gained custody of Victoria when she was two weeks old. Sara's parents felt it was not in God's plan for them to adopt her, but connected us to a couple who attended their church. Sara and Victoria would grow up together. Just a few years earlier, both couples held hands and prayed that God would give them children. He gave them sisters.

Leah's third pregnancy resulted in another newborn in our home, eventually adopted by the second couple.

Many ask how I have been able to bear such pain, but the alternative would have been worse. I have been blessed with the special opportunity of caring and bonding with each granddaughter during her first weeks of life.

Five years later, I heard, "Hi, Nana! Hi, Nana!" as Sara excitedly waved to me during her kindergarten graduation. I sat between her mom and dad and her other grandparents, relishing our unique family bond.

Belinda Howard Smith

How I Got My Brother, Mitch

"Dan, this is hard to ask, but . . . ," Mitch hesitated and swallowed hard as his voice cracked. He wiped his nose on his red flannel shirt and took a deep breath.

That's when Dan stopped him cold. He already knew what the question was, and he couldn't let Mitch suffer the humiliation of asking it. "Wait, Mitch. Bonnie and I have a huge favor to ask you. We can't finish the house without more help, especially since I broke my leg. I know your dad wants you home, but . . ."

"Dan, my parents . . ." Mitch tried to break in, but the older man pushed on, determined to prevent the question.

"Mitch . . . wait. Let me get this out," he said with mock sternness. "Could you possibly, well, move in here so you could help me more? It's a lot to ask, I know. But school's starting soon, and the nights are getting cooler. I can't keep Bonnie and the girls living in a half-finished house much longer." Dan tried to sound impromptu, but the truth was, he'd been rehearsing this speech for hours. "We don't have an extra bedroom, but we'll work something out. And when school starts, you can catch the bus with the girls every day, and then help me at night and on the weekends."

Mitch's face brightened with relief. "I can do that. I'll get my stuff and come back later. My dad won't care."

"No, not later, Mitch. Bonnie has a roast and potatoes cooking, and she told me not to come to dinner without you," Dan laughed. "After dinner, you and I will take the Jeep to your place, and I'll wait outside while you grab some things and . . . uh . . . tell your folks."

Dan knew Mitch's parents were gone, but he'd let him tell the story in his own time. For now, the important thing was that this boy needed a real home.

It was just two months earlier that the Scott family had moved to the area with their three daughters. They'd sold the family home and Dan's business, and bought ten acres in the country. The only problem was, there was no house on the property, and no running water or electricity. But Dan had built homes from the ground up before, and with the help of Bonnie and the girls, he would do it again. Meanwhile, the Scott family would spend the summer camping out in a big tent, cooking on a Coleman stove, and hauling water from town.

About that same time, another family also moved into the area. Fifteen-year-old Mitch and his parents had taken residence in an abandoned shack, about a mile away. One day when Mitch heard the sound of hammering somewhere in the trees, he followed it.

"I'm Mitch," said the scruffy boy, holding out his hand for Dan to shake.

"Mitch, I'm Dan Scott. That's my wife, Bonnie, and my daughter, Terrie. My other two girls are playing cards in the tent. You from around here?"

"Sort of. Me and my folks just moved into a place down by the lake. Looks like you're clearing for a house. Can I help?"

Dan hesitated. It would be nice to have another male

around, and he could use some muscles, but this kid looked rough. He was smoking a cigarette, and his language was questionable, especially around the girls. Still, there was something about Mitch that touched Dan's heart.

"Grab a rake," Dan said. "I could use the help. Terrie, when you make lunch, fix a couple of extra sandwiches for Mitch, okay?"

That was only the beginning. Mitch showed up almost every day, eager to work. At the end of each day, Dan tried to pay him, but Mitch refused.

"My dad wouldn't like it," he said. But after meeting Mitch's parents, Dan suspected that if Mitch showed up at home with money, his parents would take it away and spend it.

Eventually, Dan came up with a compromise. Rather than pay Mitch in cash, he took him to town and outfitted him in a good pair of steel-toed boots for work. Then they agreed that, when it was time for school to begin, Dan would buy him all the clothes, shoes, and supplies he needed to start his sophomore year.

Everything seemed to be working out well as the house went up slowly. That is, until Dan fell off a ladder and broke his leg. That was a definite setback, though as stubborn as Dan was, it only slowed him down instead of stopping him. On crutches, he still did whatever he could, but more and more, he had to rely on Mitch.

With summer slipping away, Mitch showed up every morning right after dawn and stayed as long as he dared without angering his dad.

"Mom," complained Terrie, who was the designated family cook for the summer, "Mitch eats more than all of us. All I ever do is cook for him, and then you make him take the leftovers home."

"Terrie, you've met Mitch's parents. They don't spend

their money on food. That's why Mitch is so thin. Even if he wasn't here working, we would feed him. Not only that," said her mother, "the other day when it got hot, Mitch took off his shirt, and I saw his back. It was covered with scars. We're trying to get help for Mitch without humiliating him. We're just not sure how."

A few days later, Mitch didn't show up for work. At first, Dan thought Mitch's dad was just being difficult again. But after three days, he got worried and drove down to check on the boy. He found an empty shack, with no sign of life.

On his way home, a neighbor stopped him.

"They're gone," the neighbor said. "Pulled out in the middle of the night in that old station wagon. They didn't take the boy, though," he added. "I heard the old man yellin' . . . said the boy was old enough to take care of himself. Said he was nothin' but a burden."

Dan knew Mitch had to be hiding somewhere, embarrassed and scared . . . and hungry. After talking it over with Bonnie, they called the girls in for a family conference.

"We're going to find Mitch. And when we do, we'll ask him to live here. Later, we'll make it legal, but first, we've got to get a roof over his head."

A whole day of searching the area did not turn up any sign of Mitch. But just as Dan was going home for dinner, he saw the boy's red flannel shirt coming through the trees. Dan had been practicing all day to say the right words that would let Mitch save face. It's show time, he told himself as Mitch approached. That's when Mitch opened his mouth to ask the question that Dan was desperate to prevent.

"Dan, this is hard to ask, but . . ."

Teresa Ambord

Love Conquers All

*In praising or loving a child, we love and praise
not that which is, but that which we hope for.*

Goethe

It was such a lovely day when we brought Andy
home. The warmth from the sun filled the car. Six-year-
old Bethany sat in the back seat with her new brother.
She talked aimlessly about his new room, our house,
and how much fun he'd have living with us.

Four-year-old Andy sat staring at the back of my
seat. His brown eyes were empty. Emotionless from the
day we met him, we were all determined to lather him
in love and affection. He deserved it more than any
child I'd ever met.

Andy had witnessed the brutal murder of his mother
at the hands of his father. When he was only three years
old, he watched as his mother lay in her own blood, and
he called 911 for a woman he'd never see again.

His mother obviously taught him everything she
possibly could in those short years together.

Since I'd been unable to conceive after Bethany,

adoption became the next option to pursue. We longed to provide a child with a happy, healthy home. Our family and friends were delighted when we told them our plans to adopt Andy, though some cautioned us to be wary of taking on a child who had witnessed such an awful act of violence. They were afraid he might never be the same again.

My husband, Seth, Bethany, and I were all filled with excitement over the thought of loving another child. We'd lost three children, and Andy was the blessing my family was looking for.

When we first brought him home, he was very shy and timid, and he wouldn't let us get too close to him. If any of us tried to hug him, he'd stand straight, stiff as a board, his arms down by his side. His brown eyes were always empty.

I began to worry that maybe my cautious friends were right. Maybe we wouldn't reach inside Andy and cure him of the pain he felt. Maybe he'd never overcome the horror he had witnessed.

Seth and I tried a little bit at a time to show him the affection he deserved. Even Bethany attempted to cherish her new brother.

As time passed, Andy grew receptive to our hugs and kisses to the point that he put his arms around us, too. His arms wouldn't grip us tightly, but we were ecstatic that he attempted. Yet we were gravely disappointed that Andy never said "I love you" when we said it to him.

His eyes still looked empty.

We never gave up hoping that one day Andy would express his love for us. Each day we lavished him with words and gestures of love.

One November day, the first snowfall began. Bethany and Andy went out to play. I watched them from the kitchen window, their mouths open wide as they tried to catch the snowflakes on their tongues. A tear came to my eye at the sight of my two children playing together, laughing, and having a great time.

A short while later, Bethany came running in the house out of breath and pulled frantically on my apron. "Mommy, Mommy, Andy has something he wants to tell you."

"Okay, sweetie." Laughing, I turned to Andy, his little button nose red from the cold.

"What is it, darling?" I asked, bending down to greet him eye to eye.

Suddenly, he wrapped his chubby little arms around me and cried out, "I love you, Mommy!"

Holding on to Andy as tightly as I could, I cried, "I love you, too, baby. Mommy loves you so very much."

Tina O'Reilly

Light at the End of the Tunnel

The sweetest roamer is a boy's young heart.
George Edward Woodberry

When I was in my early thirties, single people were just beginning to adopt internationally, and I was overjoyed to be able to adopt my son, Juan. I didn't realize back in 1983 that I was not only adopting an eight-month-old, but a new way of life and a new community of friends.

I became immersed in the world of adoption, even returning to school to get my graduate degree in social work. I threw myself into my new role as parent, and even though there were sacrifices, they were minor compared to the happiness I felt in raising my son. The first dozen years of our life together were loving, placid, and uneventful. Apart from his issues with attention deficit disorder (ADD), Juan did well in school, and I was now counseling other singles interested in adoption.

I knew the teen years could be particularly challenging for adoptive families as their children go through the normal issues with identity coupled with the added layer of emotional complexities surrounding adoption. To add to this, Juan is Hispanic, and I am Caucasian. I was trying to expose him to his culture and feeling woefully inadequate as I made a point of going to Latino festivals and connecting with other families whose children were from Central America.

I often attended adoption conferences, and at one of these I heard a speaker talk about how adopted children often need to test until they feel certain of their parents' commitment to them. She related the story of a boy who was learning to drive and deliberately drove the family car through the garage door. When his mother asked him why he did this, he said, "I needed to know I could do something really terrible, and you wouldn't send me away."

That story helped me understand Juan when adolescence hit and I suddenly felt like I was living with a stranger. My cooperative, though somewhat mischievous, son suddenly turned into someone I didn't know. By eighth grade, he was drinking, smoking pot, and stealing money from my purse. He started dressing in baggy pants and black sweatshirts. People crossed the street when they saw him approaching. I remember one morning looking in my purse and finding all my bills gone. I drove my car down the street to catch up with him riding his bike and I confronted him. "I'm sorry, Mom. I don't know why I did it. I won't do it again." He often seemed as perplexed by his behavior as I was. I was heartsick because I felt the close relationship we'd shared for so many years was fraying at the edges, and I had no way to mend it.

I tried everything I could think of, including therapy, a wilderness program for troubled teens, a boarding school from which he never matriculated, and an alcohol treatment center. At the end of this program, when it was time for him to graduate, his counselor called me to say, "I don't think Juan will make it if he returns to his old environment. There are just too many temptations."

What was I to do? I had also adopted a daughter by then, and she was only in first grade. I decided to take a drastic step. I moved cross-country and started a new life for our family in California.

Things didn't miraculously change overnight, but slowly began to improve. Juan graduated from high school—something I had given up hoping for—and eventually got a job he enjoys. He achieved a stability I never dreamed possible.

Something wonderful happened, too. I found my son again, or maybe we found each other. The relationship we had when he was young was not lost. He began to really talk to me again. And I began to listen and share my life with him. Our conversations were not accusations and anxious questions on my part or resentful defensiveness on his. I stopped prying, and he stopped clamming up. Al-Anon helped. We both grew.

I can't pretend there weren't some despairing times, some frightening times, some times when I felt I'd lost my son forever. But with each year that goes by, those memories fade.

When we began talking again and I asked Juan about this chaotic period, he said, "Maybe I just needed to crash the car through the garage door. And, Mom . . . you passed the test."

Lee Varon

Special Son

If there be one thing pure, where all beside is sullied, and that can endure when all else passes away—if aught surpassing human deed or word or thought, it is a mother's love.

Marchioness Spadara

Through our tears of joy and words of gratitude to an exceptionally brave and beautiful teenage birth mom, we barely heard the nurse say, "9.9 on the APGAR."

We did, however, hear the doctor's voice loud and clear two years later declaring, "Autism. Your son has a pervasive development disorder."

For years, he could speak only with his sea-blue eyes. In those days, his laugh sustained me, and I was certain that, if bottled, it would further the cause of world peace. It started in his perfect toes and bubbled its way up to his porcelain cheeks. When released, he would forget the noisy world around him and actually look into my eyes. Otherwise, face-to-face contact was simply too painful for him.

Life was always loud for our little buddy. Like

sunburned skin, his precious heart was ultra-sensitive to the rhythm and rawness of the world around him. He felt it intensely, but could not interpret it fully.

Analytical, intensely creative, and spatially brilliant, there was a mysterious neurological disconnect in his brain regarding relationships and communication. The intuitive ability to grasp social interactions and interpret nonverbal language entirely eluded him.

His inner frustration was painfully visible. You could actually feel the unresolved tension between his strong mind and uncooperative tongue. "Special needs," the doctor said, and all of the specialists nodded their heads.

Though correct, the professionals failed to mention that special needs always sing a delightful duet with special strengths. My son's perspective on life is both profound and unique.

When he was a toddler, I ached to hear him speak. Then, as he turned three, one by one, words started falling slowly like thick, magnificent raindrops:

Strawberries were called "Elmos" (for red reasons).

"O" was bologna because it was shaped like an O (of course).

Our slightly ditzy kitty, Mittens, was simply called "uhm" (which is how I felt most of the time I watched her).

And vacuums were known as "dadoos" (because it is something that *daddies* should *do*—a catchy, reasonable notion. I even considered contacting Webster's . . .)

Then, around age four, our beloved son began piecing words together. His first original sentence brought me to tears. "Daddy is amazing," he declared. So true.

Later, he announced, "I have a free will!" Yes, my young philosopher.

When he was five, he turned to me and whispered,

"Mommy, my nose stopped running."

"Good!" I said, grateful that his red nose might have a chance to recover. Then he added with all seriousness, "Yes, now it's just walking."

My son has always had an artist's eye for colors. I am Mexican and American Indian, my husband is of German descent, and our baby girl is biracial. One day when he was six, my son looked at our skin tones and explained, "Mommy's red. Daddy's green. Baby's purple. And I'm golden delicious!"

Around six and a half, he started being able to hold brief conversations. Here is one of his first:

"Mommy, what shape is free will? Is it like a circle?" he asked one night as we snuggled together for cuddle time.

"Yes, it's sort of like a circle," I replied cautiously.

"Is it like a car?" he pressed.

"Well, it's like gas in a car. If a car has gas, it can choose to turn left or turn right. But if the car doesn't have gas, it can't choose to turn. Free will is like gas. Because we have it, we can decide to make good choices or bad choices."

"Oh." He paused. "Sometimes I get a flat tire."

That night, I fell asleep with a grin, pondering the theological significance of flat tires.

But our most touching conversation to date occurred recently around a campfire. The talk started with a few concerns I shared about being careful near fire. My son asked what would happen if he accidentally fell into the fire, and I responded that he would be badly burned.

"Would I die?" he asked.

"You might," I said quietly.

"Then I would go to heaven?" he continued.

"Yes, but it's not time for you to go to heaven yet. Mommy needs you here."

My son paused for several minutes, deep in thought, and then he said, "Mommy, when you are dying and God comes to take you to heaven, I will carry you. I will hold you."

I could barely speak. Even now, I can barely type. Staring into his sea-blue eyes, I realized that I was the one with special needs. I desperately needed to be more like my special son.

Something in his words that day capsulated our love as mother and son. Over the years, his special tenderness has transformed me. So when I do enter heaven one day, I will be able to say with sincerity, "My son helped carry me here."

Alicia Britt Chole

8

HEALING

*P*ain is the deepest thing we have in our
  nature, and union through pain and
  suffering has always seemed more real
  and holy than any other.

Arthur Henry Hallam

The Boy

The voice of parents is the voice of gods, for to their children they are heaven's lieutenants.

William Shakespeare

The boy arrived three years ago in the back seat of a police car on a warm summer evening just before the sun set behind the trees. He came with a few clothes, all too small, and nothing else. We were his tenth family, and everything he owned could be scrunched inside a paper sack.

I look around his room, now piled high with toys, clothes, and books he can barely read.

I've come to say good night, and I find him crying again.

"Am I ever going to see my dad again?" he asks, through hiccups and deep, struggling breaths.

"Someday, maybe," I answer.

I lie down beside him on the bed and stare up at the bottom of the top bunk. The floral print of an old mattress shows between gray metal bars, pressed and squished through from the years of children who've slept on that top bed.

That first day in our home, the boy was eight years old. Clear blue eyes and sandy hair. Small for his age, a bit too skinny. At bedtime, he came to me, looking up for a moment as if he had something to say, but wasn't quite sure I was okay to say it to.

"I don't let nobody under my covers anymore," he finally said. Just in case I was a "nobody."

"Well, that's a good idea," I told the eyes that knew too much.

"I don't like beds."

And so he slept in a chair. A big, round easy chair with soft cushions and a back that reclined. He slept there for three weeks. In his clothes. He wouldn't change, wouldn't undress, wouldn't do anything involving bedtime.

When we finally moved him into a bedroom, we found out about the windows. He said there were things looking in. I assured him nobody could get up that high on the second floor, but reason is not a part of fear. And it was a fear. I could see in his eyes there was no bargaining with treats, as we had to get him into the bed. And so I put a curtain over the glass. Not good enough. The edges moved in the air current and that would never do. Somebody could peek in through the gaps, he told me. So I pressed the edges of the cloth against the wall and duct-taped it closed. No more window. Problem not solved, only the symptom.

On his third day in our home, the boy said to me, "Can I live here a long time? Like three months?"

"Well, three months isn't very long," I said, not realizing his history.

He narrowed his brows in thought. "How 'bout till I'm thirteen?" he asked, apparently thinking he'd come up with a bargain, something we could both live with.

He had no concept of family. The term "forever" had

no meaning to this boy. I made a phone call to see about his plan for permanency. There wasn't one. "I'll keep him," I said. And they didn't argue because nobody else wanted him.

Now, as I lay beside him, a cat leaps onto the bed, fat and shiny black. He's called Fraidy. The boy named him. They came within weeks of each other, the cat and boy. The boy arrived on the porch, the cat underneath, both abandoned, wild, and afraid. The cat, frail from neglect and too young to be away from his mother, hissed and roared at us. Much like the boy. Fraidy would come to nobody. But he came to the boy. Walked right up to him and rubbed his leg. He must have seen himself, his history, his pain. Each night at bedtime, the boy wanders the house. "Come here, Fraidy," he says, as he searches until he finds the fat black cat. The cat comes to him like a dog does. The boy doesn't pick him up; he doesn't have to. Just turns and walks to his room. Fraidy follows, and together they sleep, cuddled and warm.

I pet Fraidy, but he's not interested. He's checking on his boy.

"Why didn't they just do it?"

I wait, unsure of the question.

"If I ever had kids and they said stop doing drugs and I can have them back, I'd just do it."

"You're a stronger person," I say, and I know it's true. "Some people weren't made to be parents. Some were. You'll be an amazing father some day 'cause you know what it's like to be you."

"But they just didn't care what I was doing. They didn't be parents."

"Your mom and dad aren't bad people, just weak people." I cross my fingers behind my back. "The drugs got hold of them and wouldn't let go."

"I'm never going to do a drug," he says.

"No," I tell him. "You'll never do drugs. You know what it can do." And I pray I'm not lying. Statistically, he will. Some day, he'll forget how he feels now. He might wash it all away with whatever he can get his hands on. I hope I'm wrong.

I took the boy to see a specialist a while back, to assess his future. It's bleak, I was told. Drugs and alcohol affected his ability to learn, to reason, to make good decisions. There's too much brain damage. He'll never go to college, says the man. He'll likely not make it through high school.

Just wait, I told the well-meaning doctor, *you'll see.*

The boy couldn't read, so I taught him.

He's impulsive, so I guide him.

He gets scared, so I hold him.

He is not a lost cause. He is *my* cause.

Now I rise from the bed to leave the room and hope he falls asleep before he has a chance to think more about what made him cry in the first place. It's that thinking time that gets to him.

As I rise, he speaks again. "How long have I been here?"

"Three years." I pause in the doorway. "You were with us three years on August twelfth."

"It seems like longer," he says.

"It does," I agree as I turn out his light.

"I'll see you in the morning, Mom," says my son from his big bed next to the open window.

"Okay," I reply, shutting his bedroom door. "I'll be here."

Keri Riley

Bring It On

A mother understands what a child does not say.

Jewish Proverb

It was two o'clock in the morning when I was slowly aroused from a deep sleep by noises coming from across the hallway. Sniffles and sobs. Someone was crying, but who . . . and why? I arose from my bed and threw on my robe as I tiptoed to the closed door. I put my ear to the door and listened. The sobs were accompanied by mumbled words and sounds of a pillow being pounded. I took a deep breath and whispered a quick prayer before knocking on the door.

"Derek," I said as I knocked lightly, "may I come in?"

There was no reply, but the noises stopped. I waited and knocked again. "Do you need to talk?" I asked through the closed door.

Only silence greeted my entreaty. I considered allowing Derek his privacy and going back to bed. "You know, I'm a good listener, and I care," I told him.

No response at all—until I shuffled toward my bedroom, then once again I heard his voice.

It was louder, and there was no mistaking the anger and hurt, even though the words themselves were not clear.

I had been in this exact spot many times with many children, but for this particular one, it was a first. He had been placed with my husband and me for almost two years and not one tear. In fact, other than arrogance touched with indifference, Derek had showed little emotion one way or the other since entering our home.

His sister, Tina, was just the opposite. She wore her emotions for all to see and to share. Those are the easy ones. Those you can actually get to and help them heal their wounds.

Derek was convinced he needed no one. He was twelve, almost thirteen. He wouldn't cry when we grounded him or disciplined him by taking away an item or a privilege. His anger would surface, and he tightened his jaw and tried his best not to let us see it. Yet, not one teardrop fell.

Derek showed no sadness when he came to live with us, or when his parents' rights were terminated. Anger was always hidden right under the surface of his demeanor, and it affected his grades, his performance in sports, and every relationship he attempted with others.

So, here at last were the tears. If he would just open up to me, perhaps the healing could begin. It could go either way. Derek could push me further away and withdraw more into himself, or he could do just the opposite. I was unsure what to do. I knew how important it was to allow each child to hold onto his sense of privacy and dignity when possible. *Please, God, let me make the right decision,* I prayed. Finally, in the still of the night, I realized what I had to do.

I really only had one choice. This is why I became a foster parent. Taking a deep breath, I opened the door as I prepared myself for anything he could throw at me.

Bring it on, Derek. I'm here, and I can take it. I'm not going anywhere. Ever.

Christine Smith

"You may be a free agent, Son, but I'm not sure you'll be able to sign with any family you want."

Top Gun

*You cannot teach a child to take care of himself
unless you will let him try to take care of himself.
He will make mistakes, and out of these mistakes
will come his wisdom.*

Henry Ward Beecher

Some time ago, I happened on a television program
that caused me to question what I could believe. The
speaker insisted that music had the power to change lives
and that God gave us music to help change the world. He
related a story about a troubled youth who encountered
a family of musicians. Through his association with them,
the young man went from a troublemaker to a hard-
working, exemplary student. The speaker insisted it was
the music that made the difference. He went so far as to
say that the boy was powerless to resist.

I was intrigued by his unshakable belief that ". . .
music could make a man." I wished I could believe
what he said as much as he did. But the story wasn't
enough to convince me. "Too weird," I muttered.

Our oldest son, Jeff, was the kind of boy described by

the speaker, restless and troubled. We had adopted him when he was twenty-one months old. He'd lived in Korea with his birth mother until the age of twelve months, when she left him with another family where he stayed for three months, and then he went to an orphanage for six months before we adopted him.

It was obvious from the first that Jeff struggled with life. It was like he was put into his skin sideways. If you said "black," he said "chartreuse." If you said "up," he said "sideways." But he had the vocabulary of a sixteen-year-old by the time he was five and became a voracious reader. An incredible artist, he frequently drew with both hands at the same time.

Jeff seemed frustrated and mostly angry with people. Someone told me if I held him close, and he could feel the beat of my heart, I could communicate calmness to his spirit. We spent long hours connected physically but . . . always he struggled.

Jeff did everything with intensity and focus. As a ten-year-old, he was fascinated by the movie *Top Gun* and watched it over and over. He memorized every line and went around the house repeating the dialogue to himself as the soundtrack boomed.

But . . . always he struggled.

Adolescence was turbulent; the years that followed were worse. The anger festered. He grew too large for me to protect physically.

I worried constantly, prayed always.

He turned eighteen, then nineteen, and graduated from high school with the lowest grade point in the class. He turned twenty, then twenty-one. We dared not let him go. He was so vulnerable; the ways of the world too harsh. But all the time his presence was like a large thumb pushing on my heart.

I worried constantly, prayed always.

He left home at the age of twenty-two and smiled as he said, "You tried. Don't blame yourself. I'll probably never be back."

The Navy became his life. He struggled, completing boot camp twice. Then silence.

He called as his ship departed for the Persian Gulf. "Hello, Ann, this is Jeff, your son. I'm headed for Afghanistan. The ship stinks. Say hello to the family."

A month later was his twenty-sixth birthday. I had just watched the speaker on TV, with his claims about the power of music. I remembered *Top Gun* and bought the soundtrack on CD. I packaged it carefully, thinking it would be a miracle if this small parcel connected with its target amidst the sea of international chaos.

Jeff called from the *USS Kittyhawk*. His voice was excited. It reminded me of the year he got the GI Joe jet for Christmas. He was convinced he wouldn't get one because they were on back order everywhere. On Christmas Eve, in desperation, and feeling like he was betraying himself, he skeptically wrote a letter to Santa and propped it up on a plate of cookies. The memory of him discovering the elusive gift under the tree burned into my mind forever. Leaping into the air, he screamed, "I believe, I believe, I BELIEVE!"

He sounded like that now as his words tumbled over each other. "Mom, Mom! *Top Gun!* I got it! It played in my headphones as I stood on the flight deck. I figured it out. I am living my dream. I am Top Gun! And you are my family, and I love you. I choose you. The only thing stopping me from being happy is me. I choose to be happy. I am Top Gun!"

I remembered the "weird" music man from the television show and knew that now I believe. I believe. I BELIEVE!

G. Ann Potter

Blood Ties

There is no friendship, no love, like that of the mother for the child.

Henry Ward Beecher

The slamming of the door reverberates through the house with a level of teenage angst that you can almost see. I stand there, feeling my daughter's presence on the other side of the door. She's in her room now, muttering and stomping over the latest bout of "total unfairness" we have inflicted upon her. I move closer, resting my hand against the closed door. I press my fingers gently into the wood, and I can sense her there, full of pain and confusion. I close my eyes and wonder, as I have so many times, if I am doing this right. If my parenting is going to help her grow into a wonderful person, or damage her beyond repair.

Thirteen is a hard age. Most of us can remember that. And my daughter has a bit more on her plate than the average teen. Taylor is not my biological child. She is my husband's child from a previous relationship. He was raising her almost completely on his own when he met me. Taylor took to me right away, and I to her. I always say I fell in love with her long before I fell in love with her daddy. A beautiful, loving, sunny child, she stole my heart from the moment she placed her little hand in mine. We used to play dress-up, make cupcakes, giggle and talk, and share secrets. Taylor was my maid of honor when her father and I married. When she was ten, her biological mother agreed to allow me to adopt her. I am forever grateful for that decision. I never felt like Taylor was anything but my child. The bond we developed over the years was as deep and true as any blood tie.

Yet our path is not without its mishaps. I'm a control freak who didn't have children prior to Taylor. Now that we have another child, I've learned that kids will be kids, and doing things my way all the time isn't necessary or even good. They have to learn in their own way, at their own pace. But poor Taylor had to live with me before I learned this. We had many a battle over silly things like clothes or taking a bath. I realize now that wearing a Disney princess dress to the grocery store is not the end of the world, but it took me awhile to get that, and Taylor, like many eldest children, had to suffer through it.

Now when I look at her, I forget sometimes she did not come from my womb. She is of me, my heart. Sometimes I feel our bond is deeper than a mother and daughter because we *chose* to love each other. She didn't have to love me. I could have just been her father's wife. Yet she and I were drawn to each other, like two souls separated long ago and finally finding home—which makes this time of her life even more difficult for us than the average mother and daughter.

In the throes of figuring out who she is and where she is going, it's normal for her to reject her parents a bit, to reject me. And I try not to let it bother me. She wants to know where she came from, wants to see her "real" mother (whom she does still see). I've sometimes heard her say rather scathingly to her friends, "Oh, that's my STEPmom." And I want to protest, "No! I am your MOM!" But I don't, of course. She gets annoyed if anyone says she and I look alike. It happens sometimes since we are both blonde, and she has picked up many of my mannerisms and speaking inflections. I feel very proud when people say this, but it usually earns an eye roll from her.

There's that old saying that blood is thicker than water. But is it really? When it comes down to it, is she going to remember who held her forehead while she threw up during a bout of the flu? Is she going to remember me standing in the pouring rain, watching her play soccer? Is she going to remember who made her lunches every day and then brought them to school when she forgot them? Will she see me with different eyes when she becomes a parent herself? Will she realize that my love for her is as deep and true as the love I feel for the child who did come from my body, because she is the child who came from my soul?

I am more sensitive to her growing away from me than other moms may be. While my logical mind knows that her rejection is normal and part of growing up, my emotional mind is cut to the quick. I wonder if this rejection will be permanent, if she will never truly see me as her mom, but just some lady who took care of her. I am unsure of my parenting skills with her, worried that my fumbling around will ruin her. Or worse, make her indifferent to me and my love for her.

And then, I hear her moving toward her bedroom door. I step back as the door opens, and she and I stand there, looking at each other. She's been crying. I open my arms, rather tentatively, and she steps into them. She clings to me like I am her anchor, her ship, while she struggles through the ocean of growing up. I hold her tight, noticing that she is almost as tall as me, that she isn't that little girl anymore. Yet she still needs me, and when times are rough, I am the one she clings to. I can feel her heart beating in tandem with mine. I can feel our blood pumping simultaneously. I understand suddenly that no matter what the future brings, she and I are bound together forever. Blood ties. Mother and daughter. Her childhood is full of me; her memories will find me. She will know, despite my imperfections and mistakes, that my love for her has never faltered.

I am her mom.

Jody Ellis-Knapp

The Man of My Dreams

*The words that a father speaks to his children in
the privacy of home are not heard by the world,
but, as in whispering galleries, they are clearly
heard at the end and by posterity.*

Jean Paul Richter

I was six when my three sisters and I congregated in
the craft room. Construction paper, paint, yarn, and
magazines peppered the room. Each girl pursued her
own project. I finger-painted on a canvas and on myself
in the center of the room. Tara sculpted clay on a long
table decorated with paint stains, glue, and the refuse
from dozens of art projects. Mary sewed a wraparound
skirt at the trusty Singer machine. Yolanda lay across
the daybed in the corner behind me and wrote busily.

"What ya writing?" I asked.

"A letter to Dad."

"Paul's my dad," I said as if it were a matter of fact.

"No, he's not. Emory's your dad." I blinked in disbelief. My other two sisters nodded.

Emory and Mom divorced just after my first birthday.

Mom never hid the fact, but I didn't come to the realization that Paul was not my dad until that day in the craft room. Mom and Paul married after I turned two. Paul was the only dad I remembered.

Cold indifference described Paul's treatment of me. He never slowed as I followed him astride the white banana seat of my cotton-candy pink Huffy bicycle, pedaling as fast as I could to keep up. Streamers flew outstretched from white handlebar grips. I spent hours massaging his callused runner's feet. I attended his marathons. A consummate mimic, I cheered the Pittsburgh Steelers on television when he did, even though I hated football. I tried everything I could to break through his cold shell. I failed.

He and my mom divorced when I was eight. The only father I'd ever known left. Security evaporated. Paul disappeared, never to be seen or heard from again.

Mom remarried, and this man was so different from Paul. George talked to me and listened to what I had to say. He took my mother dancing and on trips to islands in the Caribbean. He was fun. Too much fun. He drank excessively. About six months into their marriage, money problems surfaced. He lied constantly about money. The Internal Revenue Service and numerous creditors clamored for payment.

Whenever he and Mother argued, he took us kids shopping. We saw through his manipulations, but we enjoyed the fruits of them, and the debt increased. Mother was determined to make the marriage work. She tried for a few years. No matter what she did, though, she couldn't change him. An alcoholic is an alcoholic. Until they decide not to drink anymore, they will do and say anything to feed their addiction.

After my mother and George divorced, I never saw

him again. Once again fatherless (not that he was much of a father), I was bereft.

I attempted to initiate a relationship with my biological father, but he was resistant. I thought I would never have a dad.

Without a daddy, I prayed for a man's unconditional love. As a teenage girl, I thought the answer to my prayers was to be found in the arms of teenage boys. I desperately clung to their words of love. Their love was temporary; when the sex act ended, so did their feelings. Each encounter failed to fill my aching need.

At age seventeen, we met. I think he was forty-five, with silver hair and kind, laughing eyes. The day I met him, I began putting up walls to protect myself. Mother's husbands had not provided me with the daddy I craved. My sisters and I looked at this new man and assumed he was like his predecessors.

I guarded my heart and refused him entrance. With words and deeds, I pushed Steve away. Regardless of how poorly I treated him, he repaid me with kindness. The years passed, and his even-tempered constancy began to win me over.

All my sisters had families of their own. Steve was an excellent grandpa. He tickled, teased, and shared his cookies with each grandchild. They adored him. We all started to love him. I found a man I could trust with my injured heart, one I could believe in unreservedly.

I remember days with fondness that he spent patiently teaching me how to play golf. I never mastered the game. His time, patience, and enthusiasm were what I prized. He wanted and enjoyed spending time with me. He pursued a father-daughter relationship. This was a first.

Four years after we met and one week prior to my twenty-first birthday, I helped him take out the trash

so I could talk with him alone. I had never wanted anything this badly. I took a deep breath and tried to pool
my courage. "I know what I want for my birthday."

"What?"

I stuffed my bag into the large, rolling green trash can
and tried to swallow the fear. "I'll understand if you say
no." That was a lie; if he had said no, the words would
have crushed me. Other possible questions flitted
through my mind. *Can I borrow your truck for a camping trip,
get a laptop computer, or money?* Any of these would have
provided a believable replacement for my true request.
He had no idea what I really wanted. I closed the green
lid and plunged ahead anyway.

"Will you adopt me?"

I glued my eyes to the trash receptacle and held my
breath as I waited for his answer. When he didn't
respond immediately, my heart lurched fearfully in my
chest. I turned slightly toward him, and my eyes lifted
to his tear-drenched, smiling face.

"I'd love to." His arms came around me, and tears from
a lifetime of disappointments from men were spilled for
the last time. Years of heartache washed away.

Months later, we sat on a wooden bench together,
our fingers intertwined. He squeezed my hand.
Terrified he would change his mind, I waited, smoothed
my simple white dress, and chewed my bottom lip. I
wondered if the judge could refuse us. Would they
allow me to be adopted at this age? After they called
our names, I went through the motions in a fog of
happy disbelief. The judge congratulated us. I couldn't
believe my luck.

Twenty-one years old, in a courtroom in Placerville,
California, my dream came true. I had a daddy . . . the
best daddy.

Jessica Kennedy

Running To

The interests of childhood and youth are the interests of mankind.

Edmund Storer Janes

On a fall day in Kansas, expecting a daily check-in call from my mom or last-minute instructions for my sons' Halloween parties, I picked up the telephone to hear "crackle . . . crackle . . . come get . . ." and what sounded like, "She's seven." Even with a bad connection and thousands of miles between us, the caller could only be Sister Rita, an American nun who'd lived the past fourteen years in a tiny Brazilian village. She had news we'd waited years to hear, "You have a daughter!"

It took several more calls to learn that our six-year-old daughter, Diana, lived sometimes with her blind grandmother, sometimes with her retarded mother. But, mostly, this little girl usually ran about in the jungle taking care of herself.

Over the next weeks, we placed return calls, then we waited for replies. Diana's Brazilian family of three—

scorned, ridiculed, or ignored—lived in their one-room, windowless, doorless hut on fifteen dollars a month. Diana's survival technique was often to run away, steal when she needed to, and disobey rules or grown-ups who didn't please her. She often went without food, and sometimes her grandmother left her alone in the jungle for days at a time. Yes, she knew about us. And we could come get her, these quiet nuns promised hopefully, "as soon as the Brazilian government gets around to doing her paperwork."

Sister Rita added, "Diana adores animals, especially dogs."

Immediately, we adopted Miranda, a twelve-week-old beautiful golden retriever, whose first family found her to be a little too headstrong and hyper.

While our family waited for the "Come immediately!" phone call, it became therapy for my husband, sons, and me to attempt to train Miranda, a most energetic bundle who did not like to stay put. Her first family was right. As months passed into a year, then two years, waiting for Brazilian courts to act on Diana's behalf, Miranda, naughty as she was, became the family dog.

We taught Miranda to eat dog chow and rawhide bones rather than Nathan's soccer shoes. We took turns standing in the corner of the backyard during Kansas rainstorms and scorching summer afternoons, teaching Miranda to potty there, not on the bear rug by the TV. While we lined the shelves of an illiterate girl's room with pre-readers and games like Speak-and-Spell, we stepped over Miranda, picked up her messes, and often had to run out to look for this wayward pup.

On days we searched out the perfect school for Diana, and sat through meetings with teachers who vaguely understood early-childhood loss and third-world adoptions, Miranda insisted on riding along, merely curious, we thought, about the broader world.

We shopped for dresses and nighties and noted, with pleasure and overdue relief, how Miranda diligently watched while we put away Diana's belongings in her closet and drawers. But as soon as we finished "Diana tasks," Miranda usually ran off again, and one of us would charge out after her and haul or shame or trick her home.

Normally, when suitcases appeared, Miranda went into big-time dog-funk. She'd become vigilant and tailgate us so that we could barely pack. But when the final call came from Brazil, Miranda lay in the corner of Diana's room while we stuffed suitcases.

My mother, the most loving, organized woman I know—and probably the reason I wanted to adopt a daughter in the first place—agreed to live at our home and care for our sons while my husband and I flew to Brazil to bring home our girl, her only granddaughter.

Miranda, now fully grown, was potty-trained and no longer eating footwear daily. But she was still highly charged, needed attention, stole food, and ran away whenever she could. When we arrived in Brazil and phoned home to ask, "How's everyone doing?" we learned that even Miranda was behaving. "I don't know what you mean about this lovely dog running off," my mother, never a dog lover, reported. "She hasn't run off once."

Brazilian law required that we live with Diana in the back of a clinic for six sweaty weeks. Once there, we found that this half-grown child, while interested in the toys and candy in our suitcases, ran off whenever she wanted. There were moments in each day—bathtime, bedtime, pick-up-your-toys time—when we weren't sure Diana would even stay with us. If she stuck with us as her new parents, she would have to stand before a scary judge to say good-bye to her family and first country.

When the worrisome Brazilian court date arrived, we scrubbed river dirt from our new daughter, strenuously corralled her black curls beneath a hopeful pink bow, and made her wear a freshly ironed dress and shiny shoes. She stood before the judge and declared a most grown-up decision, after which we called home to say, "All three of us are flying home!"

My mother stepped over a dozing Miranda to do final preparations in Diana's room. In the week between our happy phone call and our plane touching down, Miranda snoozed there on the pink carpet, a patient, golden friend. Waiting.

"Miranda knew," my mother said.

And I believe she did. From the first day Diana came home, Miranda never slept in any other room, but neither did she get up on Diana's bed. No need to drink from toilets or steal steaks from the table because her dutiful forty-eight-pound mistress carried bowls of food and water to her several times a day. Together, Diana and Miranda planted flowers all over our yard to make it "more Brazilian." Wherever Miranda dug her holes, Diana followed her, dropping in daisy seeds and what would become hollyhock blossoms in the most unusual places.

And Diana never ran away from her new home. She learned to speak English like lightning, learned to read, and settled into being a good family member and United States citizen. For years to come, often using her Girl Scout flashlight, Diana read bedtime stories to her beloved dog.

The only times Miranda ran away were times Diana wasn't home. Then we didn't need to shout "Miranda" throughout the neighborhood or tape "Lost Dog" signs on the bank window. We simply drove to wherever Diana played. In later years, as Diana grew into a beautiful American teenager, we'd find Miranda wherever Diana practiced soccer or babysat.

No need to keep running. Girl and dog had each found their home.

Chalise Annett Bourque

Buster

Childhood shows the man, as morning shows the day.

John Milton

It was nighttime, and the rain was coming down as though forced from a fire hose! Lord, it was nasty out! Through the storm door, I saw the pair of them. I traced their figures with my squinted eyes. I pushed the door open against the wind.

"Get in here. You must be frozen wet!" I yelled.

The big woman moved through the doorway. "I almost didn't find this house. It's so dark up here in the forest."

Lightning flashed, and I saw the eyes of the little boy clinging to her hand. They were somber, scared pools of black, filled with puddles of liquid sorrow. *So, he's a crier, I thought. This must be the one—the boy who was thrown out of his foster home for indecent behavior.* It was the perfect excuse to get rid of him.

They'd called me from Social Services. They said it was an emergency placement for a few days until they could find a suitable black family where he would feel more comfortable. Now that I looked at him, I got it. He couldn't have been more than six. His teeth were missing in the front.

I bent down, and we looked at each other. I took his hand. It was frail and cold. The skin was dry. His nails were raggedy. I could feel all the little bones under the skin.

"I have puppies here," I whispered. "Do you want to see my puppies?"

His oversized head bobbed up and down slightly. Beneath a swollen stomach, chicken-like legs with lumpy knees protruded from his too-large shorts. I took him to the puppy nursery and sat him down on a blanket on the floor. I put two yellow pups on his lap. They began to lick his face and snuggle into his arms. His eyes grew wider, and his mouth opened slightly. For some reason, even the pups understood that this was no time to chomp with their sharp milk teeth. They joyously tumbled in his lap, kissing him and blowing hot puppy breath into his nose and ears.

That spring, it rained and rained, and we played with puppies. Buster, my ancient yellow dog, took to Billy. He knew about Billy. He knew everything I didn't know and had to discover. Buster's big head would rest itself on Billy's shoulder while they watched TV together. If Billy moved away from him, Buster would scoot closer, and even though this old dog had never been allowed in a bedroom in his life, he sauntered boldly into Billy's room that first night and parked himself next to the bed. He looked at me, and with perfect clarity, without a sound, he said: "This is where I need to be."

I tucked the boy in at night, hugged his stiff body, and said, "I love you." He didn't know what to do with that.

Buster was vigilant. He insisted on touching. Billy moved away, and Buster moved forward, his big, soft ears flopping into Billy's lap, and a paw resting on Billy's arm. "Trust me," he said with his eyes.

I taught Billy to read because they said he couldn't learn. I discovered Billy hated bananas. Buster told me, and then dumped the bananas in the trash can!

"Do you like raspberries?" I asked Billy. Buster said "yes" with his lips dripping in purple juice, so Billy ate them for the first time. They were warm and sweet. Buster took him to the wild berry patch and showed him how to pick the best ones off the bottom of the bushes where the birds hadn't pilfered them. Buster could make big purple doggy lips and pluck the berries off the stems without getting stuck by thorns.

They never found a black family where he would "feel more comfortable," so Buster and I kept him—so we could eat raspberries together, and read stories to someone who hadn't heard them 100 times already.

After a few years, Buster had to leave; it was time, you know. We cried, but Billy got his own puppy. I think Buster must talk to that pup sometimes because he rests his floppy ears on Billy's lap and puts his paw on Billy's arm—and he loves raspberries and hates bananas. And, he tells me about Billy—only the things I need to know.

Sometimes, I still tuck Billy in at night and say, "I love you."

"I love you, too, Mom," he says in his deep high-school voice.

And sometimes I still buy raspberries, and we eat them with his dog.

Sylvia Smart

9

GRATITUDE

*Gratitude is born in hearts that take time to
count up past mercies.*

Charles E. Jefferson

Mrs. Usher

You save an old man and you save a unit; but you save a boy and you save a multiplication table.

"Gipsy" Smith

I was twelve years old when I was released from reform school in Florida. I was locked up in the juvenile hall because I refused to ever return to the orphanage where I'd spent most of my life. I was never going to return there, even if I had to spend the rest of my life locked in a small cell. I'd flatly refused to even walk out the front door of the juvenile hall to help them clean up the streets, for fear they would take me back to that awful orphanage.

It was a Wednesday morning when a man named Burt, who worked for the court, came into my cage-like cell and asked if I wanted to go somewhere special for Thanksgiving dinner. I told him that I did not want to go outside the juvenile shelter. I liked Burt because he was a nice man. Burt kept on and on about that dinner and how a kid should not be locked up on Thanksgiving, so I finally told him that I would go.

Later that afternoon, an older woman named Mrs. Usher came to the shelter. She talked with me for about ten minutes and said she wanted to take me to her house for Thanksgiving. She said no child should be locked up in a cage. Before we left, I made her promise she would bring me back the next day. She and I walked out together and drove to her home.

As we walked into the house, I was surprised at what I saw. It was really small, not like the big dormitory house that I lived in at the orphanage. You could sleep thirty or forty people in our house at the orphanage.

I was really surprised when I went to their bathroom. I saw right away that they were not rich at all. They only had one toilet and one sink in their bathroom; they were really poor, and they did not even know it.

Wednesday afternoon and evening were very difficult for me. I wanted so badly just to get out of there and be back in my cage. There must have been fifty people going in and out of that house, getting ready for the big Thanksgiving dinner the next day. I was really scared. I didn't like people very much, especially grown people. They can do some really bad things to you when you're a kid. I never moved out of the chair, until almost all those people were gone later that afternoon.

Mrs. Usher came into the living room and asked if I wanted to have a Coke in the small bottle. I told her "thank you," but that I did not care for anything. I wanted that Coke really bad, but was just too scared to take it. Late that night when everyone was asleep, I snuck into the kitchen really slow and quiet-like, and took a cold Coca-Cola out of the refrigerator. I drank it real fast, in about five seconds, and hid the bottle cap behind the refrigerator. After that, I pressed the cold bottle against my stomach so it would be warm like the other ones. Then I put it in the carton so no one would ever know I drank it.

The next day was almost as unbearable for me. I would have rather died than have gone through that big dinner. All those strange people were laughing, joking, and making all kinds of noise. I have never been so embarrassed and so scared in all my life, and that is the God's honest truth. I hardly ate anything that day, even though I had never seen so much food in all my life. I sure was glad when it was finally over.

Later that night after everyone else had gone to bed, Mrs. Usher took me out onto her front porch. I really didn't want to go out. I knew that I would be asked a bunch of dumb questions, questions that I could not possibly answer. I just wanted to be left alone until I was returned to the juvenile shelter the next morning. Nevertheless, I got up and walked out onto the porch.

We talked for hours and hours. She was a real nice lady. I had never once sat and talked with anyone before that in my whole life. It was my first "nice and slow time," as she called it, and I really liked it.

I will never forget her kindness and her warm smile. But what I could not understand was why she did all of this for me. Why would anyone be kind to me? So I always kept one eye on her all the time.

Mrs. Usher got up from her chair and went into the kitchen. When she returned, she brought a small bottle of Coke for each of us. She smiled and handed one to me. I will never forget that either. That was the best Coke I ever drank in my whole entire life.

The next morning, we ate some breakfast together. Then she told me to go into the bedroom and get my things so she could take me back to the juvenile hall like she promised. When I was in the bedroom, I heard her in the hallway talking on the telephone to the authorities. She asked them why I was being sent back to the reform school. She wanted to know what I did that was so bad that I had to be sent back there. They told her that I did nothing wrong, but they had nowhere else to put me. I heard her get very mad at them and say, "I'm not going to bring him back to the juvenile hall to be locked up again like an animal!"

God knows I loved that woman for saying that!

It was the most wonderful thing anyone ever did for me as a child. That, of all the things in my life, is the one thing that made me want to become somebody someday. That one little sentence which came out of her mouth was the small and only light guiding my life for the next forty-five years.

I stayed with Mrs. Usher for several weeks, then left to go out on my own at the age of thirteen. I told her, "I have to make it on my own now 'cause I'm a man."

I continued to see the Usher family on and off for the next twenty or thirty years, until their deaths. I know they would have adopted me, but when it was discussed, I told Mrs. Usher that it was too late for me. She placed her hands over her face and cried.

I just wish I could have shown her how much I really loved her before she died, but I didn't know how to show love. I didn't even know what love meant or what it felt like.

So I tell her now, on quiet nights on porch swings, *Mom, now that you are in heaven, I hope you know how much I love and respect you. I hope you know how much you added to the life of one lonely, little boy who nobody else in the world wanted. I love you, Mom.*

Roger Dean Kiser

Tea in the Afternoon

*So much has been given I have no time to pon-
der ever that which has been denied.*

Helen Keller

I was born cold, small, and underweight in a country
in South America, at a time when incubators were
unheard of and the mortality rate for premature babies
was devastatingly high. Lacking strength to even swallow small amounts of nourishment, I was not supposed
to survive twenty-four hours. Everyone was resigned
to let nature take its course . . . everyone except my
grandmother. She had great faith, fierce determination,
and bold ingenuity, an unbelievable mix of virtues for a
simple woman who didn't write or read.

Lovingly, she took me to her home, tucked me in a
shoe box, and placed light bulbs around it to keep me
warm. She slowly and constantly fed milk to me with
an eye dropper.

Under her care, I not only survived, but flourished
physically, mentally, and spiritually.

For years, I thought she was my mother. Even today,

when "mother" is mentioned, it is her I think of. She, however, would often remind me, "No, I am your grandma. Your mother is that lady who comes on Sundays and brings us groceries. Talk to her; she is lonely. Someday, you will have to live with her."

For me, it was unconceivable that such a severe-looking lady could be my mother. I felt as if I was the victim of fraud. When she visited, I would hide behind a couch. In my child-mind, if she didn't see me, I didn't exist, and then I would not have to go with her. I wished life with Grandma would never end.

Even under that cloud, however, I lived a happy life. Our small family consisted of three: my grandmother, our dog, and me. My grandmother was a frail, spirited, clever, small woman with worn-out hands, a sweet grin, easy laughter, crow's feet deeply carved into her temples, and brown eyes that resembled mine. Her thinning white hair was pulled back in a tight bun. Most of the time, she dressed in a white shirt or sweater and brown skirt and shoes. My playmate was our old dog. Patient and almost blind, he would let me pull his tail at my will. I completed our family, a skinny little girl about four or five years old, who liked paper dolls, picture books, pretty clothes, and had lots of simple questions requiring complicated answers. We were all snug in our humble home in a small town near the Andes mountains. We didn't have many material conveniences, but always had enough food and a place to live. Our life was peaceful, quiet, and predictable.

Tea in the afternoon was our favorite routine. My grandmother, the perfectionist, enjoyed setting the best stage for our tea. It was not just the tea, but the position of the table holding the tea. It had to catch the sunlight coming in from the only window in the room. Together, we placed the small round table in the best location. On sunny days, we put it to the south and delighted in the brightness and warmth while shadows projected into our teacups. On cloudy days, we opened the worn-out window to maximize the light coming in. The sunlight made us feel special, fancy, and mischievous. Then, only when everything was just right, we would begin our very own tea ceremony.

My grandmother made my tea in her own special way. A half-cup of tea, a half-cup of warm milk, and two teaspoons of sugar. She called it *tecito*, Spanish for "little cup of tea." Our dog sat at our feet, lazily wagging his tail in quiet approval. Grandma sat in front of me with a twinkle in her eyes, sipping her tea ever so slowly.

I preferred to make it last longer, getting tiny teaspoonfuls, one from the lighter side of the cup, another from the darker side. I savored her company and the feeling of closeness, security, and love. I eagerly looked forward all day to that time of nourishment and affection. A very religious woman, Grandma talked to me about God's goodness and the angel assigned to protect me all my life. Graciously and wisely, she was preparing me for the jagged road ahead.

We didn't have a heater, and during winter our home was bitterly cold. Always worried about my health, she put me to bed early to prevent my catching a cold or worse. Then she brought me *tecito* in bed with her small, trembling hands. The warmth and the smoothness of the tea going down my throat, as well as her presence and devotion, warmed me body and soul.

Then, one day when I was nine years old, without any warning, Grandma peacefully died. My world crashed, and my life was forever parted into two: before and after Grandma.

I never realized how strong I had become under her guidance; her teachings kicked in, and I continued believing in God, my guardian angel, and sunshine.

Years have passed. Places have changed. People have gone. Painful memories have faded. But happy memories continue to live in me.

I live now in a different and faraway place. I honor her memory by living my life by the values she taught me. In return, I have been blessed with children, grandchildren, health, and life. And I am not cold anymore.

Sometimes, when I need to talk to Grandma, I wait for the afternoon and then deliberately, leisurely, playfully, and lovingly set myself a little table near a sunny window and pour myself a cup of tea. Then, I feel her love softly comforting my soul. It's the two of us again, and I secretly whisper, "Thank you, Mother."

Nancy Bravo Creager

What It's Like to Truly Have a Mother

All that I am or ever hope to be, I owe it to my angel mother.

Abraham Lincoln

Plenty of people say that your birth mom is the only mother you can love beyond doubt, no matter what. But that's not true. They always forget about the fact that there are mothers out there who don't love their children like God intended them to, thus they do things to those children like abuse them, stop loving them, or trade them for things that will benefit them more.

"How's it possible to trade your own child for anything else in this whole entire world?" you may ask. But it's quite possible, and alcohol was what was more important to my mother than me.

I was born in Bryansk, Russia, a midsize town about six hours west of Moscow. The first few happy years of my life, I thought no one existed except my mommy and me—until I was about five years old. Then I started to realize that my mom and I stopped spending time together, and it was constantly my grandmother and me—not that it was a bad thing.

One day, after I got home from playing with my friends, I found my mom arguing with my grandma. When she turned around to look at me, I didn't see the same woman who once had given me birth and the woman who once loved me like I was the only one existing in her life. Her eyes were bloody red, her once-beautiful smile was now a gigantic frown, and she kept rocking back and forth like a tree blowing in a stormy wind.

"Let's go!" she yelled at me as she grabbed me by the arm.

Right away, I started to cry because I didn't know, anymore, this lady who was screaming and pushing me.

"Help!" was the last and only word that came out of my mouth before she pushed me down to the floor and started to kick me like I was just some dirty soccer ball.

I lived like that, with her hurting me, my grandma, and herself, for two years. One day my grandma promised she would do everything in her power to get me out of that abusive and unloving home—and she did. She made her promise come true, and for the next three years I lived in an orphanage.

There wasn't a night when I didn't go to bed thinking about how alcohol could do such a thing to my once sweet, caring, and loving mom. But the biggest question I was carrying in my head was, *Will I ever have another woman who can love me just as much or even more than the one who traded me like I was some baseball card?*

Every morning and night, I prayed to God that maybe he would send me an angel who could take me under her wing, an angel I could call "Mother" like I once used to.

When I was twelve, my prayers were answered. I

strolled into a room and saw an exquisite, smiling, full-of-grace-and-kindness woman who I began calling my mom right away. From the moment I saw her, I realized I could forget about everything bad that had ever happened. I could now envision that only she and I exist in this world.

My mom is always there for me, whenever I'm in trouble or I just need a little cheering up. Whenever I'm sad or happy, she can tell, not because she can look at my face and say, "Oh, she must be sad," but because she can feel it. That's what real moms do. They feel their children's pain, happiness, success, or failure.

I never imagined that I could ever find another woman who I could love as much as I did my birth mom, but I proved myself wrong. I love her way more then I ever loved anyone or anything in this whole entire world.

God sent me an angel to take under her wing . . . an angel I call Mother.

Maria Ervin (age 17)

Love Transcends Blood

In 2000, when my husband and I told my aged Chinese parents that we had filed the application to adopt an orphaned girl from China, their responses were less than enthusiastic. Adoption in China, where they live, bears a heavy stigma. The main concerns are not only about carrying on the family bloodline, but also the deep-rooted fear one might not love a child who was not of their own flesh and blood.

We got our little girl, Anna, from China, when she was seven-and-a-half months old. She was a pretty, feisty little thing. As we began our lives together, we formed a bond so deep and a love so palpable that we were often too overwhelmed for words. Love does transcend blood. Our experience with Anna was evidence of that, but would it be enough to convince my parents?

In 2004, when Anna was two-and-a-half, we took her to China to visit them for the first time.

When Anna saw my parents at the doorway in the light of the setting afternoon sun, she ran toward them, calling out, "Grandpa and Grandma!" in Chinese. My father hunched down and picked her up, and my mother touched her tender cheeks. Faint smiles spread over their faces. I held my tears and breath.

We spent an exciting month in Beijing. Although she was too young to really appreciate these places, we took Anna anyway to visit Tiananmen Square, the Great Wall, and the Summer Palace. She had fun, especially at the Summer Palace where we rented a boat. Anna insisted on pedaling it herself and nearly tipped over the boat. When she was not out touring the city, she stayed home, playing hide-and-seek with her cousins and watching Chinese cartoons with fascination. She also helped my parents make dumplings and noodles, making progress with her fine motor skills as well as a complete mess.

During the second week of our stay, she caught the flu and had a high fever. On her one day of bed rest, my parents took turns taking care of her, feeding her boiled ginger soup, touching her forehead every so often to assure her that her fever was receding by the minute. When Anna felt better, she wanted to go out with my father to the nearby local market. My mother insisted that Anna should not go out since she had just gotten better. My father insisted that she should. They had a serious argument that resulted in both of them taking Anna to the market, bundling her up in layers of clothing in the scorching Beijing August weather.

The day before we were to leave, as my mother sat at the table with Anna, she looked at me and said, "What difference does it make if you gave birth to Anna or not? We were all wrong. You can love a child not related by blood as though you gave birth yourself."

My father, who was sitting nearby, added, "When you miscarried, your mother asked heaven what we did wrong for you to deserve this fate. Now she asks heaven what we did right for you to deserve Anna."

Linda Zou

Nine Months in My Heart

A baby is God's opinion that the world should go on.

Carl Sandburg

We walked out of the office, misty-eyed. After seven years of marriage, another phase in our lives peeked on the horizon. Soon, my husband and I would stop our adult chatter just to hear our baby coo. Our hardwood-floored hallways would become the runway for Tonka trucks or the pathway of a baby doll in its stroller. Our evenings would soon be filled with basketball prac-tices—or would it be ballet recitals?

We marked our calendar days. We ended each day with prayer and praise.

Soon, the plain white, junked-up, spare bedroom became a pristine, pastel nursery. Months zoomed by while we dreamed of the sweet smell of our soft baby. We anticipated the baby's burps. We stacked diapers in the corner of the closet, waiting for the blessing of changing our baby's gooey diaper. The quiet nights of our waiting would have been traded gladly for a night of holding our crying baby in the folds of our arms.

One hot September afternoon, I stood before my fourth-grade classroom. I had my back to the class, writing math equations on the board. It was a normal afternoon, quite routine. The hot sun beat through the tall windows while the fan in the corner circulated the hot air.

But the normalcy was about to end. My principal opened the classroom door and peered in. The students and I stopped our work to see what he needed. "Mrs. Phillips, I have some news for you," he announced. All ears perked. His eyes sparkled. I grasped my desk.

He walked into the classroom toward me. "Mrs. Phillips, we just received a phone call."

Oh, no, something had happened to my husband, my parents. But he was smiling. Maybe a good report from a parent?

"We just talked with a nice lady from an adoption agency. They wanted me to let you know that you are now in labor." Twenty mouths dropped open. I'm glad I had a desk to steady myself. That day would be the day, perhaps. That day, *the* baby of my heart would become the baby of my life. My students and I never did get back to our mathematics.

Ashley was born shortly before I arrived home from work. The adoption agent gave me a dramatic report of the details of her birth. The birth mother had held our daughter in her arms. She lovingly kissed her and patted her face with her young hands. But she knew her decision was final. It was for the best, she still felt in her heart. Ashley would be afforded a happier life with the family she'd already handpicked—my husband and me. Ashley became ours.

It had been nine months almost to the day since we'd walked out of the adoption agency. No, I did not carry her physically in my body, but for nine months she grew and was fertilized in me, emotionally and mentally. For nine months, the dream of having her as my daughter was sometimes larger than life itself. Nine months. Just like a normal pregnancy.

That September day, she jumped right out of my swollen heart and straight into my life.

Rhonda Lane Phillips

"We may not appear as family from the outward package, but we're tied together by our heartstrings."

Children of Our Own

God sends us children for another purpose than merely to keep up the race—to enlarge our hearts.

Mary Howitt

After a couple of years of "trying," and having tests and drugs and procedures and more tests and more drugs, a fertility specialist told us it was very unlikely we would be able to have a child of our own.

After much discussion and the realization that having biological children wasn't our motivation to be parents, we decided to adopt. The adoption process was eye-opening, soul-moving, and time consuming. It was close to three years of application forms, weekend workshops, and visits with our caseworker before we got the phone call.

"Leah, there are two-year-old twin girls I think you should meet." Two days later, we met them. The possibility of these gorgeous little girls becoming our daughters had both Keith's and my heart racing. After one more visit, they were living at our house.

Keith and I decided to be very open with the girls about how they came into our lives. We started talking about adoption long before they knew what the word meant. We wrote our own little book about their adoption and talked about our adoption journey with them often.

They loved to hear the story about the first day we met them. It tickles them to hear that we fell in love with them the very first moment we laid eyes on them and how they hid behind the door and peeked at us.

I always ended these little adoption talks with, "Thanks for being mine."

As the girls have grown older, they seem to have fewer questions; adoption is simply the thing that brought the four of us together to be a family, no big deal.

Then, a few days ago, the girls and I were talking about writing a letter to their birth mother and sending her some pictures. At the end of this little chat, I said, as always, "Thanks for being mine." Then the best moment of my life happened.

My sweet little Madison said, "I wouldn't have it any other way, Mom. Thanks for adoptin' us!"

My other sweetheart, Brooklyn, came running over. "Me, too, Mom!"

And to think that the fertility specialist said we wouldn't have children of our own.

Leah Cook

Dear Mom

Dear Mom,
Dear Virginia,
Dear Ginny,
None of those names sounded right.
Dear Birth Mother? Maybe.

Dear Birth Mother,
 This is Karen. I have wondered where you might be
for a long time, but didn't think I could actually find
you. Then, my father died. I mean my adopted father.
 Before the burial service began, I had enough time to
retrieve the contents of his safe-deposit box. Inside,
there were several envelopes, all labeled, and all in my
mother's neat handwriting, in my adopted mother's
neat handwriting. Deed for the house. Life insurance
information. Adoption papers.
 I was already running late, but I had to see what was
inside. I took a deep breath and removed the contents
of the envelope. Inside there was a bundle of papers.
Written on the outside was this note: "We may not be
around when you read this, but always remember you

brought us great joy. Love, Mom."

Well, Mom was still around. I shrugged and continued.

Inside were papers with attorney letterheads, a thick folded manila paper labeled, ORDER OF ADOPTION BABY GIRL BENSE, and a folded yellow scrap of paper.

Wait! BABY GIRL BENSE? Was that me? Would they have used the real name? I was expecting Jane Doe or something plain. What about secrecy and sealed records? I was startled by the capital letters. I felt like someone was yelling at me.

My heart was pounding. I needed to finish getting dressed for my adopted father's burial. Part of me wanted to read more. Part of me wanted to forget all about it.

I read more.

I unfolded the yellow scrap of paper revealing a list hurriedly written by my adopted mother. I could tell by the awkward abbreviations and the choppy phrases. Very bright. Artistic talent. More phrases. Mat GranF. Born Germany. Her Grandmother-Eng-Sec.

Her grandmother. "Her" meant you! My mother! My birth mother! These phrases about family origin were about you!

I couldn't believe it! And there were more phrases. *Hazel eyes. Light complexion. Light red hair.* Red hair! My daughter has red hair! Neither my husband nor I have red hair. We have been asked hundreds of times, "Where does the red hair come from?" It comes from you!

And more. My eyes were glued to that scrap of paper. A faint picture was forming in my mind. *April 1934.* A date of birth?

There was more to read, but I couldn't see it. My eyes were welling up with tears, and my heart was breaking. I never thought this information existed. I never thought my adopted parents would have kept it from me. I felt betrayed. It was too much. Too much for a thirty-six-year-old woman to receive on the way to the cemetery. It would have been just right for an eighteen-year-old woman to receive on her birthday. This was eighteen years too late.

And it was too much for my adopted mother to know and not let on. Why hadn't she told me? She had written it, and she had kept it. She had stood next to me while the red-hair inquiry repeated itself. She had known the answer.

And it was too much to handle that day. So I buried the envelope, I buried him, and I tried to bury my emotions.

But I couldn't. Anger, hurt, shock. I felt them all, and a few weeks later I focused them all on my adopted mother.

I confronted her with the envelope and asked why. She said she was sorry. I asked why she hadn't said anything about the red hair. She said she had forgotten. This wasn't acceptable. But nothing would be. I wanted something that she couldn't give me. I wanted the envelope eighteen years earlier. Still hurt, I cut her out of my life.

And as hurt as I was, the silence afterward hurt worse. But I didn't know how to break that silence. Then the silence fed upon itself until a whole year had passed.

And then, while sorting through papers, I came across the envelope, and I took out the scrap of yellow paper again. I felt a need to look at it again.

There they were. All of those hurriedly written phrases that I had read before. *Light complexion. Light red hair. Chose name.*

What? I hadn't seen that before. *Chose name.*

I needed to find out who chose my name. You? My adopted mom? How could I find out? I could try to get my adoption records unsealed and find you, but that would take too much time, and I had to find out now. I knew one person who could answer me.

So, I did what I had not done for a year. I called my adopted mother.

She said, "Well, hello, Karen. How are you?" as if it had only been a few days since our last conversation.

"Fine, but I need to ask a question."

"Of course. What is your question, Karen?"

"That's it," I said. "Karen is the question."

"What?"

I took a deep breath and asked more clearly, "Did you name me Karen?"

She hesitated. "We wanted to name you Karen. It was Daddy's and my favorite name. When we got a phone call learning that a little girl was available, we were so excited. We didn't need to talk long to decide. We called right back and said we would take you. Then they told us that your birth mother had already named you, and that name was Karen. We knew you were meant to be ours.

"You know," she continued, "you didn't grow in my womb, but you grew in our hearts. Maybe your other mother named you Karen, but you were *our* Karen."

With the silence broken and those few words spoken, my heart was healed.

And when that reunion was complete, I felt it was time for our reunion.

I took the envelope and sat in front of my computer. I found you in thirty minutes.

And in a heartbeat, I lost you.

Virginia Bense. Born April 10, 1934. Died May 15, 1988.

It usually happens the other way around, lost and then found.

But I decided to find you again.

And I have. Again and again.

I have found you in the radiant *light red* halo of my daughter's *hair*.

I have found you in her inquisitive *hazel eyes* and her glowing *light complexion*. Her *artistic talent* seeps out every pore and *very bright* is a mild compliment.

Dear Mom,

This is still Karen. Thank you.

Karen C. Helmrich

Hallelujah Baby!

There is a sweet joy that comes to us through sorrow.

Charles Haddon Spurgeon

"Miss Batty (I sometimes think the name fits me well), where is Mr. Beel?" Nurjahan was standing in the kitchen with one hand on her hip while waving her finger at me. "I missy his!"

"I missy his too, Nurjahan," I said. "He will be calling here soon, though, and you can talk to him."

"No!" the ten-year-old declared in her sternest voice. "I cally him now!"

I tried to explain that Mr. Beel was on the road, and his cell phone was not charged, but she did not understand. "I cally him on the leetle phone," she persisted. "His answer and talky to me. Why he not here?" She put up her hands and shrugged her shoulders. "When he coming home?"

I stopped stirring dinner and looked at her as she stood staring at me with her determined expression. I realized that she was really missing Mr. "Beel," and I better give her satisfactory answers before she head-butted me (something she does to Mr. Beel on a regular basis).

I explained to her that Mr. Beel was visiting his dad in Washington and would be back on Thursday. We counted on our fingers to figure out how many days it would be until his return. She was not happy to see it was a full five days away. I had to laugh when she told me she missed head-butting him. Nurjahan insisted that the top of her head was lucky, so gentle head-butting, in her eyes, was a sign of great affection.

It was not all that long ago when Nurjahan, who came to live with us from Bangladesh, would not even be in the same room as my husband, Bill. In her culture, it is considered inappropriate to be in the company of a man who is not a relative. Initially, Nurjahan would not go in the car with Bill or even talk to him unless I was there with her. She would not look at him when he spoke to her. I cannot say there was a precise moment when she finally felt comfortable around Bill; it just happened. They started by teasing each other, and then Nur began this head-butting thing, and they have been best buddies ever since.

Nurjahan keeps us laughing. One morning, she came into our bedroom and cried, "Miss Batty, my nose is stopped, and my hole is running!"

I tried not to laugh, but could not help myself. Soon, she too started to giggle. Then Bill joined in. It's hard to explain this phenomenon to the casual observer. Nurjahan has a hole in her forehead from acid burns, which leads to her sinuses. So, when she gets a cold, her forehead runs. We have learned over the months of living with her that she takes all of these oddities in stride. She is the kind of kid who, when handed a bunch of lemons, will make lemonade. We have lots of kids who have been handed lemons, so to speak.

Like our newest arrival, Paola, who arrived four days ago from Haiti wearing a pretty little blue dress with patent-leather shoes and frilly little socks. She showed up on our doorstep with her bottle and two diapers. The folks who brought her were volunteers for Mercy and Sharing, an organization that helps children in Haiti.

Paola has a double cleft lip and a cleft palate, as well as some other birth defects. Her mother gave her over to the orphanage because in Haiti, where voodoo is a way of life, a child with such defects is considered cursed. She weighed a measly sixteen pounds at sixteen months old. She will have to undergo numerous surgeries to correct her problems. But, like our Nurjahan, it is not the imperfections you see when you look at this little bundle of joy. Instead of seeing a baby expected to be sad and cranky, you see gorgeous brown eyes and a ready smile that lights up her whole face. She laughs and interacts with everyone and everything around her, and has already won over the hearts of our whole family.

Yesterday, all the children—our three, and six (of our eventual forty-three!) foster children—were gathered around Paola, breathlessly waiting for her to throw her arms up in the air and yell, "Hallelujah!" When she finally did, the noise was deafening as they all clapped and laughed.

I watched this celebration and wondered to myself, *How does a baby with all these problems have reason to rejoice?* Then I thought about the country she came from where you are considered lucky if you end up in an orphanage. In Haiti, many of the children live in rat-infested streets where raw sewage runs freely. At least in the orphanage, they have someone to care for their basic needs. In

the orphanage, they rejoiced over simple things that we
take for granted in our country of plenty. In the orphanage, they yelled "Hallelujah!" when diapers or formula
arrived. They yelled "Hallelujah!" when a baby went to
a new home. They yelled "Hallelujah!" when they had
fresh water. They yelled "Hallelujah!" when a doctor or
nurse came to minister to them. I suspect that some
may have even said a silent "Hallelujah" when the sick-
est little ones stopped suffering and returned to God. I
am sure they all said "Hallelujah!" when little Paola left,
because they knew that she would thrive and be loved
unconditionally.

So now we have our little "hallelujah baby," and
together we celebrate smiles, laughter, crawling, standing, clapping, and swinging. We celebrate smelling
flowers, picking up the telephone, and sleeping on
freshly washed crib sheets. We celebrate toes that wig-
gle and fingers that point. We celebrate the sunrise and
the sunset. We celebrate rocking chairs and rocking
horses. We celebrate baths and baby powder. We celebrate arms that hug and voices that soothe. You name
it, we celebrate it!

Hallelujah, hallelujah, hallelujah!

Elizabeth Henderson

10

REUNION

Absence, with all its pains, is, by this charming moment, wiped away.

James Thomson

Searching

It is the slowest pulsation which is the most vital. The hero will then know how to wait as well as to make haste. All good abides with him who waiteth wisely.

Henry David Thoreau

Digging through the piles of heaven knows what on my desk, looking for the school lunch forms I need, I once again run across the paperwork to start the process to find my birth parents—holding them as if the papers alone can give me answers I need. It's only paper, assembled, waiting for a signature—a couple hundred bucks and a stamp to follow through. It needs my action to become more than the pulp of a ground-up tree with ink decorations. Tears start a trail down my cheeks, wetness without awareness. I always put the papers back. I need to make a decision and stop living in limbo—waiting. Do I sign and send, or delay until it's too late and I am filled with regret?

My sister found her birth parents. She turned in the forms, waited for the follow-up calls, hired an intermediary, and had a joyful reunion. I cannot bring myself to follow in her footsteps. Oh, I got my non-identifying information years ago and the paperwork that would start the process, but I have never followed through. It seemed there was always a bill, always an excuse, always something. The truth is I have been putting it off.

At forty-two years old, the mother of two adopted children as well as two living birth children, you would think that sending a simple form would be easy. I want to set a good example for my boys, to do the "right thing." I am just not sure what the right thing is.

"Hi, I'm Nancy, and I will be playing the part of your birth daughter. I am not the perfect person you may have imagined, if you thought of me at all. And here I am on your doorstep. What do you mean your family doesn't know about me?"

No matter how many times I play it out in my mind, it never has that Hollywood ending I hoped for when I was a child and life was less complicated.

I remember those fantasies, pretending my birth parents were famous or exotic. I can sing, so maybe they were famous singers. I would tour with them, and they would be so proud of me. Any dream to stave off the nasty voice in my head that whispered, "They gave you up."

I know the reasons I was placed for adoption, some altruistic, some probably not so much, and I am accepting of them. I would not want to have been reluctantly raised by someone who struggled to do a good job but lost part of their youth because of my birth. I love my adoptive parents dearly. My mother was a wonderful and caring woman, once terribly depressed by her inability to have a baby, and overjoyed by my adoption. My father was remote, proud, a typical sixties bread-winner. My parents were always honest about my adoption. I cannot remember them sitting down for the "big adoption talk," but I always knew. I have followed that example with my own children; they have always known.

So if I have a good life and am a good mother, why am I so reluctant to find my birth parents? Why do I balk and shake when I look at those forms? I wish making this choice, once and for all, was cut-and-dried. I almost hope some weird thing will happen that would force my hand, but that could be a genetic disease that threatened my boys, and I would never wish that on them—us. It would, of course, be easier if my birth parents just knocked on my door. I am in all the match databases. Once a year, I do an Internet search to see if they are looking for me. They aren't. I have been told most people who placed their kids for adoption are willing to reunite. They actually hope the birth children will come to them, and here we are, many of us, wanting for them to come to us. Is a second rejection really that frightening? Why do I feel like I am underwater and cannot breathe when I think about this search?

What if I'm not pretty enough, smart enough, happy enough, sad enough? What if they have been miserable or scared or really happy without me? What if they never thought of me, not ever? If they never told anyone about me, would I really exist? What if? It swirls around me in a big cloud of pain-filled fear, need, and regrets, no matter which path I take. Is the search for my birth parents a betrayal to those people who raised me? Oh, who am I kidding? It's not my parents I am afraid of hurting; it's me. I love my father, and if he forbade my looking, I would take his fear into consideration, but he never has. That's saying a lot for his growth. I had a private baptism so my birth mother would not find me and grab me back. A little overdramatic, but very much Daddy.

There is the specter of my boys' birth parents. I want the boys to search someday, but there is a small secret part of me that wants their mom-love all to myself. It's selfish and needy, and I am ashamed of it. I fear that maybe they somehow got the short end of the stick. I am a good mother, but perfect? Hardly. I know the dreams, especially when you are punished for some pint-sized transgression that your "real" parents would not have punished you for. Birthdays with presents stacked to the ceiling from your birth parents, Lady and Lord Bountiful.

So here I sit. Staring at a sheaf of papers that could or could not change my life, and I don't know what to do. Strange for me. I am usually so decisive. I jump into choices with a certainty, a lightness of heart that covers all fear of mistakes. This should be easy for me. It isn't. It's bigger than me alone.

I put the papers back on the pile and cover them as if I am hiding a precious prize, or a dark secret. My decision is once again on hold. Just for a little while, until I am stronger, tougher, more desperate. When I am more ready. I am not ready to change our lives—yet.

Nancy Liedel

Two Paths for Two Daughters

The joy of meeting, not unmixed with pain.

Henry Wadsworth Longfellow

In May 1974, in the summer heat of El Paso, Texas, I became a birth mother to a daughter.

In May 2003, in the still frozen air of Palmer, Alaska, I became an adoptive mother to a daughter.

Dichotomies—that's how my life has played out. I've been overweight and out of shape; I've been thin and trim and a competitive gymnast. My college degree started me on a career teaching schoolchildren; later, I was an investigator for crimes against them. Those dichotomies brought me wonderful and painful lessons.

When I had my daughter in 1974, I was put on a surgical ward away from the babies. I insisted on seeing and holding her though I'd made the decision to put her up for adoption. Before I left her, I slipped her ID bracelet off her ankle and hid it in my pocket in a desperate attempt to hold onto some link to her. Leaving the hospital without my daughter left me numb and asking, "Will I ever know her?" A social worker came by my apartment days later, and after taking some of my family history, left me with a nugget of information that I mentally embraced and absorbed . . . and then repeated over and over to myself. They're calling her "Amy."

The days, the seasons, and then the years came and went, but, for me, the calendar year began and ended with May. My daughter and I shared a birthday in May, and as I thought about her, I tried to picture her face, her eyes, her hair. Eventually, moving to Alaska put me miles from my former life in Texas. My husband and I raised a daughter and a son, and I became an investigator for the Alaska State Troopers, where I worked Crimes Against Children. Seeing the plight of these children motivated me to do more, so my husband and I looked into becoming foster parents. As we took classes, we discovered we both wanted another child, even though ours were out of high school. We researched agencies and chased paper like there was no tomorrow. We moved like a tornado through the multiple tasks and bureaucracies, knowing in that calm eye of the storm was our heart's desire—our daughter in China.

In May 2003, we traveled to Jiangsu, China, to hold our fifteen-month-old daughter, Gianna Qingruo. Gianna latched onto me and stared hard into my eyes as if to say, "What took you so long?" After an incredible two weeks, we returned to Alaska and enveloped Gianna with family.

There is a Chinese belief that states: an invisible red thread connects those who are destined to meet, regardless of time, place, or circumstance. The thread may stretch or tangle, but will never break. Initially, I looked at this belief as a charming saying. That is, until

I realized that somehow, in the cacophony of voices pleading to be adopted from China, we were matched with Gianna. She was simply meant to be ours. That "charming" belief took on more meaning in March 2006 when a connection through time and place further stretched that red thread.

I received an e-mail from an odd address, but opened it anyway. The woman identified herself as an intermediary and said she was attempting to find a woman who lived in El Paso in 1974 regarding an adoption. I immediately knew it was about my daughter. The urgent desire to know more overwhelmed me, and then I read her name . . . Amy . . . and that she worked in the Texas Department of Corrections.

They offered Amy's phone number. There was no doubt, no uncertainty, no hesitation. I grabbed a pen and paper and went to the phone.

A young voice with a Texas twang answered, and I simply said, "Amy? I'm your mother."

We talked, cried, laughed, and shared our lives for over two hours. Later that night, we talked some more. Computers allowed us instant gratification as we shared photos of ourselves. Looking into her eyes and . . . hers into mine . . . we knew. DNA tests could only result in a big ol' "I told you so!" The similar and parallel lives we've led defy logic. Genetics explains the matching eyes, smiles, and sassy personalities, but only the word "surreal" describes the choices of careers, the patterns of relationships, and the shared dreams.

In May 2006, the thread through time brought together Amy, Gianna, and me. As the three of us hugged, meeting for the first time in the Lubbock, Texas, airport, strangers stared, as if somehow knowing and feeling they were seeing a unique moment unfold. Amy explained that somehow, in her heart, seeing that

I loved and adopted someone else's child, she was released from her past question wondering if her birth mother gave her away out of love . . . or lack of love. We both talked about our freedom from being bound to the past. We were now simply mother and daughter.

Gianna is only five years old now, but one day she will have questions, and she will need look no farther than her sister and mother to start down that trail of inquiry.

We've walked the path.

Ruthan Josten

It Was You

Standing beside my birth mother's hospital bed, I noticed that her glazed eyes had suddenly become lucid. Turning to see what she was staring at, I looked at the white wall directly behind me.

"Renora," I whispered to her sister-in-law, "Anita is seeing something."

Peering from her vantage point at the end of the bed, Renora craned her neck. "Oh, honey," she spoke softly, "she's been staring ever since she stopped talking."

Convinced Anita was seeing something beyond the white wall, I turned again. An avid *Touched by an Angel* fan, I had come to believe that angels appear to those in need, and surely to those who are dying.

It was noon on Sunday. I had arrived in Duluth the day before. Renora was standing outside Anita's hospital room waiting for me. Having taken the first morning flight from San Francisco to Minneapolis, I had driven the 180 miles northeast to Duluth on a cold, sunny, snow-covered morning. Renora saw me exit the elevator. She rushed toward me, greeted me, and ushered me into the sixth-floor waiting room.

"I thought it'd be best if we took a moment to get acquainted and for me to explain Anita's prognosis to you," Renora said. Her kind demeanor comforted me. I was nervous, unprepared for this first meeting with her and my birth mother.

"When I spoke with you on Wednesday, Anita was still able to speak, and we thought that she might be getting better. But since then, she's taken a turn for the worse. They've given her morphine for the pain, and she hasn't spoken a word since Thursday."

"Do the doctors think she'll make it?"

"I'm not sure at this point."

A nurse popped her head into the waiting room, and Renora introduced me.

"It's so nice to meet you. I'm sure Renora has told you your mother is not well. And, actually, the other nurses and I aren't sure what's keeping her alive." The nurse smiled sweetly, as reassuringly as one can when delivering disconcerting news.

My head dropped. I stared into my hands. "I'm glad you came," Renora continued. "We did not tell Anita that you were coming. As I told you over the phone, we begged her to let us tell you she was in the hospital. She was adamant about not wanting you to come, but I think it's best that you did. When we called, we wanted you to be able to choose. I hope this won't be too hard on you." She paused. "Let's go see her."

I walked up to the bed and looked down upon the woman who had given birth to me. An oxygen mask obscured most of her face. Her hair, tousled from lying in bed, was a dark shade of brown, with only a touch of gray at age fifty-nine. Sitting on the chair next to her, I stared through the siderails into her glassy eyes.

"You look like her," Renora said, reading my mind.

I spied Anita's hand cupped under her chin. "Look,

Renora. Her hand is just like mine."

"It's time you told Anita who you are." She smiled reassuringly while nodding her head.

Breathing deeply, I stared into my birth mother's big brown eyes, the exact color of mine. "Anita," I hesitated, "it's Ana, and . . ."

Anita began to shake violently. Terrified, I looked at Renora. "I think she's having a seizure!"

"Please don't think it's because of you."

But I knew that it was.

Renora turned to the door. "I'll get the nurse."

I took Anita's hand. She looked up at me, meeting my eyes, then became still.

Now what? What do you say to the dying woman who birthed you, but you've only just met? Gathering my wits about me, words began to flow. "Anita, I'm Ana. I know you didn't want me to come. But I wanted to meet you, to thank you for giving me up for adoption. I have a wonderful family and a nice life. I want you to know that I am happy and that I love you for your courage." I paused. There must be something else. Then I remembered the wall and a story my adopted mother had shared with me about my grandmother at her death.

"Anita, I know you're seeing something, and I want you to know that they are angels. And that one of them is your mother. She's waiting for you. Don't be afraid."

Three hours later, with Renora and me by her side, praying for the angels to come and take her, Anita died. Standing over her body, I marveled at her peacefulness and the soul I had felt leave the room.

A nurse came to prepare her for the move. As she bathed Anita's face with a washcloth, she turned to me.

"Now I know why she stayed alive as long as she did. She was waiting for you."

Ana Hays

Life, What a Precious Gift

Occasionally in life there are those moments of unutterable fulfillment which cannot be completely explained by those symbols called words. Their meanings can only be articulated by the inaudible language of the heart.

Martin Luther King, Jr.

Patti was born in Germany to a very young, unmarried woman who had two other children, both boys. Although her mother loved this new baby, she was financially unable to feed and clothe her, so she held her little girl once after she was born. Within days both the baby and one of her little brothers were taken to an orphanage. The mother intended to get a job, and when she had enough money to take care of her family, she would bring them back home with her again.

Many months later, her mother told the people at the orphanage that she couldn't come up with the money, and that, if her children were adopted, she wanted them sent to the United States so they would have a better chance for a good life. Still, she struggled day and night to raise the much needed funds to retrieve them.

The orphanage didn't tell Patti's mother when they found a couple in the States willing to take both children. Her mother never got a chance to tell her babies good-bye. At age two, Patti, and her three-year-old brother were put on a plane by themselves, and were adopted and raised by a very loving and caring couple.

A few years after Patti was adopted, the orphanage contacted her adoptive parents to tell them there was still another little boy in the family, and asked them if they wanted him, too. They declined.

Patti and her brother remained very close. They did everything together. She loved Danny more than anyone else on earth. When he died of cancer at the age of twenty-nine, she felt a major part of herself had died too.

Perhaps that's why, when she reached her thirties, Patti became obsessed with finding and meeting her birth mother. This obsession became her life's biggest dream. She was determined to do all in her power to make that dream come true.

She contacted Catholic Charities and within six months she knew the town where she had been born and her mother's name. Scared, yet thrilled to possibly be so close to so many answers, she got in touch with her birth mother. After a brief conversation, she knew she had to meet her in person, and she saved enough for her trip to Germany.

Patti's mother didn't speak English, but words weren't necessary. A touch, a soft hug, a gentle kiss spoke louder than any voice on earth. Her mother had an English-speaking stepdaughter who interpreted for them.

The next ten days they spent getting to know each other. Pattie showed her mother pictures of her own two children, both adopted.

Patti and her mother had a lifetime of questions.

Patti's was, "How could you ever give your children away? Did you ever think about us?

Her mother started to cry. She got up and left the room momentarily, then returned with a little plastic bag clenched in her hands. She opened it and pulled out a tiny T-shirt. "This was yours the day you were born. That was all I ever had of yours to remember you by. Do you really think that a mother could ever forget her child? Oh, Patti, every day since you were born, I have used this shirt to wipe away my tears. See the stains on this shirt? Those are the ocean of tears I have shed for you. Not a day has passed that I have not thought of you, not one day."

She brushed the little shirt softly against her cheek, gently caressed it, then kissed it. Refolding it neatly, she placed it back into the plastic bag and handed it to her daughter. "I believe this now belongs to you."

They rocked gently in each other's arms.

Before Pattie left Germany, her mother promised to keep in touch, and Pattie believed her. A dream of a lifetime had come true, and she felt a peace she'd never known.

October came, and on her thirty-second birthday, Patti received a card from her mother, her very first! On the card she told Patti she would call her on Christmas Eve.

Patti waited for December with a passion. She was more enthused than ever, preparing for the holiday. As she wrapped gifts for her children, she realized for the first time what a gift her birth mother had so unselfishly given to her adoptive parents. Her mother had known she wouldn't be able to give her tiny daughter a good life, so she tried to detach herself, giving away a large part of her own heart as well.

On Christmas Eve, as she watched her children open

gifts, she nervously waited for the phone to ring. She waited up most of the night, but the call never came. She was a little disappointed, but she reassured herself that it would come on Christmas Day.

It didn't.

How could her mother forget her so soon? Did she have second thoughts about the reunion, and decide to part ways again? It just didn't make sense. Patti's beautiful, long awaited Christmas suddenly became an inner holocaust.

Two days after Christmas, using every bit of courage she possessed, Pattie dialed her mother's number. Her half-sister answered. "Our mother died of cancer," she mourned.

Patti couldn't remember the rest of the conversation, or even if there was any. Placing the phone back on the receiver, she ran for her room and retrieved the tiny shirt from her dresser drawer. Throwing herself onto the bed, she cried for hours. As her own tears fell onto the fabric, they blended in with the stains already there. Tears of the deepest love known to mankind . . . the love of a mother for the child conceived within her womb, a child to whom she had given life, a child she had loved so long from afar, and now a child that she would love for an eternity.

Her tears were a mixture of "lost love found," and "found love lost." Lost to the world, but forever—like her dream come true— alive in her heart.

Barbara Jeanne Fisher

The Answer

*I know no blessing so small as to be reasonably
expected without prayer, nor any so great but
may be attained by it.*

Robert South

After years of trying to start a family, and the loss of
several babies, my parents were elated to learn there
was a six-day-old baby girl waiting for them!

My mother had an arthritic condition, and because of
this they had just about given up hope of ever being
able to adopt.

The year was 1941, and Pearl Harbor had just been
bombed. Within two short years, my father enlisted in
the U.S. Navy and left his little family for training camp
in Idaho. A few weeks later, at the age of twenty-nine,
he collapsed after a forced march and died of a heart
attack. Letters addressed to his "little angel girl" were
all I had to remember him by.

My early memories are of my mother crying and
going away to the hospital. I vividly recall being
awakened in the middle of a cold December night and

rushed to her bedside. She told me to be a "good girl for Grandma," waved good-bye, and later that day joined my father.

At the age of two, I was an orphan. I went to live with my paternal grandmother. I remember missing my parents so very much. Photo after photo, in a timeworn album, showed the proud new parents holding me. The looks on their faces radiated love. As a small child, I knelt in front of a large crucifix which hung on the wall in my grandmother's bedroom. I promised to be a "good girl" and begged God to give my parents back to me. "If I can't have both of them, then please, just give me one!"

My pain lessened with the passing of time.

One day when I was about twelve years of age, my grandmother, who was illiterate, asked me to help her sort through some papers that had belonged to my parents. In doing so, I found my adoption records! To this day, no one knows how she acquired them. As I read the information, which included my birth mother's name, family history, and last known address, I knew that someday I would find her.

I married shortly after graduation and became a mother myself. I looked at my baby and thought how difficult it must have been to give birth and then have to give the baby away.

Several days before my twenty-first birthday, I decided to try to locate my birth mother. I called directory assistance and, using her maiden name, got the phone number of my maternal grandfather, still living at the same address listed on the adoption records.

My hands shook as I dialed the number. I told him I was a long lost friend of his daughter and asked for her phone number. I called the number, and when she answered, I said, "You don't know me, but I believe that twenty-one years ago you gave birth to me."

"I always knew that someday you would find me!" she exclaimed.

She wanted to know if I was given a good home and was devastated when she learned of my parents' deaths. Within an hour of our phone conversation, she was at my front door. Tears filled her eyes as she reached out and wrapped her arms around me. Her words echo in my memory to this day. "Oh, you're beautiful!"

We developed a special bond, and she became my best friend. We were blessed with years of sharing laughter and love. I could always depend on her to be there for me. When she passed away at the age of eighty, I sat looking at her for the last time. I remembered the prayer I had said as a child, when I begged God to give me back one of my parents. I realized at that moment that my prayer had been answered.

Priscilla Miller

"Yes, This Is My Sister"

Ah, me! The world is full of meetings such as this—a thrill, a voiceless challenge and reply, and sudden partings after.

Nathaniel Parker Willis

In the 1920s, in rural Tennessee, Emmett Lee Jones died from influenza, leaving his young wife with six children. Two years later, she died from tuberculosis. Having no one to give them a home, the orphaned children went to various social agencies in Tennessee. The oldest four were boys, ages seven, ten, twelve, and fourteen. The younger were girls, ages four and two. The beautiful four-year-old cherub-faced child was my grandmother. This is her story, and I tell it to you with love.

In the fall of 1922, Mr. and Mrs. Willie Rayburn of Columbia, Tennessee, were taking a stroll one evening when they saw a group of children accompanied by a matron from the orphanage. Bringing up the end of the group was a small angel named Media. The Rayburns must have been melted by the little cherub, for Mrs.

Rayburn, after discussing it with her husband, was at the Tennessee Orphans Home first thing on Monday morning. Media May Jones, my grandma, went home with her mother that afternoon.

As Media became acquainted with her new surroundings, she began to cry. Mrs. Rayburn held Media and asked her what was wrong. Media went to the small bag she had brought with her that contained all of her belongings and pulled out a small dress, too small to be her own. "This is my baby sister's."

Mrs. Rayburn didn't waste any time, and after some inquiring found that Emma, Media's sister, had been sent to Nashville to a home for orphaned babies. The boys were sent to work on separate farms, not being truly adopted, but given room and board and the last name of the foster father, a common practice then.

Mr. and Mrs. Rayburn went to Nashville to try to adopt baby Emma but were too late. Emma had already been placed. All records were sealed, and no information could be obtained.

So Media began a new life with the Rayburns, who went on to have two boys and a girl. Growing up a Rayburn was a beautiful gift, and no one told Media that she was adopted. My grandmother had a very happy childhood and was deeply loved.

In 1931, the Rayburn family moved to Florence, Alabama, when Media's father was transferred with the railroad. When Media was fifteen years old, a neighbor told her that she was adopted, and she ran away from home for a while. The neighbor asked her not to tell her parents that she knew, so this was a very difficult time for her. But her upset turned to joy when her biological brothers, Earl, Claude, and Clayton, located each other, then found her. This brought her an everlasting peace and a joyful relationship with them, as well as with her adopted family that always supported her. It must have been hard for her to learn that her brothers had not been as fortunate as she; one of her brothers had been hit over the back with a rake and was permanently crippled.

Now five of the six Jones children were reunited, but what about baby Emma?

As the years ticked by, Media and her brothers grew to adulthood, married, and continued to search for their sister with no success. My "Nana," as I called her, and my grandfather made their home in Florence and had two daughters.

Media and her brothers began to think they were never going to find Emma, for all roads would eventually lead to dead-ends because the records were unavailable to them.

When I was growing up, my Nana would take the tiny lavender dress out of an old cedar trunk and tell me the story of herself, her brothers, and baby Emma. Always, I would ask, "Do you think you will ever find her?" To which she would answer, "I think I might. I hope I will."

Tennessee adoption laws were changed in the 1980s, and sealed records were made available to those who desperately wanted to know about loved ones. On September 9, 1985, Emma Jones was located in Johnson City, Tennessee. Four days later, Nancy Worley (Emma) received a phone call, and a woman's voice asked, "Do you know who you are speaking to?"

She replied, "Yes, this is my sister."

A joyful reunion took place in Nashville, with Media, her three living brothers, and Emma (Nancy) as well as lots of family. I was there that sunny day when my grandmother first saw the sister she had been searching for those forty-three years. Imagine the awe when my grandmother told her sister about their biological parents, Emmett Lee and Susie, about whom Nancy had no information, not even their names. After recovering from this information, Nancy very emotionally told all who were gathered, "My two daughters are named Lee and Suzy."

Nana had eleven precious years with her beloved Emma. She died in 1996, but not before giving Nancy (Emma) her little lavender dress.

I married, always carrying with me the plan to adopt at least one child, a dream that took root because of Nana. Today, I share her story with my three children, one adopted.

Lisa Cobb

Lessons from the Trees

In the darkling wood, amidst the cool and silence, he knelt down and offered to the Mightiest solemn thanks and supplication.
                                    William Cullen Bryant

In agriculture it's not uncommon to graft a branch from one tree to another. That newly grafted branch grows and flourishes, getting nurtured by the main trunk of the tree, just like all the other branches. Yet the branch does not lose its identity; it remains part of the original tree that it came from.

That story was told to me by my parents over and over when I was growing up. I was adopted, and it was my parents' way of explaining how I was different and always would be, and that I was loved like all the other family members (branches). I was adopted (when I was eight days old) by a military family. I was born in Panama City, Panama, and my name then was Don Louis Martinez. While I was growing up, within me grew the seed of yearning. I thought some day I would visit Panama and find my tree (family). My parents encouraged me, but had limited information, which they had already shared with me.

I was nurtured and blessed in many ways growing up in the United States. I received a college education, got my MBA, and married my wonderful high-school sweetheart, Ladonna. I was a partner in a firm, and it was there that my life would forever change.

My firm hired a young man whose wife was from Panama. One night after work, the young man gave me an Internet site, and a pop-up came to look at about retiring in Panama. Since I was fifty-three, I looked at the site, and a pop-up came on the screen and caught my eye. It was a private detective stating that he could help buy land in Panama and even find a person if needed. I noted the initials after the detective's name and did not think any more of it. Later that week while attending a function, I met someone who had experience in this field, and he assured me that those initials proved credibility. With this information, I contacted the detective at once.

The first thing he wanted was money. I paid it. And waited and waited and waited and waited over a year.

Then one day, my wife called and said, "Read your e-mail!" When I did, my eyes got big and swelled with tears. The detective said he had found my family. I had two brothers and one sister. And my mother was alive. It went on to say that my brothers and sister did not know of me until then. My sister set my mother down and asked her the question. She fainted, and they took her to the hospital. When she recovered, she told the family that the reason she fainted was that, as a devout Catholic, she had been lighting a candle daily, praying that before she died, she would receive a message that I was okay. Her prayers were answered. The detective had previously explained that if any member of the

family did not want to contact me, I would be told the
family was not found. But it was the opposite—they all
wanted to see me.

So my son and I arrived in Panama City on
September first, one day after my birth mother's birthday. Over fifty people were at the airport cheering and
waiving their hands, welcoming us with hugs and
kisses. The crowd parted, much like the Red Sea for
Moses, and up stepped my birth mother, showering me
with hugs and kisses. She blessed me and my son.

The next day, she and my sister took us to a mission
and showed us one of the oldest items left standing at
the mission, lasting over 100 years, a tree called the
Panama tree.

I looked at the tree and its branches and remembered
the story my adoptive parents had told me. I'd found
my tree, my family.

Edward Dow Bartling Martinez

"So, because I'm adopted, does that mean
my branch was grafted to the family tree?"

She Held Me for the Longest Time

There is in all this cold and hollow world no fount of deep, strong deathless love save that within a mother's heart.

Felicia Hemans

All of my life I had wondered about my birth mother and thought of many questions I'd ask her if I ever got the chance. I had my heart set on meeting her, and although I tried to tell myself not to get my hopes up too high, I still felt that she wanted to meet me, too.

My friends and family cautioned me, not wanting me to get hurt, but I didn't like to consider that my dream of seeing her would never come true. There were just too many things I needed to know, too many questions left unanswered.

One time a friend of mine asked me what my number-one question would be if I could only ask her one. I thought about it long and hard and finally said, "I would like to know if she ever held me."

Too often I'd seen on TV shows a teenage girl giving birth, and when the doctor asked if she wanted to hold the baby, she cried out something dramatic like, "I don't want to see it!" I knew sometimes this was just Hollywood dialogue, but still I hated to think that there was a possibility that I might be the baby that the teenage girl didn't want to hold.

Despite all these fears, I still longed to find my birth mother, so began the countdown. With each passing year, I told myself, *Only three years until you're eighteen and can meet her,* then it became, *Only two years . . .* and finally, *Just one more year.* I was preparing myself for anything. Or at least I thought I was.

When I turned seventeen, during my spring break, I was up late, bored and unable to sleep. Inspired by a TV show that I had been watching, where a boy searched for his birth mother, I got onto my computer and searched a few adoption registries. I found three postings that matched my adoption exactly. The same woman, by the name of Shelley, had posted all three.

I kept these findings to myself for the remainder of the break, but finally I got up the nerve to tell my parents. They pulled out the information they had on my adoption and, sure enough, my birth mother's name was Shelley.

The next day we contacted the adoption agency, and by the end of the week I had already received my first e-mail from my birth mother. I couldn't believe she had been searching for me and wanted to meet me, too.

From that day on, Shelley and I e-mailed each other almost every day.

About a week or so after our first e-mail, Shelley sent me a package. It contained a baby blanket she had made for me, a few pictures of her son and husband, and three or four pictures of herself. She was so beautiful, and I noticed that we both had the same eyes. Then I noticed something else . . . a letter addressed to my birth father, but apparently never sent. In it, Shelley talked about having me and giving me away. She described every detail, from going to the hospital to signing the final papers. It made me cry to read about her feelings during all of this. I stared at page three where she'd written, "I held her for the longest time." A smile spread across my face. She had held me after all.

For the next three months, Shelley and I continued to e-mail each other and send packages back and forth. It turned out that she had saved a lot of stuff, including my hospital bracelets and even a sonogram picture of me.

Finally, after what seemed like forever, the special day came. That morning, Shelley e-mailed me, saying, "I'll be there . . . with butterflies." And she was. A stream of people flooded into the baggage-claim area. Then from across the way I saw her wave at me and smile. I ran and wrapped my arms around her.

The rest of the time we spent talking, shopping, and laughing. She was so funny and wonderful that the time passed by very quickly, and before I knew it Sunday had arrived. It was time for Shelley to go back home. About fifteen minutes before we had to leave, Shelley gave me a copy of *Chicken Soup for the Teenage Soul.* Inside she had written, *I realize your teenage years are almost over, but hang on to them as long as you can. Time goes by so fast, like this weekend, so take your time and enjoy each day like it's your last. Sweet dreams for the sweetest girl in the world.*

That's when I realized that Shelley had never let go of me. She'd been holding me all along, in her heart. I ran to hug her, and while in her embrace, she cried the words, "I love you, Amy." And after I said, "I love you, too," she held me for the longest time.

Amy Tolleson

What Happened to Those Babies?

He who wishes to secure the good of others has already secured his own.

Confucius

Being adopted can make a child feel unique compared to her peers.

Being adopted and part of a U.S. military operation brings a whole new level of complexity to the question, "Where are you from?"

I was part of Operation Babylift out of Vietnam in 1975. I was born the year before in Bien Hoa, one hour northeast of Ho Chi Minh City, formally Saigon. My orphanage was home to twenty-nine orphans and a handful of Vietnamese Catholic nuns and caregivers. Children were left at the orphanage for a variety of reasons, usually because their parents lacked money or the child was of mixed race.

I left Vietnam on a Pan Am flight and arrived in the United States on April 28, 1975. I was adopted by a wonderful family in Oregon, and was raised with love and encouragement.

Growing up, I lived in a wonderful neighborhood with a lot of kids. We spent our days playing and inventing great adventures. One day when I was five, we were all outside and a neighbor lady came out. She told all the kids that she had just made some cookies. "Come inside and have some." Then she turned to me and said, "Bree, it's time for you to go home now."

I ran home crying, thinking I had done something bad to deserve her rejection. I threw myself onto the couch and sobbed. My parents came rushing into the room. "What's wrong?" they asked.

Trying to catch my breath and cry at the same time, I managed to stutter out what happened and told them what the neighbor had said. A sad look passed between them, and they heaved a sigh. They sat down on either side of me. "Bree, we're sorry that happened to you. You did nothing wrong. You need to understand that some people in the world may not like you because you are oriental."

I was shocked! I stammered, "Why wouldn't they like me if I was a flavor of Top Ramen Noodles?"

That event was a turning point. I realized I was different in appearance from my peers. As I grew older, I began to wonder about my birth country. I spent hours at the local library looking for information on Operation Babylift, though I was embarrassed when people saw me looking through magazines about the Vietnam War. Sometimes my heritage was a burden. I was always hesitant to offer up my ethnicity because I was unsure how people would react.

Many people expect me to be an authority on the war. Others ask my insight on the cause of the conflict. For some Americans, that time in history represents sadness, loss, and anger, and I am the physical representation of many things . . . the war, the sexual exploits of soldiers, and the face of the enemy that killed U.S. troops.

In early 2000, I traveled back to Vietnam for the first time to do work for those less fortunate. I instantly fell in love with the country and its people. For the first time, I experienced pride in being Vietnamese; it was very emotional for me. The people welcomed me into their homes and were anxious to hear of my life in the United States. Many attempted to teach me the language during my two-week stay.

It was also in 2000 that I attended a reunion of Vietnamese adoptees that changed my life. For the first time, I met others like me from Operation Babylift. Our shared experience created an instant bond. We wanted to capture and maintain that special connection, and some months later the Vietnamese Adoptee Network (VAN) was formed. As adoptees, we find strength in each other and serve as a resource to our generation and the next of Vietnamese adoptees. As I meet more people and tell them my story, I am often greeted with statements like, "I always wondered what happened to you."

My work with VAN allows me to meet other adoptees and families and aid them in exploring topics around adoption, especially transracial adoption.

That's when I say, "Do you know about Top Ramen Noodles?"

Bree Cutting Sibbel

Helping and Loving Orphans

*It is one of the most beautiful compensations of
this life, that no man can sincerely try to help
another without helping himself.*

William Shakespeare

BETTY:

In the sweltering heat of Saigon, I walked into the An
Lac Orphanage, filled with 400 babies and toddlers, and
knew my life as a "swinging single in New York City"
was over as I searched for my true destiny. My eyes
took in the rusty cribs, with chipped enamel and no
sheets. Hammocks made of rags were strung between
cribs, two and three babies to each crib, their bodies
covered with sores, their bony fingers reaching out
to . . . me? I could not erase them from my mind and
heart, and so began the lifetime of "babies."

Many people have others in their lives who have
inspired them to do things they ordinarily would not
do. Dr. Tom Dooley was that inspiration for me. A naval
doctor, he set up jungle medical clinics throughout
Cambodia, Laos, and Vietnam, and established An Lac

Orphanage in Saigon. Dr. Dooley wrote books and raised money to support his medical camps and orphanage. I first met Dr. Dooley while I was working for Senator Jacob Javits in New York. Encouraged by his books and philosophy of helping others, I visited him in his hospital room while he battled cancer. I offered my services and volunteered my secretarial skills in helping to open and answer his mail. When Dr. Dooley passed away from cancer one day after his thirty-fourth birthday, I took over supporting An Lac Orphanage.

I visited the orphanage at least once a year, and I helped Madam Ngai, a brave Vietnamese lady who traveled south from North Vietnam during the Vietnam War. She collected the abandoned and neglected children and cared for them with the help of Dr. Dooley. It was at this orphanage that I met Dr. Patrick D. Tisdale, a colonel in the United States Army. Dr. Tisdale was widowed and had five boys ranging from five to twelve years old. At age forty-nine, I married him, and I had quite a family!

I guess you could say I was orphaned as a child. My father died when I was young, and my mother had tuberculosis and was placed in a sanitarium. My three sisters and I were spread out among different family members, and I lived with my aunt. Maybe that's why, even with an instant family of five children, I felt compelled to adopt a girl.

One night, I stood in the An Lac Orphanage nursery, feeding a baby. Then, as if a searchlight stopped over one crib, there lay a little two-month-old baby girl. She looked up at me with laughing eyes, with lashes like black satin fans and round cheeks, and hair so black it looked almost blue. I scanned the room and realized this was the only baby awake. Walking quietly to the side of the crib, I scooped her up while she looked directly into my eyes, and I knew at that very moment this was my daughter. My mind raced at all the things I needed to do to bring Mai, the name Madam Ngai gave her, home. As I held Mai and cooed, Madam Ngai brought me another child wearing a ragged dress.

"You take Lien, too," stated Madam Ngai. "She will be good at helping you." I had discovered that Madam Ngai very seldom asked, but rather insisted. However, in this case, she was right. I would take Lien home. There was no way I could turn my back on this severely malnourished four-year-old girl with sores and disease covering her body and hair ridden with lice. Her head was flat from being left in her crib on her back too long as a baby. Where Mai had shiny onyx eyes, Lien's were dull and emotionless. As I cleaned her up, I could see what a beautiful child she was.

That was only the beginning. After bringing Mai and Lien home and seeing how the boys took all this in stride—babysitting, changing diapers, playing with their new sisters—I knew I needed to help more children. In a subsequent visit, I sat on the floor feeding a three-month-old who was so tiny she looked three weeks old. Her entire length extended from the crook of my elbow to the tips of my fingers. I knew she would die if she stayed at An Lac. At that time, Madam Ngai and I put our little babies who passed away in shoe boxes to be buried by the local hospital. I could not see my little one in a shoe box, so I took her to a friend of mine at the British Embassy and left her there until I could complete the paperwork. Three months later, Thu Van became the third baby girl in our ever-growing family.

The following year, when we delivered van loads of supplies to the orphanage, we adopted two more girls:

Xuan, a healthy, beautiful seven-year-old girl, and Kim
Lan, a very sick baby. Like ThuVan, I knew she would
also die in the orphanage if I left her there. I made
arrangements for Kim Lan and Xuan to fly out with Pat
and me. While in the Philippines, Kim Lan's stomach
began to balloon, and Pat rushed her to the Army hospital, where she died, connected to multiple tubes in an
incubator.

Devastated, yet never discouraged about saving
more children, I immediately called Madam Ngai and
asked her to find me another child. Three months later,
I brought home another baby whom we also named
Kim Lan. She was so incredibly malnourished that
people cried when they saw her. She looked like a
skeleton covered by a thin layer of skin. Like ThuVan,
she looked only a few weeks old instead of three
months old, yet she flourished into a healthy child.

I did not adopt any more children after Kim Lan.
Whether it was because there were no more rooms in
our house or because I finally had an even number, I
realized my family was complete. But my work with An
Lac continued as I made what would be twenty-seven
trips to Vietnam.

In 1975, when Saigon was falling, I left my ten children and headed for Vietnam, determined to rescue the
children at An Lac. I had no idea how, but that had
never stopped me before.

Because I was not an adoption agency, I did not have
access to military planes provided for Operation
Babylift. I called Pan American Airlines, but the fee was
cost-prohibitive. And where would the babies go when
I got them to the States? Because Fort Benning was in
my home state of Georgia, I called the general there.
He did not return my calls, so I called the Secretary of
the Army. He did not return my calls, so I called his

mother! I told her I was leaving for Vietnam in the morning and begged her to help me.

When I got to An Lac, I promised Madam Ngai that I would save our children. I went to the office of the ambassador and begged for their lives. He said that if I gave him a list of names, and if each baby had a birth certificate and a legal name, he would get me an Air Force plane. I said, "No problem," and raced to the local hospital to get some blank birth certificates. Since orphans were denied legal birth certificates and didn't even have legal names, we made up both! Frantically, two days later, we loaded 219 children onto two planes and headed for the Philippines for a layover. It was only there that I heard from the general's mother that a school in Fort Benning had been converted to care for the children. In the United States, I contacted Tressler Lutheran Adoption Agency. They eagerly provided stacks of applications of waiting adoptive parents, and within thirty days, every one of the children was in their new home.

For more than fifty years, I have tried to make a better life for "my" babies—in Vietnam, Mexico, Colombia, and now Afghanistan through my organization H.A.L.O., Helping And Loving Orphans. Far from a "swinging single" in New York City," I have found my destiny.

Betty Tisdale

ThuVan:

My pen flies as my poetry and deepest thoughts flow onto the pages of my journal. It was late at night in my hotel room in Kon Tum, Vietnam. This was my first trip back to Vietnam since I was left on the doorstep of An Lac Orphanage, Happy Place, and later adopted as the war in Vietnam raged on in 1971. Raised in Georgia, and later in Washington State, I've always considered myself an American and nothing else. I have a loving husband, supportive family, and two beautiful daughters. My life was complete . . . or so I thought.

My trip to Vietnam was supposed to be a vacation/humanitarian trip with my adopted mother, Betty Tisdale. I was there to distribute the donations collected by Oceanway Elementary School, where I taught fifth grade. Like so many who visit this beautiful yet very poor country, Mom and I toured the main cities, such as Ho Chi Minh City and Hanoi, then we traveled to Kon Tum and visited three orphanages and a leper village. Yes, that's right, a leper village.

I had never wanted to look back into my past, preferring to be grateful for who I was and what I had, never wanting to learn what I could have become if I'd stayed in Vietnam.

As I picked up a baby at the Vinh Son Orphanage in Kon Tum, she put her small head on my shoulder. Like a dam breaking under the pressures of a river, my tears welled up and fell uncontrollably. God, how I wanted to take this five-month-old baby home and sweep her away from the bleak life I was sure she would face. Looking around the orphanage, the floors are swept spotless. Lined along the walls are celery-green, paint-chipped metal cribs. On top of a piece of plywood on the bottom of each crib is a half-inch mattress and thin blanket rolled up at the foot of each crib. At that moment, it was very clear to me why my mother evacuated those babies and my sisters all those years ago.

As I cried and watched the toddlers run around wearing cloth diapers pinned around their malnourished waists, I wondered if my mother felt this strongly when she first held me at An Lac where there were literally hundreds of babies just like me. During the war, there were so many babies, often two to three to a crib. How did she pick me out of the hundreds of war orphans?

Going back to Vietnam and seeing the disparity and devastation in the provinces outside the ever-growing tourist cities provided me closure to a part of my life that lay dormant and opened a door to a chapter in my life I did not know existed, but now embrace.

I could not walk away from Vietnam without looking back. I came home once again to be a teacher, but with many new lessons to teach. I will never live another day without trying to teach the values of compassion, caring, and voluntarism. I now understand who I am and what I have become is because of my past.

I could have been that little girl I held in my arms.

ThuVan Tisdale DeBellis

COLLEEN:

In April 1975, I was watching the news. A planeload of Vietnamese children died in a C-140 transport plane crash! I broke down, crying. I had just found out I could not have children—and here was a whole plane full of children dead.

I ran outside and told my husband, Jerry, "We're going to adopt a Vietnamese child!" He looked at me strangely, and I proceeded to tell him about the story I had just seen.

I did a lot of research and found out about Tressler-Lutheran Adoption Agency. I told them we were interested in adopting a Vietnamese child. I felt that I struck gold when I was told that all I needed to do was fill out the proper paperwork . . . mounds and mounds of paperwork.

Then we waited. We finally got a call saying a woman named Betty Tisdale had another plane filled with children who would soon be coming in an organized evacuation to Fort Benning, Georgia, a couple of hours from where we lived.

The next week we received another phone call from Tressler-Lutheran saying our paperwork had been completed correctly, and we could pick up our newborn child the next day!

On the way, we stopped at K-Mart and picked up a blanket, an outfit, and a bottle. Once on base, we discovered the army had turned the school into a makeshift hospital/dorm area. While waiting in the hallway we saw children with scars, wounds, missing limbs, and big sores on their little bodies. Each tiny child had his or her own crib. I picked up some of the babies, thinking how precious each of them was. Finally, our number was called, and we were ushered into a room.

There, an army doctor handed us some paperwork. After signing the papers, we were handed a tiny baby. His armband read Vu Tien Do II. The baby was in a diaper and wrapped in a pale yellow quilt. The doctor said he estimated his age to be about six weeks. Overjoyed, we named him Robert Loran Ballard, or "Bert" for short.

When we returned home, the entire house was filled with everything you could ever want for a baby—a crib, a dresser, blankets, diapers, food, bottles, toys, baby bathtubs, washcloths, bibs, shoes, and much more! Our friends had brought over everything. I was overwhelmed!

Soon, the local Department of Family and Children Services came to the house and said we needed to do more paperwork. We had to pretend we didn't have a baby and go through the entire process as if we were going to adopt through their agency. They did the usual family studies. They questioned our parents, our friends, and our places of employment. Documentation of our income was needed. They even went through the entire house with a fine-toothed comb to see if we were fit to be parents. Jerry and I had to be finger-printed and checked out.

There was some speculation that some of the babies in Operation Babylift were not orphans. We had to go to Atlanta to the main immigration office to apply for a green card. After several months, we got it, and I guarded it with my life!

One day when Bert was about five months old, an FBI agent came to the front door. "I need to see Vu Tien Do II."

I panicked!

"Bert is his name, and he is asleep."

"Wake him up," he ordered.

I went to get Bert, and the man proceeded to take off my baby's clothes and diaper. He told me that he needed to check for any identifiable marks "in case somebody would lay claim to him at a later date."

"Sir, please leave," I said as I opened the front door. "Nobody is *ever* going to take Bert away from us! I'll move to Canada if I have to!"

After all the paperwork, investigations, and agents, the FBI, the INS, the local Family and Children Services, and Tressler-Lutheran approved us for the final adoption on May 7, 1977. Bert belonged to Jerry and me forever.

I truly believe that God spoke to me through the evening news program when the plane crashed. Just when I thought all hope of being a parent had been taken away from me, he gave me his greatest blessing: Bert.

Colleen Bonds

BERT:

I tried to focus. I was waiting to reunite, after twenty-five years, with the woman who brought me out of Vietnam. I didn't know what to think. I didn't know how to react. What do you say to the woman who saved your life? How do you prepare for a reunion you have been looking forward to all of your life? In the brief moments before Betty walked through the gate, I recalled how I came to be waiting in the Denver airport.

Like many in the early 1970s, my parents watched pictures of orphaned Vietnamese children on the evening news and decided to adopt. In their research, they found Betty Tisdale, an extraordinary woman who was singlehandedly supporting an orphanage in Saigon called An Lac—"Happy Place" in Vietnamese.

An Lac was operated by a woman named Madame Ngai, a former northern Vietnamese aristocrat who had a heart for children. When she moved those she cared for from North Vietnam to Saigon in South Vietnam, a United States Navy doctor named Tom Dooley assisted her. His guiding philosophy was to provide an "education and healthy body" to orphaned children. When Dr. Dooley passed away, he passed his legacy onto Betty.

When it was time to evacuate the children from An Lac in April 1975, right before the fall of Saigon, Betty, Madame Ngai, and others created names and birthdays so the government would allow us to leave the country. In fact, only children under ten years of age were able to go; 181 were left behind. I was given the name Vu Tien Do II.

I was approximately three weeks old when I was evacuated. I had a made-up name, a made-up birthday, and no past. I had no known ties to my birth family. I don't even know how I arrived at the orphanage.

In May 1975, my new parents received a phone call

that they could pick up their new infant. It was an exciting time for them, but a scary one as well. I can only imagine the nervousness and anticipation they were feeling as they drove to see me for the first time. When they first held me, they knew it to be true. They named me Robert Loran Ballard after my two grandfathers.

I always knew my life and story were unique, but it wasn't until college that I became serious about understanding my story. During my junior year of college, a friend of mine introduced me to LeAnn Thieman and Carol Dey, two extraordinary women who traveled to Vietnam and helped bring out babies at the end of the Vietnam war. Meeting them, reading their book, and hearing firsthand about their experiences as they brought out babies and children during the last days in Saigon spurred me on even more.

In June 2000, I attended a twenty-five-year reunion of Operation Babylift children. For me, it was like finding long lost brothers and sisters. It was finding a group of people who related to my experiences growing up. It was being around others who could understand the uniqueness that came with being multiracial and multiethnic. It was being around others who also didn't know their parents.

That's when I learned Betty Tisdale was coming to Colorado.

And so, standing at the gate on a cold November morning in 2000, I held my breath as the seconds felt like years. Twenty-five years ago, I was separated from Betty; in a few moments, I was going to be reunited.

She walked into the airport terminal. I recognized her. She recognized me. We embraced. It was like coming home. It wasn't an overwhelming feeling of emotions or elation. It was subtle, like God whispering his comfort in my ear.

Over the next few days, I spent a lot of time with Betty. We held hands and hugged like a mother and son. We laughed and joked like family. She told a lot of stories. I learned where my name came from and why I had the birthday I did. I was told about why I have nerve deafness in my ears and why she thought my birth parents dropped me off at An Lac. I got to hear firsthand of the last days when she evacuated the children from An Lac and how Dr. Dooley inspired her to become involved. I heard her sadness regarding those she left behind and how they were living in Vietnam today.

As we spent time together, I realized that this is what Dr. Dooley and Betty had strived so hard for.

I think often of Dr. Dooley and the inspiration he provided and how proud he would be of Betty's courageous efforts in rescuing 219 children. And me.

Dr. Dooley passed on this legacy to Betty Tisdale. Today, I have an education. Today, I have a healthy body. Today, I have countless opportunities beyond what either Dr. Dooley or Betty ever imagined.

I will continue their legacies.

Bert Ballard

Who Is Jack Canfield?

Jack Canfield is the cocreator and editor of the Chicken Soup for the Soul series, which *Time* magazine has called "the publishing phenomenon of the decade." The series now has 105 titles with over 100 million copies in print in forty-one languages. Jack is also the coauthor of eight other bestselling books, including *The Success Principles: How to Get from Where You Are to Where You Want to Be; Dare to Win; The Aladdin Factor; You've Got to Read This Book;* and *The Power of Focus: How to Hit Your Business and Personal and Financial Targets with Absolute Certainty.*

Jack has recently developed a telephone coaching program and an online coaching program based on his most recent book, *The Success Principles.* He also offers a seven-day Breakthrough to Success seminar every summer, which attracts 400 people from fifteen countries around the world.

Jack has conducted intensive personal and professional development seminars on the principles of success for over 900,000 people in twenty-one countries around the world. He has spoken to hundreds of thousands of others at numerous conferences and conventions and has been seen by millions of viewers on national television shows such as *The Today Show, Fox and Friends, Inside Edition, Hard Copy,* CNN's *Talk Back Live, 20/20, Eye to Eye,* the NBC *Nightly News,* and the CBS *Evening News.*

Jack is the recipient of many awards and honors, including three honorary doctorates and a Guinness World Records Certificate for having seven books from the Chicken Soup for the Soul series appearing on the *New York Times* bestseller list on May 24, 1998.

To write to Jack or for inquiries about Jack as a speaker, his coaching programs, or his seminars, use the following contact information:

The Canfield Companies
P.O. Box 30880 • Santa Barbara, CA 93130
Phone: 805-563-2935 • Fax: 805-563-2945
E-mail: info@jackcanfield.com
Website: www.jackcanfield.com

Who Is Mark Victor Hansen?

In the area of human potential, no one is more respected than Mark Victor Hansen. For more than thirty years, Mark has focused solely on helping people from all walks of life reshape their personal vision of what's possible. His powerful messages of possibility, opportunity, and action have created powerful change in thousands of organizations and millions of individuals worldwide.

He is a sought-after keynote speaker, bestselling author, and marketing maven. Mark's credentials include a lifetime of entrepreneurial success and an extensive academic background. He is a prolific writer with many bestselling books, such as *The One-Minute Millionaire, Cracking the Millionaire Code, How to Make the Rest of Your Life the Best of Your Life, The Power of Focus, The Aladdin Factor,* and *Dare to Win,* in addition to the Chicken Soup for the Soul series. Mark has made a profound influence through his library of audios, videos, and articles in the areas of big thinking, sales achievement, wealth building, publishing success, and personal and professional development.

Mark is the founder of the MEGA Seminar Series. MEGA Book Marketing University and Building Your MEGA Speaking Empire are annual conferences where Mark coaches and teaches new and aspiring authors, speakers, and experts on building lucrative publishing and speaking careers. Other MEGA events include MEGA Info-Marketing and My MEGA Life.

As a philanthropist and humanitarian, Mark works tirelessly for organizations such as Habitat for Humanity, American Red Cross, March of Dimes, Childhelp USA, and many others. He is the recipient of numerous awards that honor his entrepreneurial spirit, philanthropic heart, and business acumen. He is a lifetime member of the Horatio Alger Association of Distinguished Americans, an organization that honored Mark with the prestigious Horatio Alger Award for his extraordinary life achievements.

Mark Victor Hansen is an enthusiastic crusader of what's possible and is driven to make the world a better place.

Mark Victor Hansen & Associates, Inc.
P.O. Box 7665 • Newport Beach, CA 92658
Phone: 949-764-2640 • Fax: 949-722-6912
Website: www.markvictorhansen.com

Who Is LeAnn Thieman?

LeAnn Thieman is a nationally acclaimed professional speaker, author, and nurse who was "accidentally" caught up in the Vietnam Orphan Airlift in 1975. Her book, *This Must Be My Brother*, details her daring adventure of helping to rescue 300 babies as Saigon was falling to the communists. An ordinary person, she struggled through extraordinary circumstances and found the courage to succeed. LeAnn has been featured in *Newsweek*'s "Voices of the Century" issue, on FOX-TV, BBC, NPR, PBS, PAX-TV's *It's a Miracle,* and countless radio and TV programs.

After her story of adopting their son was featured in *Chicken Soup for the Mother's Soul*, LeAnn became one of *Chicken Soup*'s most prolific writers. Her devotion to thirty years of nursing made her the ideal co-author of *Chicken Soup for the Nurse's Soul*. She went on to coauthor *Chicken Soup for the Christian Woman's Soul, Chicken Soup for the Caregiver's Soul, Chicken Soup for the Father and Daughter Soul, Chicken Soup for the Grandma's Soul, Chicken Soup for the Mother and Son Soul, Chicken Soup for the Christian Soul 2, Chicken Soup for the Nurse's Soul: Second Dose,* and now *Chicken Soup for the Adopted Soul*.

As a renowned motivational speaker, she shares life-changing lessons learned from her airlift and nursing experiences. Believing we all have individual "war zones," LeAnn inspires audiences to balance their lives, truly live their priorities, and make a difference in the world.

LeAnn is one of about 10 percent of speakers worldwide to have earned the Certified Speaking Professional designation.

She and Mark, her husband of thirty-seven years, reside in Colorado where they enjoy their "empty nest." Their two daughters, Angela and Christie, and son Mitch have "flown the coop" but are still drawn under their mother's wing when she needs them!

For more information about LeAnn's books, CDs, and DVDs, or to schedule her for a presentation, please contact her at:

LeAnn Thieman, CSP
6600 Thompson Drive
Fort Collins, CO 80526
Phone: 1-970-223-1574
E-mail: LeAnn@LeAnnThieman.com
www.LeAnnThieman.com

Contributors

Diana M. Amadeo received the 2006 Catholic Press Association Book Award for *Holy Friends: Thirty Saints and Blesseds of the Americas* (Pauline Books and Media). She has 450 publications with her byline, yet she humbly and persistently tweaks and rewrites her thousand or so rejections with eternal hope that they may yet see the light of day.

Teresa Ambord makes a living as a full-time business writer from her home in rural northern California. When she's not writing for her employer, she enjoys putting together creative nonfiction stories, assisted and inspired by her posse of small dogs. You can e-mail her at ambertrees@charter.net.

Maresa Aughenbaugh is a homeschooled sophomore. She lives in Colorado with her parents and seven siblings. In her spare time, Maresa enjoys debate, soccer, acting, and music. She has been writing fiction and nonfiction stories for several years and hopes to publish a book soon. Please e-mail her at maughenbaugh@yahoo.com.

David Avrin is a successful marketing, public relations, and branding strategist, professional speaker and executive coach. Aside from his "real job," he is also the author of the very popular book: *The Gift in Every Day— Little Lessons on Living a Big Life* (2006 Sourcebooks). Reach him at david@visibilitycoach.com.

Aaron Bacall's work has appeared in most national publications and has been used for advertising, greeting cards, wall calendars, and several corporate promotional books. Three of his cartoons are featured in the permanent collection at the Harvard Business School's Baker Library. He continues to create and sell his cartoons. He can be reached at ABACALL@MSN.COM

Bert Ballard was three weeks old when he was evacuated from Vietnam. He is married with two girls, Adria (five) and Kyla (three). He is pursuing a Ph.D. at the University of Denver and is active in the international adoption community. He can be reached at bert@van-online.org.

Edward Dow Bartling Martinez, born Don Louis Martinez in Panama, is an American citizen. He received his bachelor's degree from Wayne State University, CLU from American College, and MBA from National American University. Edward resides in the Black Hills of South Dakota and enjoys camping with Scouts, swiming, racquetball, and traveling to Panama. E-mail him at godfather@prodigy.net.

Coni Billings is currently pursuing her teaching degree and hopes to teach art at the elementary-school level. Coni enjoys hiking, camping, drawing, and carving. She plans to write historic novels and children's stories. Please e-mail her at coni@elkcreekcc.org.

Martha Bolton was an Emmy-nominated writer for Bob Hope and the author of more than fifty books, including *Didn't My Skin Used to Fit?* She has also written for Phyllis Diller, Wayne Newton, Mark Lowry, Jeff Allen, and numerous others. Martha co-wrote the *New York Times* bestselling book, *The Rick and Bubba Code.*

Colleen Bonds was born in Sacramento, California, and earned a degree in business administration. She adopted Robert Loren Ballard, a Vietnamese orphan, in 1975. She is married to Philip Bonds, and she is currently an administrative assistant at a high school in Kremmling, Colorado. Hobbies include golf, bike riding, and scrapbooking.

Chalise Annett Bourque grew up in Manhattan, Kansas and graduated from Kansas State University. She writes from home in the Kansas City Plaza. She's published a children's book, *Rain Forest Girl,* about her Brazilian daughter. Chalise has two sons, three grandchildren, and a cat, who share and make up her life stories.

Sharon Beth Brani is a licensed professional counselor, life coach, and freelance writer. Her greatest joy is being the mother of two daughters who were adopted from Russia. She is currently writing an inspirational book titled *Walking Toward the Sunrise.* Her website is Always Life Coaching at www.sharonbrani.com.

A former atheist **Alicia Britt Chole** is now known for the portraits of truth she paints with her words. Wife, mommy, author, and speaker, Alicia and her fun-filled tribe of five live off a country road in a home devoted to reflection and writing. Learn more about Alicia at www.truthportraits.com.

Amanda Brown Houk is a freelance writer and editor. She teaches high-school literature in Colorado Springs, where she lives with her husband, Pete, and their two daughters. Mandy was born in Georgia and returned to her southern roots when writing her first novel, *Cloud Hunting.* Please visit her website at www.mandyhouk.com.

Martha Campbell is a graduate of Washington University of St. Louis School of Fine Arts and a former writer/designer for Hallmark Cards. She has been a freelance cartoonist and book illistrator since 1973. She can be reached at PO Box 2538, Harrison, AR 72602 or at 870-741-5323 or marthaf@alltel.net.

Barbara S. Canale is a freelance writer. Currently, she writes for local newspapers and magazines. She has been published in *Chicken Soup for the Veteran's Soul, Women's World,* and other magazines. She is the author of *Our Labor of Love: A Romanian Adoption Chronicle.* Barbara volunteers in her church, the schools, and community.

For more about the life that "Almost Adopted" depicts, visit **Nancy Canfield's** website at www.StAgathaHome.org and order *Home Kids: the Story of St. Agatha Home for Children.* All profits from the sale of the book are donated to the children of St. Agatha Home Services.

Virginia Chaney lives in North Carolina where she is a substitute teacher and full-time mother. Virginia has also written a humor book enititled *Stupid Stuff! How Did All of This Get in My Head?* Please e-mail her at virginia@virginiachaney.com or visit her website at www.virginia chaney.com.

Laura Christianson is the author of *The Adoption Decision* and *The Adoption Network*, and writes the award-winning Exploring Adoption blog. She founded a ministry that supports adoptive families and is a presenter at adoption events. She lives with her husband and two sons in the Seattle area. Visit her at www.laurachristianson.com.

Bryan Clark is a fire inspector/investigator. He is an alumni of Oklahoma State University's School of Fire Protection. He lives with his wife and two daughters, adopted from China, in Northern California.

Cherie Clark was instrumental in implementing Operation Babylift to help rescue 3000 orphans from Vietnam in 1975. From there she journeyed to India where she worked with Mother Teresa. She returned to Vietnam in 1988 where she continues to minister to needy children today. Visit her at www.cherie.clark@gmail.com.

Lisa Cobb is a happily married army wife of twenty years, a registered nurse, and the mother of three terrific children, one adopted. She loves Jesus, traveling, gardening, writing, and being with her family. She would be pleased to have you contact her at valitehaus@yahoo.com.

Bridget Colern is a grandmother. She lives in Southern California. She likes reading and spending time with family. Bridget has been writing since winning a school essay contest in the sixth grade. She hopes to publish a book of her inspirational stories and poems. You can e-mail her at BridgeBKnT@yahoo.com.

Erin Conroy received her bachelor of arts degree from Concordia College in Moorhead, MN, and her juris doctorate from the University of North Dakota in Grand Forks, ND. After several years in private practice, Erin is now in-house counsel at Integreon Managed Solutions, Inc. Erin enjoys spending time with her two children, Nicolas and Michael, and plans to travel soon with them to Colombia.

Leah Cook is the mother of twin girls. She would like to write children's stories, particularly adoption stories. Leah and her husband, Keith, live with their children in Alberta, Canada.

J. M. Cornwell is a nationally syndicated freelance journalist, editor, award-winning writer, and book reviewer who lives in the Colorado Rockies. Her work has appeared in *Columbus Monthly*, *The New York Times*, *Ohio Magazine*, *The Celebrity Cafe*, *Haunted Encounters*, and *Cup of Comfort*. Please e-mail her at fixnwrtr@gmail.com.

Nancy Bravo Creager was born and raised in Chile. She lives now in Washington State. She is a wife, mother, and grandmother. Nancy enjoys reading the classics; her favorite poet is Neruda, and her favorite writer is Steinbeck. She experiments with writing inspirational prose and poetry. She can be contacted at nancreager@Comcast.net.

Cathy Cruise received her bachelor of arts in English from Radford University and her master of fine arts in creative writing from George Mason University. She is a freelance writer and editor, and is currently working on a novel. Please e-mail her at ccruise@cox.net.

Ruth Curran, a vocational nomad, has been a teacher, vocational counselor, YMCA manager, and director of a not-for-profit organization. Now retired, she hopes to spend more time writing, traveling, and being with her friends and family. Please e-mail her at r.curran@shaw.ca.

Melody Davis received her master's of education degree from the University of Missouri in 1985, and taught for eighteen years before becoming a full-time mom. She loves to read, write, hike, and travel. She hopes to publish several of her children's books someday. She can be reached at mcdavis@kc.rr.com.

ThuVan Tisdale DeBellis received her bachelor of arts in psychology from the George Washington University in Washington, D.C. She is a fifth-grade teacher living in Jacksonville, Florida. Thu Van was recently appointed to the Board of Helping and Loving Orphans (HALO), whose mission is to support orphans throughout the world.

Cheryl Dieter is a UNLV graduate who has traveled throughout the world. She is the lucky mom of five children, three of them adopted from South Korea, and married to David, the Saint of Patience. Cheryl writes at 2 AM while her children sleep. She is always tired. Contact her at reyes-dbd@hotmail.com.

Jody Ellis-Knapp is a freelance writer living in Alaska. She enjoys travel with her family, running, hiking, and her four crazy dogs. She may be reached via her website at www.writersblocfreelance.com.

Maria Ervin is an eleventh-grade student who enjoys creative writing, journalism, and participating in her school's varsity track and cross-country teams. Maria was born in Russia and lived in an orphanage before being adopted at the age of eleven. She lives with her mother and sister in Michigan.

Barbara Jeanne Fisher has a degree in creative writing and teaches writing online for Writer's College. She owns the Open Book Store in her town. She has published two novels and several children's books. She enjoys reading, writing, and spending time with her large family. E-mail her at mentorsfriend@cros.net.

Renée Friedman, originally from Brooklyn, New York, now lives off the west coast of Canada from where she travels the world, teaches, mothers, kayaks, hikes, and indulges in her lifelong fantasy of becoming a writer. She can be reached at rjf12156@yahoo.ca.

Kim Gaudiosi received her master's degree in elementary education with honors from Queens College of New York in 2003. She is currently retired and awaiting her first child from China.

Sharon Gibson and her husband adopted four teenagers from poverty backgrounds and started Hopeful Hearts Ministry for children in poverty in Brazil and Colombia. Sharon is a writer/speaker, raised in Africa by missionary parents. She served in the Kansas legislature and owned two Christian stores. Her e-mail address is sharongibson@cox.net.

Dave Gorden and his wife, Beverly, have been foster parents for fifty-seven children. They have two adopted children and one biological child. Dave is a member of the Speakers Hall of Fame and past President of the National Speakers Association. Please e-mail him at www. davegorden.com

Diana Green is writing a book about her life after a tragic car accident left her paralyzed. After visiting Haiti in 2003, she followed her heart by returning in 2004 to care for a child she is adopting. She has returned home to raise funds to build orphanages in Haiti. She can be reached at alexndiane@hotmail.com.

Cheryl Gromis is a wife and mother of four great kids. She works both as Children's Pastor of her church and Supervisor for Special Education intern teachers in Los Angeles County. She gives thanks to God for his abundant goodness, and to her husband for his unconditional love and support.

Valerie Kay Gwin, a freelance writer and administrative assistant, enjoys writing inspirational short stories and poetry. She is an active member of a Christian writers group in central Nebraska. Valerie and her husband have been blessed to be adoptive parents for the past nineteen years. Please e-mail her at vgwin@charter.net.

Debra J. Haralam has been blessed with hundreds of children through her work as a teacher's assistant in a local Christian elementary school. Her adopted son continues to bless her every day with his delightful ponderings and witticisms.

Jonny Hawkins dedicates the cartoons in this book to his cousin Faith, who lives by her name, her wonderful husband, Steve, and their rainbow of adopted children. Jonny's works, such as *Medical Cartoon-a-Day* and *Fishing Cartoon-a-Day* calendars, along with *A Joke a Day Keeps the Doctor Away*, are available everywhere. He can be contacted at jonnyhawkins2nz@yahoo.com.

Ana Hays lives in the San Francisco Bay Area where she writes and leads writing workshops for aspiring writers and works at cancer centers and healthcare institutions providing wellness programs for their members. She is also the associate publisher, editor, and columnist for *Maui Vision* magazine. Visit her at writeonwriters.net.

Karen C. Helmrich, RN, BSN, RYT, has been teaching group fitness since 2001. She currently teaches yoga to her family and friends, travels the United States in an RV, and homeschools her children. She is working on additional stories about her adoption journey. Please e-mail her at karen.helmrich@gmail.com.

Elizabeth (Betty) Henderson grew up in New Jersey. She graduated with a bachelor's degree in special education from Georgian Court University. She and her husband Bill now reside in Florida where Betty teaches autistic children. The Hendersons have two biological daughters and an adopted son, and are currently adopting another daughter.

Brenda Henn, aside from her top priority of being a mother, is Director of Small World Adoption Foundation of Missouri, having helped nearly

1,800 orphans find loving homes. She resides in Missouri and loves family, friends, reading, and sports. She is writing the detailed story of her life.

Peter Hesse is a freelance cartoonist, a WWII vet, and a graduate of R.I. School of Design. He and his wife, Liz, live in Denver. Check out his website at www.cartoonsbyhesse.com.

Stefanie Johansson is a freelance writer living in Florida with her three amazing daughters. She is currently working on her first novel. She dedicates this story to the little boy who captured her heart. She can be reached by e-mail at stefaniedurham@comcast.net.

Ruthan Josten is a mom/grandmother/police officer/teacher/college graduate/tap dancer who lives in Alaska and dreams of retiring to the warmth of the Southwest. She has four children, ages six to thirty-three, and was blessed in 2006 with a reunion with her oldest daughter.

Bev Jaundrew (Schellenberg) is a freelance writer, writing instructor, high school educator, choral director, and parent. Her articles have appeared in anthologies and the *Globe and Mail*, and she writes for backofthebook.ca. Through nonfiction she preserves memories, and in fiction, she flies with dragons and unites people separated by centuries. Contact her at me@bevschellenberg.com.

Cindy Kauffman is a graduate of Bowling Green State University, Bowling Green, Ohio. She is the mother of four children. She has been published in Leader Publication newspapers for eleven years. Other publishing credits include: "Chocolate for the Soul" series and "Glencoe's Literature, Reading with a Purpose, Course 2"

Jessica Kennedy received her B.A. from the University of California at Davis. At twenty-six, she had a stroke and became a ventilator-dependent quadriplegic. A guest speaker at classes for respiratory therapists and a writer of inspirational articles and children's stories, she foresees a bright future. E-mail her at jessicakennedy1971@yahoo.com.

Jean Kinsey, now retired, resides in Brooks, Kentucky. She is devoted to her church and family and loves to travel. Her nonfiction stories have appeared in *Nostalgia, Live,* and Chicken Soup books. She's authored several profile articles and is currently writing an historical inspirational novel. E-mail her at kystorywriter@yahoo.com.

Published author **Roger Dean Kiser**'s stories take you into the heart of a child abandoned by his family and abused by the system. Through his stories, he relives the sadness and cruelty of growing up an orphan in the early 1950s. Roger's stories and CDs are available at www.geocities.com/trampoline/survive/srv080.htm.

Mimi Greenwood Knight is a freelance writer living in south Louisiana with her husband, David, four kids, four dogs, four cats, and one knuckleheaded bird. She is proud to have stories included in ten Chicken Soup books as well as other anthologies, national parenting magazines, and Christian websites. E-mail her at djknight@airmail.net.

Nancy Liedel is an author, wife, mother to four boys, and triathalete. She enjoys belly dancing for fun, and loves to read and travel. She writes in southeast Michigan. Please e-mail her at nancy@liedel.org.

Elizabeth Mallory founded the not-for-profit organization No Child Left Out (NCLO) after adopting from Cambodia. NCLO provides food, medical care, education, and supplies to orphaned and impoverished children. Visit www.nclo.org to learn more. Elizabeth now resides in New Zealand with her husband and their three children. She may be contacted at mallory@nclo.org.

Cathy McIlvoy is a mother to four boys by birth and adoption. She is a freelance writer and is currently writing a middle-grade novel. She loves going on long walks with her husband and appreciates a good, clean, stand-up comedian. Please e-mail her at cathymcilvoy@gmail.com.

Kim McKinney has a degree in psychology and a master's in counseling. She currently works at a child advocacy center in southeast Texas. However, her greatest joy is being the mother of her beautiful daughter, Kendall.

Priscilla Miller is a wife, mother of four sons and one adopted daughter, and has thirteen grandchildren and four great-grandchildren. At sixty five, faced with loss of vision due to Age-Related Macular Degeneration (ARMD), she is realizing her life's dream when her human-interest stories appear weekly in a small northern Michigan newspaper.

Diana M. Millikan was born in England and grew up during the Second World War, where she lost her home to bombing. She is a retired nurse and lives with her husband and pets on a small island in Puget Sound. She enjoys her grandchildren, gardening, and photgraphy.

Nancy Morse grew up in Illinois but now lives in North Carolina with her husband, Dave, and their children, Nathan and Heather. She enjoys spending time with her family, traveling, reading, and volunteering at school and church. Her passion is writing poetry and short stories inspired by life experiences.

Eric Myers currently resides in Austin, Texas, with his wife, Jennifer, and daughter, Lydia. They are currently approved for another adoption. Eric received his B.S. from Harding University and a B.S. in physical therapy from the University of Oklahoma.

Kelli Myers-Gottemoller received her master of social work degree from Smith College School for Social Work and has been working in adoptions with Lutheran Children and Family Service of Eastern Pennsylvania since 1992. She and her husband have three children, including a daughter who was adopted from Cambodia in 2001.

Nancy O'Neill met her husband, Michael, in Pakistan in 1968. In 1974, they packed up their two children and moved to Ireland, followed by tours in Nigeria, Kenya, and Eritrea. Nancy presently works with her daughter in their personalized gift business and enjoys helping with her three grandchildren.

Tina O'Reilly lives in Rhode Island with her husband, three children, and two Labrador retrievers. She is a freelance writer who enjoys reading, traveling, and the ocean. She loves getting lost in her characters' lives. She can be reached at tmoreilly68@aol.com.

Ellie Porte Parker, Ph.D., is a licensed psychologist and a writer. She adopted her son, Dmitry, from Russia when he was six years old, and he and his brother, Franklin, as well as the dog, Maverick, are all grown up and doing well. The story, "Pet Connections," is excerpted from the manuscript *Bringing Up Dmitry*, which she is seeking to publish. You can e-mail her at ellieparker@hotmail.com.

Rhonda Lane Phillips is a certified reading specialist, with a love for writing. She teaches reading full-time in an elementary school and part-time for Virginia Tech. Two years after her daughter came into her life, she and her husband adopted a baby boy—again, nine months in her blessed heart. Rhonda can be reached at readwrite@verizon.net.

Stephanie Piro lives in New Hampshire with her husband, daughter, and three cats. She is one of King Features' team of women cartoonists, "Six Chix." (She is the Saturday chick!) Her new book, *My Cat Loves Me Naked*, is available at bookstores everywhere. She also designs gift items for her company, Strip T's. Visit her website at www.stephaniepiro.com or contact her at stephaniepiro@verizon.net.

G. Ann Potter is the mother of four children. She received an M.A. in family studies from Michigan State University. She's happiest with her family at the beach. She currently teaches middle school in Florida. She loves being able to inspire her students to reach out and embrace the world.

Kathy Pride is a mom, wife, friend, encourager, and writer who loves to live life passionately and with one foot over the edge. She enjoys traveling and scuba diving, and lives in Pennsylvania with her husband and two daughters. Please e-mail her at kathy@KathyPride.com.

Rhonda Richards-Cohen is a graduate of Greenville College and Stanford University. She lives and writes in Dallas, TX.

Keri Riley received a bachelor's of creative writing from Linfield College in Oregon. She is a full-time foster/adoptive parent living in Kasilof, Alaska, where she writes for fun and runs a photography business from home. She can be reached at www.northernexposureimages.com.

Lisa J. Schlitt lives in Kitchener, Ontario. She has been married to Patrick for sixteen years. Together they have four children and are in the process of adopting number five. Lisa hopes to have "The Race" illustrated and published for the children's literature market. You may contact her at p.schlitt@sympatico.ca

Heidi Shelton-Jenck is mom to four children. Two of her daughters were adopted from China. Heidi enjoys hiking, skiing, and camping with her family in the Rocky Mountains where she lives and works as a reading specialist and curriculum writer.

Bree Cutting Sibbel left Vietnam as an infant on Operation Babylift. She was adopted shortly after arriving in the U.S. on April 28, 1975 and was raised in Baker City, Oregon. She began traveling back to Vietnam in 2000. Bree is very active in the Vietnamese Adoptee Network.

Sylvia Smart is a nonfiction author, video producer, and grandma. She lives with her two youngest adopted sons, three dogs, and five cats in Arizona. Her motto is: "If you don't like your life, change it!" She currently has a book under contract and another one in development. Contact Sylvia at keepsakekats@mchsi.com.

Belinda Howard Smith lives in Austin, Texas. She and her husband, Steve, have a blended family of six and three granddaughters. Belinda teaches faithbooking at her church, and enjoys writing, scrapbooking, crafts, and reading. She homeschools her youngest daughter, Kellyn, age sixteen. Please e-mail her at Belinda@belindahowardsmith.com.

Christine Smith is married and resides in Oklahoma. She is the mother of three, grandmother of thirteen, and foster mother to many. Her stories have appeared in magazines and local newsletters, and she is a frequent contributor to the Chicken Soup for the Soul book series.

Sarah Jo Smith holds a master's degree in education from Santa Clara University. She writes narrative essays and fiction. A mother of three children, one biological and two adopted (she just can't remember which two!), she lives with her family in Los Gatos, California.

Joyce Stark lives in Scotland and has completed her first book about traveling around the United States. Her second book about fictional characters in Spain aims to teach Spanish to very young children. She is now working on a collection of her short stories. E-mail her at joric.stark@virgin.net.

Kimberly Hee Stock received degrees from both the University of Nebraska–Lincoln, and Penn University. In 1998, she cofounded the Boston Korean Adoptees. She resides in Delaware with her husband (also a Korean adoptee) and children. She is working on a screenplay about a Korean adoptee woman. Contact her at kimberlyhee@comcast.net.

Anthony S. Tessandori is a husband and father. Currently, he is working toward his Ph.D. in anthropology. He enjoys teaching scuba diving, writing, and playing music, and the Los Angeles Dodgers. He is interested in writing science-based fiction novels in the future. Please e-mail him at atess@u.washington.edu.

Michelle and Stacy Tetschner are the proud parents of three boys, including five-year-old Raymond, who has Down syndrome. You can contact them and learn about inspirational stories of other children with Down syndrome at www.windowsintoheaven.net.

Betty Tisdale was born in Pittsburgh, Pennsylvania. After moving to New York City with U.S. Steel, she then became the New York secretary to U.S. Senator Jacob K. Javits. She left to marry and become the mother of ten children, five from Vietnam.

Amy Tolleson is a psychology major at Southern Methodist University in Dallas, Texas. In 2003, she met her birth mother, Shelley, and that event inspired her to write about it. Amy hopes to eventually write a book about her adoption experience. She dedicates this story to Shelley, Marywood (the adoption agency through which she was placed), her father and brother, and, above all, her mom, Debbie, who showed Amy what it was to be strong during this whole process.

Kim Toms runs a university writing center. On weekends, she and her husband build their dream shack in the mountains. They regularly join her biological family for vacation and Southern barbecue. Kim shares her mother's passion for rocks and laughs just like her sister.

Lee Varon adopted two children as a single parent. She is the author of *Adopting on Your Own: The Complete Guide to Adopting as a Single Parent*. Please contact her at LsVaron@aol.com.

Patti Wade Zint writes newspaper columns, faith-based relationship articles, short stories, and service articles. Married with three children, she resides in Arizona. Patti is currently working on an inspirational historical romance novel set in the South. E-mail her at pwzint@cox.net.

Colleen Wells received her master of arts in English from Butler University in 2001. She lives with her husband, two sons, and four dogs. Colleen enjoys working with the elderly and traveling. She plans to use her writing in advocacy for the environment. Please e-mail her at colleen-wells@earthlink.net.

Pamela D. Williams is a mother, pastor's wife, and freelance writer, and has been published in various cat magazines and Christian periodicals. Her work also appears in *Traveling Calvary's Road* and *Chicken Soup for the Soul: Stories for a Better World*.

Linda Wood left her job as an interior designer to stay home full-time with Parker and to help manage her husband's appraisal business. To learn more about Parker and his amazing story, you may visit his website at www.Parkersstory.com

Sandy Wright received her teaching degree from Baylor University and a GT endorsement from UNT. She teaches in Texas where the west began. While completing her first novel, she enjoys intricate painting, hiking, traveling, attempting to be a wanna-be tool chick, and playful family time. Her e-mail address is wrightonsandy@yahoo.com.

Sharon M. Yager has enjoyed writing stories and poems, and journaling since childhood. She recently helped her father edit his memoir on his service in Vietnam. Sharon and her husband, Will, are currently working to reunite their daughter with her two birth siblings who had to be left behind in Russia.

Linda Zou received her bachelor of arts from Northwest University in China and her Ed.D. in higher education administration from Oklahoma State University. She recently finished her novel, written in Chinese, titled, *She Is Not My Flesh and Blood*. She lives with her husband and daughter in Fort Collins, Colorado. She can be reached at lmark@comcast.net.

Permissions

Improving Your Life Every Day

Real people sharing real stories—for nineteen years. Now, Chicken Soup for the Soul has gone beyond the bookstore to become a world leader in life improvement. Through books, movies, DVDs, online resources and other partnerships, we bring hope, courage, inspiration and love to hundreds of millions of people around the world. Chicken Soup for the Soul's writers and readers belong to a one-of-a-kind global community, sharing advice, support, guidance, comfort, and knowledge.

Chicken Soup for the Soul stories have been translated into more than 40 languages and can be found in more than one hundred countries. Every day, millions of people experience a Chicken Soup for the Soul story in a book, magazine, newspaper or online. As we share our life experiences through these stories, we offer hope, comfort and inspiration to one another. The stories travel from person to person, and from country to country, helping to improve lives everywhere.

Share with Us

We all have had Chicken Soup for the Soul moments in our lives. If you would like to share your story or poem with millions of people around the world, go to chickensoup.com and click on "Submit Your Story." You may be able to help another reader, and become a published author at the same time. Some of our past contributors have launched writing and speaking careers from the publication of their stories in our books!

Our submission volume has been increasing steadily — the quality and quantity of your submissions has been fabulous. We only accept story submissions via our website. They are no longer accepted via mail or fax.

To contact us regarding other matters, please send us an e-mail through webmaster@chickensoupforthesoul.com, or fax or write us at:

Chicken Soup for the Soul
P.O. Box 700
Cos Cob, CT 06807-0700
Fax: 203-861-7194

One more note from your friends at Chicken Soup for the Soul: Occasionally, we receive an unsolicited book manuscript from one of our readers, and we would like to respectfully inform you that we do not accept unsolicited manuscripts and we must discard the ones that appear.

Chicken Soup for the Soul

Our 101 BEST STORIES

On, Being A Parent

Inspirational, Humorous, and Heartwarming Stories about Parenthood

Jack Canfield & Mark Victor Hansen

edited by Amy Newmark

Parenting is the hardest and most rewarding job in the world. This upbeat book includes the best selections on parenting from Chicken Soup for the Soul's rich history, with 101 stories carefully selected to appeal to both mothers and fathers. This is a great book for couples to share, whether they are embarking on a new adventure as parents or reflecting on their lifetime experience, with stories written by parents about children and by children about their parents.

978-1-935096-20-7

Chicken Soup for the Soul.

New Moms

101 Inspirational Stories of Joy, Love, and Wonder

Jack Canfield,
Mark Victor Hansen
& Susan M. Heim

Becoming a mom is the most amazing event. This book celebrates the physical, emotional, and spiritual experience of having a child and creating a family. New and expectant moms will delight in this collection of stories by other moms, sharing the wonders of early motherhood, from waiting for the baby, to those early weeks and first few years, and everything in between! A great baby shower and new mother gift.

978-1-935096-63-4

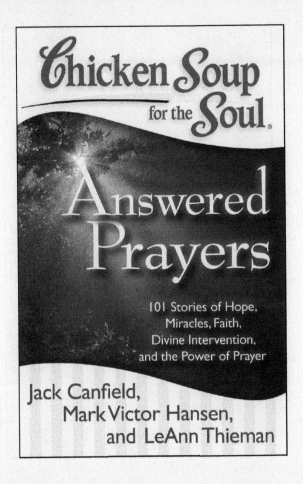

Chicken Soup for the Soul®

Answered Prayers

101 Stories of Hope,
Miracles, Faith,
Divine Intervention,
and the Power of Prayer

Jack Canfield,
Mark Victor Hansen,
and LeAnn Thieman

We all need help from time to time, and these 101 true
stories of answered prayers show a higher power at work
in our lives. Regular people share their personal, touching
stories of God's Divine intervention, healing power, and
communication. Filled with stories about the power of
prayer, miracles, and hope, this book will inspire anyone
looking to boost his or her faith and read some amazing
stories.

978-1-935096-76-4

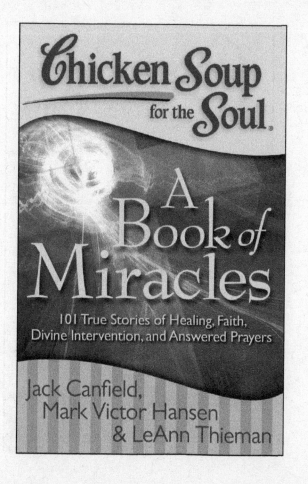

Chicken Soup for the Soul

A Book of Miracles

101 True Stories of Healing, Faith, Divine Intervention, and Answered Prayers

Jack Canfield,
Mark Victor Hansen
& LeAnn Thieman

Everyone loves a good miracle story, and this book provides 101 true stories of healing, divine intervention, and answered prayers. These amazing, personal stories prove that God is alive and active in the world today, working miracles on our behalf. The incredible accounts show His love and involvement in our lives. This book of miracles will encourage, uplift, and recharge the faith of Catholics and all Christian readers.

978-1-935096-51-1

Chicken Soup for the Soul
for the Soul

Think Positive

101 Inspirational
Stories about
Counting Your Blessings and
Having a Positive Attitude

Jack Canfield,
Mark Victor Hansen & Amy Newmark
Foreword by Deborah Norville

Every cloud has a silver lining. Readers will be inspired by
these 101 real-life stories from people just like them, taking
a positive attitude to the ups and downs of life, and
remembering to be grateful and count their blessings. This
book continues Chicken Soup for the Soul's focus on
inspiration and hope, and its stories of optimism and faith
will encourage readers to stay positive during challenging
times and in their everyday lives.

978-1-935096-56-6

Chicken Soup for the Soul: Find Your Happiness

101 Inspirational Stories about Finding Your Purpose, Passion, and Joy

Jack Canfield, Mark Victor Hansen & Amy Newmark

Foreword by Deborah Norville

Others share how they found their passion, purpose, and joy in life in these 101 personal and exciting stories that are sure to encourage readers to find their own happiness. Stories in this collection will inspire readers to pursue their dreams, find their passion and seek joy in their life. This book continues Chicken Soup for the Soul's focus on inspiration and hope, reminding readers that they can find their own happiness.

978-1-935096-77-1

Chicken Soup for the Soul

for the Soul

Grandmothers

101 Stories
of Love,
Laughs,
and Lessons
from
Grandmothers
and
Grandchildren

Jack Canfield,
Mark Victor Hansen
& Amy Newmark

The moment a grandchild is born, a grandmother is born too. This collection of stories by grandmothers about being a grandmother, and by grandchildren about their grandmothers, celebrates these special relationships. Personal stories about legacies and traditions, grandma's wisdom and lessons from grandchildren as well as the joys and challenges of grandparenting, will touch the heart of all grandmothers.

978-1-935096-64-1

Chicken Soup for the Soul
for the Soul.

Stay-at-Home Moms

101 Inspirational Stories for Mothers
about Hard Work and Happy Families

with stories by
Jane Green, Jill Kargman,
Liz Lange, Melora Hardin,
and Jodi Picoult

Jack Canfield,
Mark Victor Hansen,
and Wendy Walker

With stories by famous moms, including Jane Green, Melora Hardin, Liz Lange, Jodi Picoult, and Jill Kargman, and stories from other moms who elected to stay at home or work from home. A reissue of Chicken Soup for the Soul: Power Moms, this book contains 101 great stories from mothers who have made the choice to stay home or work from home while raising their families. This is perfect for book groups as it contains a reader guide.

978-1-935096-82-5

www.chickensoup.com